THE SHAPE OF THE FUTURE

THE SHAPE OF THE FUTURE

THE POST-COLD WAR WORLD

SECOND EDITION

DONALD M. SNOW

M.E. Sharpe
Armonk, New York
London, England

Library of Congress Cataloging-in-Publication Data

Snow, Donald M., 1943–
The shape of the future : the post–cold war world / Donald M. Snow.—2nd ed.
p.   cm.
Includes biographical references (p.   ) and index.
ISBN 1-56324-423-3.—ISBN 1-56324-424-1 (pbk.)
1. World politics—1989–
2. Cold War.
3. Security, International.
I. Title.
D860.S66   1994
327'.09'04—dc20
94-12522
CIP

Printed in the United States of America

The paper used in this publication meets the minimum requirements of
American National Standard for Information Sciences—
Permanence of Paper for Printed Library Materials,
ANSI Z 39.48-1984.

EB (c)   10   9   8   7   6   5   4   3   2   1
EB (p)   10   9   8   7   6   5   4   3   2

Contents

Preface

That the early 1990s have been turbulent, even tumultuous years, by now goes without saying. In a period of less than five years, the international system has been turned on its head; its most visible symbol, the Cold War competition between the United States and the Soviet Union, has disappeared as first the Warsaw Pact and then the Soviet Union itself disbanded. For the United States, the success of Desert Storm and the national pride it elicited inevitably gave way to a debate over whether that conflict in the Persian Gulf was the last convulsion of the old order or the first challenge of the new order. The brutal siege of Sarajevo on nightly television demonstrated international impotence as national self-determination showed its ugliest face in the breakup of the former Yugoslavia; the precedent may well apply in places as physically distant as the southern rim of the former Soviet Union and central Africa. Somalia taught the system first about the existence of failed states and subsequently about the frustration of trying to revive them, a lesson learned and applied by avoiding military intervention in Rwanda and tempering action in Haiti.

No one predicted any of this very far in advance. Communism was not supposed to collapse as an idea and form of government, but it has in all but a few isolated places. The Cold War ended without a bullet being fired. The world's attention was diverted to places most people had never heard of. The resulting image has been one of uncertainty and unpredictability about international relations and the shape of the new international order.

Will the apparent disorder continue, or is a new order emerging around which we can develop an understanding of the post–Cold War world? I think the answer is clearly that a new order is forming. Part of that order was evident and reported in the first (1991) edition of this book: the rising importance of a globalizing international economy dominated by the most advanced states and the technological motor that powers the global economy. What the first edition (and many other analyses at the time) failed to anticipate as it was written in 1990–91 was the disappearance of the old Second (Socialist) World.

What is emerging is a coherent pattern that I call a world of tiers (an idea fundamentally similar to the zones of peace and turmoil that Singer and Wildavsky developed in *The Real World Order*). It suggests, in essence, that the overall system is now dominated by two relatively distinct subsystems, the First and Second Tiers, which roughly correspond to the First and Third Worlds of the Cold War system. Each tier (especially the First) is distinct in economic, political, and military terms, and a major systemic question is how the two groups of states will relate to one another.

This is really not such a new arrangement; how the First and Third Worlds related to one another politically and economically was a Cold War system concern that simply extends into the new order. What is different is that the East–West overlay has disappeared as the Second World has imploded. What we are left with is half the Cold War system.

This system is evolving, and there are many outstanding questions about it that we will address in the pages that follow. A sample of these questions includes: Will the countries of the old Second World end up in the prosperous First Tier or the developing Second Tier? How will the economic intertwining and globalization of the First Tier proceed? Which Second Tier states will join the First Tier, and how? How will the dominant First Tier deal with violence and instability in the Second Tier?

There are many people to be thanked for their assistance in this enterprise. The first edition was researched and written while I served as Visiting Professor of Political Science within the Department of National Security and Strategy at the United States Army War College from 1989 to 1991. I want to thank the college for its material and other assistance, for its encouragement, and for allowing me the time and freedom to work on this manuscript. In particular, I want to thank my two departmental chairs, Cols. Dave Hansen and Dave Hazen, who worked valiantly to understand the needs of a person writing an academic book and to shield that process from some of the army's more intrusive diversions. Moreover, I want to thank my War College colleague, office mate, and subsequent coauthor Gene Brown for helping me fashion the idea of a world of tiers, around which this edition is organized.

Others had a constructive role too. Undergraduate classes at both my home institution, the University of Alabama, and Dickinson College served as captive audiences while I attempted to hone the original ideas. This second edition was completed while I was on sabbatical leave, and I want to thank the University of Alabama, and especially the Department of Political Science, for making the time and resources available to facilitate my work. My editor, Michael Weber, gently but firmly wrestled me to ground on both substantive and mechanical aspects of the manuscript, notably my propensity to overquote. The work was also reviewed by outside readers, whose anonymous comments were of considerable value. Joyce Kaufman offered especially valuable comments.

Finally, I would like to thank my wife, Donna, and my son, Ric. The first edition was written in original draft during 1990, and both had to endure that process. Like many authors, I am not the most communicative person in the world while writing, and they suffered that patiently. Moreover, Ric deserves specials thanks for producing the map in chapter 4 and the table in chapter 8.

1

Bloodless Revolution to New Order

"It was the best of times; it was the worst of times," Charles Dickens began *A Tale of Two Cities*, his description of revolutionary Paris in the eighteenth century. The ferment and pace of change that he described could be applied to the contemporary scene: the best of times has witnessed the virtual disappearance of global communism and the end of the Cold War; the worst of times marks the disorder of transition from one international system to another and the bloody artifacts of change in places like the former Yugoslavia, Somalia, and Rwanda.

What we have witnessed in the past decade, beginning with the rise of Mikhail S. Gorbachev to power in the then–Soviet Union in 1985, is a powerful, all-encompassing process of change that has fundamentally altered the international system and the basic relations among its members. Such transformations occur only occasionally in international relations: the end of World War II created basic change, as did the French Revolution and Napoleonic Wars, and the Treaty of Westphalia ending the Thirty Years War in 1648. Somewhat less seismic change accompanied the end of World War I.[1]

These basic systems changes share with Dickens's depiction the common thread of war and bloodshed as cause and effect. Major wars involving the most powerful political units have, through human history, been the major catalysts for basic change; usually they result in an altered balance of power that requires a redefinition of how the system operates.[2] The more basic and traumatic the war's outcome, the more the system is changed.

The change currently unfolding is utterly different from any change in the nation-state system (generally agreed to have become the basic system structure with the Peace of Westpahlia) to date in one most basic respect: it came about without a major war as its stimulus. It has, at least to this point, truly been a bloodless revolution. Although in places like Bosnia and Kuwait violence that probably would not have been allowed to occur during the Cold War scarred the transition, nonetheless the change has been achieved largely without the sword.

The key event in this change, of course, has been the disintegration of the Soviet Union into fifteen successor states, none of which officially retains communism as its political system, and the disappearance of communism throughout Eastern and Central Europe. Half the Cold War has melted away. The great ideological divide is found only in isolated pockets: a People's Republic of China wedded to Stalinist politics that recommends against Marxist economics (the system of so-called market communism); a failing Cuba for whom defection—recently of a number of its world-class athletes—is a major concern; a Vietnam that is turning westward; and a North Korea brandishing the possibility of nuclear weapons as a form of death rattle probably prefatory to reunification of the Korean peninsula under market democracy.

How do we understand this remarkable process of change? In the first edition of this book, drafted during 1989 and 1990, the author posited eight propositions about how the system was changing and the probable direction of change. Although they seem less remarkable today than they may have previously, they remain a reasonable conceptual way to begin the discussion. Having established those parameters, we will then move to a kind of cursory overview of four chronological steps in the evolution of the Cold War system to the new order. The chapter will conclude with an introduction to the evolving shape of the new system based on the concept of a world of tiers.

Eight Propositions

Predicting the past is, of course, a less perilous task then predicting the future. When these eight propositions were originally formulated, some of them looked at a past not yet fully understood and at a future whose clarity was marred by the fact that it had not yet occurred and appeared especially unforeseeable. Today, most of these propositions are about a past on which there is considerably greater perspective and on a future that is now occurring or has occurred. Luckily, the dynamics they describe are still largely accurate.

The first three propositions attempt to describe what happened in 1989 and why. The next three describe the period of transition and the forces influencing that transition. The last two attempt to identify forces in the emerging order.

1. *The events of 1989 culminated a process of change that has begun to alter fundamentally the Cold War international system and that undid much of the post-1945 organization of the world.*

The revolutions of 1989 that began in the last quarter of that year produced an enormous rush of change largely unanticipated in the West. Its visible beginning was in September, when the Polish people elected an anticommunist government that was installed without Soviet interference, an event unprecedented in itself. Hungary followed suit in October by electing a reformist noncommunist government, and the Berlin Wall was breached that same month. In November, the velvet revolution overthrew Communist rule in Czechoslovakia and brought Vaclav Havel to power, the Communist leadership of East Germany (notably Communist leader Erich Honecker) was imprisoned on charges of corruption and misgovernment, and the Berlin Wall fell, its pieces becoming the souvenir of the year. In December, Romanian Communist leader Nikolai Ceausescu and his wife were assassinated and the Communist regime destroyed. In 1990, Bulgaria renounced communism and Germany reunited.

These were turbulent days where the pace of change was "such that much of what experts write is obsolete before it gets into print."[3] As we shall see in the next section, the roots of that change go back to internal events in the Soviet Union that began to surface earlier and could have been seen if one looked hard enough and made the assumption, by no means universally accepted at the time, that change was more than cosmetic disinformation meant to delude a gullible West into lowering its collective guard.

The events of 1989 represented a watershed in the post–World War II period. As Soviet writer Sergei Karaganov said at the time, it was "the time when history is really made (as opposed to the last few years which has been history unmade)."[4] It produced a situation of fluidity in which both leaders and observers were left uncertain of the future direction of the international system.[5]

In retrospect, there are significant parallels between 1989 and 1945. In 1945, the world's largest war had ended, and the old order had been shattered. Reconstructing that order took a period of time where the central systemic question was what the relationship between the two remaining major powers, the United States and the Soviet Union, would be. By the end of the 1940s, it was clear that the wartime collaboration could not be continued and that confrontation would be the central feature. In 1945, that outcome was not so obvious.

We are at just about that juncture today. The Cold War system took nearly a half decade to become entrenched, and about the same amount of time has elapsed since the Cold War system disintegrated with the formal dissolution of the Soviet Union at midnight on December 31, 1991. Forming a new set of relationships has been more leisurely, because there has been no need to repair the destruction of a major hot war; nevertheless, a world of tiers is emerging as the dominant organizational concept in the new order.

2. *A major precipitant of the end of the Cold War has been the deadlock in East–West military affairs.*

There are several reasons militating toward the Soviet decision to end the Cold War that will be examined in subsequent pages. These include the internal stagnation of the Soviet state and society, as demonstrated by a weakened economy and a progressively uncompetitive technological sector. All these created pressures for internal reform under the banner of *perestroika* that Gorbachev unveiled in print in 1987 when he published a book with that title.[6]

The major cause was the deadlock in the military relationship, a situation caused, ironically enough, by military—and especially thermonuclear—might. By the early 1980s, and even far before, the United States and the Soviet Union had amassed such enormous arsenals of destruction against one another that, if war occurred, the result would be the likely destruction of both. At the pinnacle of this awesome destructive capacity were the arsenals of so-called strategic nuclear weapons: missile-borne nuclear bombs aimed at one another's heartland and against which neither could protect itself.

The result was *necessary peace*,[7] a situation of peace created not out of goodwill but from the realization that war was potentially suicidal and thus had to be avoided at all costs. The purpose of strategic nuclear force on each side was to deter the other. This balance, and the potential horrors it contained, became the central reality and focal point of the Cold War military confrontation.

This confrontation and stalemate were not an altogether bad thing. Gradually, both sides came to realize the impermissibility of nuclear war, which Soviet leaders back to Nikita S. Khrushchev and American presidents back to Dwight D. Eisenhower had acknowledged publicly. The unique horror of thermonuclear holocaust, however, created a kind of nuclear allergy that made the beneficial effects of confrontation and stalemate hard to recognize.

In retrospect, it is clear that nuclear weapons stabilized superpower relations, made *any* war between them less likely,[8] and ultimately contributed to the decision to dismantle the competition. They stabilized relations and made war less likely as both superpowers came to realize that any war involving them on opposite sides was a potential nuclear war, wherein the probability of escalation could not be calculated in advance. As a result, *all* military conflict had to be avoided, meaning that the extensive and expensive preparations for a conventional war in Europe between the North Atlantic Treaty Organization (NATO) and the Warsaw Pact became an exercise in practicing for a conflict that had to be avoided at all costs. The military confrontation at all levels became increasingly hollow and ritualistic.

When that competition also became ruinously expensive to the Soviet Union, the stalemate made the decision to call off the Cold War all the more necessary and sensible. Both sides were losing the military battle because of the effect on their pocketbooks. Faced with the need for comprehensive reform of the economy and the devotion of all possible resources to that change, jettisoning the Cold War made good sense. The nuclear weapons did not, of course, disappear, but by 1994 the United States and Russia had agreed to retarget them from one another toward areas in the world's oceans.

3. *The major product of the revolutions of 1989 has been to complete the end of the Cold War as an institutional confrontation between the eastern and western halves of Europe (including the United States).*

The roots of ending the Cold War, as mentioned, preceded the physical revolutions of the latter part of 1989, which are as much the effect as the cause of change. In chapter 4, we will examine the dynamics of reform and change in the former Soviet Union that contributed to forming policies by which Soviet power was removed from Eastern Europe, making the breakdown of Eastern European communism possible. The effect was to begin the process of canceling the Cold War.

Two events in 1991 provided the wrecker's ball for the Cold War. The first was the formal dismantling of the Warsaw Pact on July 1, 1991, by a vote of its members in Prague, Czechoslovakia. The effect was to leave the Western alliance with no counterpart; in the current debate, the major question now is how (or if) to admit the members of the Warsaw Pact into NATO, a process begun in early 1994 through the Partnership for Peace (P4P). The second was the formal dissolution of the Soviet Union at the end of the year, a decision announced by Gorbachev on December 17, 1991, ratifying the joint announcement of December 8, 1991, by the leaders of Russia, Ukraine, and Byelarussia (now Byelarus) that the Soviet Union had been disbanded and replaced by a Commonwealth of Independent States (CIS).

We are still assessing the permanence of these changes and will consider them in some depth as we proceed. In a tentative way, however, we can assert the unlikelihood of reversion on three grounds that speak to fears that the threat might return.

First is the chance of the emergence of a reassertive, possibly Communist, and certainly expansionist Russia. This is, of course, possible and has roots in a Russian history of expansion and empire. What makes this unlikely, however, is the effect such a phenomenon would have on economic and political development in the country. A revanchist Russia would be cut off economically from an international mainstream it has desperately sought to court, and it knows this would be the consequence. Moreover, the failed coup of 1991 against Gorbachev and the effective showdown by Boris Yeltsin of the Communist-dominated CIS parliament in 1993 speaks to support for the political system. Russian elections in December 1993 did not exactly embrace reform. Their unmarred occurrence, however, is historic, and they did ratify the Yeltsin constitution that is the framework within which future change is scheduled to occur.

The second question deals with the emergence of an aggressive Russian military in opposition to the West, thus reopening the military threat to Western Europe. This, too, is extremely unlikely. In addition to the dilatory effect such a movement would have on Russian and Western economic relations, the Russians have neither the military wherewithal nor intentions for such activity. Beyond its continuing nuclear might, the Russian military is a force that can project power within the bounds of the old Soviet Union but not beyond, and it has adjusted its military doctrine to that reality. Moreover, it would have to fight its way across parts of the former Soviet Union (notably the Ukraine) and Eastern Europe before it could even get to Germany.[9]

The third question addresses the likelihood of reversion in Eastern

Europe. As we will see in chapter 5, the prospects vary among the former states of the Warsaw Pact, with democratic market conditions taking hold firmly in the northern tier states such as Poland, Hungary, and the Czech Republic, while less progress is occurring in southern tier states such as Bulgaria and Romania. Nonetheless, the dramatic rejection of the Communist model across Eastern Europe was so savage and swift that it is unlikely it could be reversed. The Communist regimes were not only economic failures, they were also clearly viewed as "an affront to the nationalist aspirations of citizens who had an intense pride in their own heritage."[10]

4. *The system is entering a period of transition and uncertainty. It will not, however, revert to its old form.*

The possibility of reversion seems less likely today than it did in 1991, when the propositions originally appeared. Political democracy remains extremely fragile in Russia and nonexistent in a number of other successor republics, some of which are ruled by people who now refer to themselves as former Communists. The old Soviet military has broken apart and been replaced by independent military forces within the successor states, many of which (notably Ukraine) openly view Russia as their primary military problem. The states of Eastern Europe look progressively westward to the general prosperity of the market democracies.

There are indeed great uncertainties about the future of the old Communist world, but one point stands out: communism as a competitor ideology to the West has simply ceased to exist. As noted, isolated communist regimes hang on in the world, but they are not evangelical, and no responsible figures extol the virtues either of Marxist socialism or of political Stalinism (although some still practice the latter). One practical effect of this ideological vacuum is an ideological agreement within the system probably unmatched since absolutist monarchism was the universal ideology during the eighteenth century. More important, the vacuum means there is no ideological rallying cry around which a return to the old system could form.

5. *As the military element of power becomes a less effective way for major states to influence one another, the application of power will be based progressively on the economic strength a nation possesses.*

Among the most salient characteristics of the emerging international system is the political and economic similarity of the major nations: all are political democracies with some form of market economy. As such, their values are overwhelmingly similar, to the point that it is impossible to think realistically of military conflict among any members of what we will call the First Tier. As the First Tier encompasses all the most powerful nations in the system, military prowess among these nations is simply irrelevant to their interaction.

Status in the twenty-first century will increasingly be gauged in terms of economic competitiveness, which will largely be measured in terms of preeminence in "high technology." A major trend and force in the world today is the internationalization of economic activity, a movement that has largely been fueled by advances in knowledge production and transmission, which collectively defines high technology. The result is a thorough intertwining of companies and nations: technologies leapfrog national boundaries; international financial markets operate globally on a twenty-four-hour basis; the subcomponent mix of goods contains so many parts from so many countries that it is difficult to put a national identity on products; and companies are owned by stockholders from many countries.

This phenomenon has transformed the locus of power in the world. The basis of change has been the mastery of high technology, the revolutionary growth in knowledge development and generation (largely the result of advances in computers and computer-related technologies), information processing and dissemination (the telecommunications revolution), and a highly diverse set of associated and derivative technologies. These technologies compose the so-called Third Industrial, or Information, Revolution.[11] Their growing symbol for the future is captured in the concept of the "information superhighway." Competition in this arena has been a primary thrust of economic policy by the Clinton administration within the United States.

6. *Because of economic internationalization caused in part by high technology, states will have a progressively difficult time regulating that activity. The consequences will include dilutions of effective sovereignty and diminished national applications of power.*

The high-technology revolution produces great changes and uncertainties. There is the distinct possibility that high technology will generate historical discontinuities such that past experience will be a poor guide for future policy decisions.[12] The race in high technology is currently triangular among the major First Tier powers (the United States, the European Community, and Japan); it is a competition that extends to the whole emerging idea of economic security.[13]

This phenomenon particularly concerns the Russians, as it did the Soviets, who are well behind in the competition for reasons discussed later. Recognition of this uncompetitiveness and its implications was a primary driver for the reformers who unintentionally began the process of the Soviet demise partly out of this concern. As one then-Soviet commentator put it, "The basic reason for this shift is the inability of the [Communist] socio-economic system to adjust to the scientific and technological revolution."[14] Gorbachev admitted as much in a major speech in 1990: "We were nearly one of the last to realize that in an age of information science, the most expensive asset is knowledge, the breadth of mental outlook and innovation. . . . Yes, there are shortages of resources and technology."[15] This recognition has dual effects. Power status in a world of tiers is largely calculated by technologically driven economic competitiveness; to fall behind is to lose status. Moreover, the application of high technology to military matters affects military preeminence, a historic Russian long suit in danger of eclipse.

There is another consequence of the international character of technology and economic activity. As both become increasingly internationalized, they move progressively beyond the effective control of national governments. Modern telecommunications compromises the control over information flow—witness China's frustration in its 1989 attempt to censor the Tiananmen Square upheaval from its own people in the face of facsimile (fax) transmission of *samizdat* newsletters from overseas Chinese students. Similarly, in an international economy, individual states will have fewer available instruments of national economic power to employ.[16] Most observers agree this problem of reduced practical sovereign control will only get worse, especially as supranational economic unions like the North American Free Trade Area (NAFTA) and the Asia-Pacific Economic Cooperation (APEC) come into existence and expand and as the technological base becomes increasingly international.[17]

The future ramifications are likely to be extensive. If states cannot effectively regulate the activities of firms operating on their own territory or owned by their nationals, they can hardly force those firms to do their bidding—a dilution of effective sovereignty. This in turn means the arsenal of effective economic levers of power is diluted. This effect is likely to be most pronounced with regard to the emerging stateless corporations—firms so thoroughly international in ownership, management, work force, and product composition that they cannot be identified with a single nation-state. As economic activity becomes more international within a system of free markets, the values of international commerce are likely to become privatized—based on the bottom line of corporate profit rather than some form of public equity.

7. Third World (what we will call Second Tier) problems will increase in salience in the new order. Regional conflict will become an important national security concern.

The so-called Third, or Developing, World—the Second Tier—has taken on a different significance in the current and future international system. During the Cold War, the developing world's importance within the international system was derivative; it was a place where the superpowers competed for influence, and interest seldom extended beyond that competition to the real problems facing the Second Tier.

The results were mixed. Positively, the overlay of East–West competition provided resources for development, the primary need of the Second Tier, that would not otherwise have been available as both sides sought to buy influence (or to deny influence to the other). Also, when the superpowers became patrons of opposite sides in regional conflicts, they tended to moderate the ferocity with which those conflicts were conducted. The motivation was not, of course, pure; the reason for moderation was to lessen the likelihood that either or both superpowers would be drawn physically into conflicts that might escalate to direct confrontation between them. Negatively, the effect was to frame problems in East–West, Communist–anticommunist terms that had very little to do with the real structure of problems in various Second Tier regions.

The end of Cold War removes that veil, revealing a Second Tier that is the source of nearly all the violence and instability in the new international system. Regional conflicts between old rivals (India and Pakistan and the Koreas, for example) are made more difficult and dangerous by the introduction of deadly weaponry such as nuclear, biological, and chemical (NBC) munitions and ballistic missile delivery systems that may eventually imperil the First Tier as well. In addition, the wave of national self-determination that has attended the end of the Cold War has produced a spate of secessionary violence that threatens to balkanize much of the Second Tier. This phenomenon is currently most evident in the crumbling Communist world in former Yugoslavia (Bosnia) and within some of the successor states of the Soviet Union (Armenia, Azerbaijan, Georgia, and Tajikistan). The phenomenon is almost certain to spread to Africa, and the problem of "failed states" (states that seem incapable of self-governance) is evident in places as distant as Somalia and as close as Haiti.

Two unrelated questions stand out about this phenomenon. The first and most basic is whether the wealthy countries of the First Tier care enough to involve themselves in the Second Tier's problems. Beyond access to Persian Gulf petroleum, there are very few interests that most of the First Tier has in the Second Tier that are vital (worth going to war over) in any traditional geopolitical sense. Moreover, it is not clear how much of the conflict, whether it is in the form of regional conflicts or internal wars, can spill over into and affect the First Tier. The other side of this issue is the assertion of universal humanitarian interests that the international community must enforce, a position most associated with the United Nations and its assertive secretary-general, Boutros Boutros-Ghali.

The second question is whether the formerly Communist states (the old Second World) will end up in the First Tier or the Second Tier. In most cases, consignment to the Second Tier seems most likely, as in the old saw that the Soviet Union was a "Third World country with nuclear weapons." The prospects for joining the political and economic mainstream of prosperous market democracies may be open to a few states in Eastern Europe such as Poland, Hungary, and the Czech Republic and in a few of the successor states such as the Baltic states. For the rest, slipping into developing world status seems more likely.

8. One of the characteristics of the new international order may be a gradual process of economic and political democratization of the globe.

A nearly euphoric glow surrounded the revolutions of 1989, as communist dictatorships fell and were replaced by putatively popular (although, reflection has shown, not necessarily democratic) alternatives.

As John Lewis Gaddis put it, "Liberty suddenly found itself pushing against an open door."[18] At the same time, democratic systems have begun to take hold in much of South America and along the Pacific Rim, allowing the conclusion that the Western ideals of economic and political freedom (market economies and democracy) may be becoming universal. Certainly with the collapse of communism as a viable intellectual alternative, there is currently no ideological alternative—with the possible and limited exception of fundamentalist Islam. With the exception of China (which justifies its stand as a means to avoid Soviet-style dismemberment), there are few open advocates of authoritarian rule, even if there are still practitioners.

There are reasons to restrain our enthusiasm for the general spread of democracy. Samuel P. Huntington, for instance, argues that democratization tends to come in waves (the current one being the third wave) that are followed by retrenchment as some democracies fail. He observes that the third wave has probably crested.[19] The probability of reversal is most likely in the so-called fragile democracies of places like South America, which lack a democratic tradition. Reversal may also occur if political democratization is unmatched with economic prosperity. This concern is particularly acute for Russia; the most plausible "horror scenario" for that country has the citizenry reaching a Faustian bargain with an authoritarian movement, trading democracy for the hope of prosperity. Finally, reflection allows us to distinguish between freedom and democracy. Freedom for much of the former Soviet Union means the absence of Russian domination and the ability to forge ethnically exclusive communities, a phenomenon quite the opposite of democratization.[20]

Evolutionary Steps

A second way to gain perspective on where we are in progressing from the Cold War system to the future is by looking at the process as a matter of evolution. To that end, the process can be thought of as having had four essential steps: the weakening of the Cold War structure; the revolutions of 1989; the aftermath of the revolutions of 1989; and the transitional period between the end of the Cold War and the emergence of its successor. Discussing each briefly will aid our perspective on the present and, hopefully, the direction of the future.

We are still uncertain of the exact time at which the march of events leading to the end of the Cold War began. The ascension of Gorbachev following the death of Konstantin Chernenko certainly represents a convenient and dramatic change point in retrospect, although it was not so evident at the time. In light of how we now view Gorbachev, it is worthwhile to remember that when he came to power, there was little evidence or speculation that he would be any different from his predecessors. That he would lead a reform movement that would dismantle the Communist state in the Soviet Union, preside over the physical dissolution of the Soviet Union itself, and ultimately cause the Cold War to end would have been laughable ideas at the time.

The genesis of the reforms that started the process go back to the 1970s, into what the Soviets came to describe as the "era of stagnation"; the Soviet economy simply ceased to grow, a flat trend line made all the more dramatic in the 1980s by the enormous expansion in the First Tier states fueled by the high-technology revolution. Even this phenomenon was mostly ignored by a West more fixated on the number of Soviet ICBMs and tanks.

The need for economic reform created an engine for change that became a runaway train, as we shall see in chapter 4. An economy progressively unresponsive and uncompetitive could ultimately only be revived by tearing down the old edifice and starting over. That was *not* what Gorbachev and his colleagues had in mind when they started what they believed was a process of "fine-tuning" socialism; the problem was that socialism simply did not work, a conclusion that Gorbachev, a believing Marxist, came to accept reluctantly. Because the Soviet state and economy were so inextricably intertwined, one could not be altered without the other being affected.

These economic woes, and particularly their intractability, made a continuing Cold War an unaffordable luxury. The Reagan administration, through its enormous military buildup, probably contributed to this conclusion by rendering the arms competition economically ruinous for the Soviets. A hemorrhaging economy and political system could also not sustain subsidizing weak and unpopular Communist regimes elsewhere. They had to be cut loose.

The result was the revolutions of 1989. During the summer, Gorbachev and his foreign minister, Eduard Shevardnadze (the current president of Georgia), visited the capitals of Eastern Europe and delivered a harsh message to the unreconstructed Communist leaderships: Come to terms with your people; there are no Soviet tanks to keep you in power any longer. Gorbachev's hope probably was that the result would be a new generation of reformist Communist leaders like himself in power. What he got, of course, was something very different.

The revolutions shocked the West. They were unanticipated, as was the absence of a violent Soviet response. Gorbachev had told the world —in *Perestroika* and in numerous speeches—that his country had abandoned the so-called Brezhnev Doctrine, which had provided the policy justification for intervening in Afghanistan and elsewhere, and he had completed the painful extrication of Soviet troops from Afghanistan. Yet, we were surprised when there was no "Warsaw Fall" equivalent to the violent crushing of the Prague Spring twenty-one years earlier.

The ease and speed with which the revolutions occurred were equally shocking. Apparently granitelike regimes were swept aside with remarkable ease, revealing Communist rule throughout Eastern Europe as little more than a Potemkin village, a false facade with no substance.

The remnants of the Cold War unraveled between the end of 1989 and the formal end of the Cold War with the dissolution of the Soviet state at the end of 1991. The reunification of Germany stands out as a most visible symbol of change. From 1945 until 1990, a permanently divided and weakened Germany had been a prime pillar of Soviet foreign policy, the bedrock that guaranteed World War II's eastern front would not be revisited on another generation of Soviets. Yet, when the largely grass-roots process of unification began, the Gorbachev leadership did absolutely nothing about it other than to reach out for economic handouts as reward for its acquiescence.

It is probably fitting that the end of the Cold War coincided with Gorbachev's fall from power as the leader of a defunct Soviet state that symbolized the Cold War's end. Gorbachev was the overarching figure of the period between 1985 and 1991. He was the catalyst of a process that produced the fundamental changes we are now trying to understand, but he could neither fully comprehend nor even come close to controlling that process once engaged. Had anyone been able to show Gorbachev an accurate picture of the world on January 1, 1992, when he began his reforms, he almost certainly would not have engaged the process. By doing so, Gorbachev will undoubtedly go down in history as the single figure most responsible for ending the Cold War—the Great Transitioner.

With the end of the Cold War, we entered a period of transition, trying to order or reorder the system. It has been a confusing task. For one thing, most of those who have tried to guide or to understand the changes are products and students of a Cold War system that we understood and that had shaped our view of the world. Suddenly that construct has disappeared, and there is little precedent for the present and future. Older constructs like bipolarity and multipolarity are not very helpful guides to the new order. For that matter, there is very real disagreement about whether there *is* a new order.[21]

The transition continues, and there is nothing like consensus about the shape of the future. It is, for instance, interesting that as of the end of 1993, there was substantial agreement over what the system is not: it is the not–Cold War, or post–Cold War, world. There was not, however, any agreement on a term to describe what the system *is*—what to call it.

A World of Tiers

While the shape and nature of the new international system are not yet crystalline, a framework is beginning to appear that suggests the new international order consists of two distinct, almost independent subsystems that are so unlike one another that they can only be described and understood separately. Max Singer and the late Aaron Wildavsky, in their pathfinding book *The Real World Order*, describe these subsystems as the zones of peace and the zones of turmoil.[22] Franz Schurmann refers to a system marked by Northern and Southern Tiers that he argues has been evolving since the 1970s.[23] Richard Rosecrance makes oblique reference to such a system in discussing what he calls a "new concert of powers."[24] Samuel P. Huntington's "clash of civilizations" is not dissimilar.[25] I call this emerging system a world of tiers.

The central contention of this formulation is that there is not a single, unified system at work in the current construction of international relations. Instead, there are two distinct subsystems, the First and Second Tiers. Each tier has its own distinct characteristics and patterns of interaction, and each pattern has different consequences for the system as a whole. Much of what is not yet settled about the new international system is how the two tiers will relate to one another.

The idea of tiers updates the way scholars have described the world to reflect the end of the Cold War. During the Cold War system, it was commonplace to divide the international system into three or four "worlds": a First World composed of the most advanced industrial democracies; a Second World made up of the Communist or socialist countries; a Third World that included most of the developing countries of the Afro-Asian and Latin American areas; and even a Fourth World composed of the most helpless, even destitute countries of the world.

The end of the Cold War requires changing those designations for the most obvious reason that the Second World has essentially disappeared. The remaining Communist countries are geographically and politically too isolated to form any coherent category, and their numbers are almost certainly going to dwindle. Of the remaining Communist regimes, only China is of real consequence, and calling China Communist or Socialist in the traditional sense strains the meaning of the term. North Korea's apparent nuclear program poses an interim threat to a South Korea poised on the edge of joining the First Tier, but joining the South Korean economic miracle is a more likely route for the North Koreans than incinerating a prosperity of which they could become part.

The designation of two tiers is straightforward. The First Tier includes the twenty-five or so wealthiest countries of the world, what has traditionally been thought of as the First World and what President Clinton calls the "ring of market democracies." All members share the political ideology of democracy, have thriving market-based economies, and participate in the increasingly intertwined global economy. The relations among these states of the "first sphere of security" are marked by "peace, prosperity, and stability."[26] Membership in the First Tier is open to any state that meets its dual criteria, similar to those for membership in the European Community (EC): stable democratic political systems and advanced market-based economies. A number of states qualify as near-members but fail on one criterion or the other: they lack a stable democracy (Korea and Argentina, for instance) or a democracy at all (China), or they fall short of the required economic status (Mexico prior to NAFTA). It may well prove that the growing phenomenon of regional trading arrangements will provide a vehicle for funneling additional states into the First Tier: the EC for some of the Eastern European countries; NAFTA for Mexico, Chile, Argentina, and, later, others; and APEC for some of the most advanced Pacific Rim nonmembers.

The Second Tier consists of all the states outside the First Tier. As such, it accounts for the vast majority of the world's population and nation-states; Singer and Wildavsky's zone of turmoil, for instance, encompasses six-sevenths of world population.[27] It also includes very diverse states under one umbrella—from prosperous near-democracies on the verge of First Tier membership (Brazil, Taiwan), to extremely destitute places (Mali, Bangladesh), to anomalies such as the oil-rich monarchies of the Middle East. As a result of this diversity, the Second Tier is further divided into six subcategories, which both facilitates differentiating among them and suggests a path of progression toward the Clintonian goal of expanding the ring of market democracies.

The division of the globe into tiers is hardly a radical departure. As already noted, similar ideas are entering the literature, and the idea simply updates depictions that go back to the 1950s, when the emergence of the Third World of "developing" countries from colonial rule created the need for new sets of descriptions. The problem then and now was how to devise categories that did not seem paternalistic or demeaning: developed as opposed to less developed or underdeveloped, for instance. The designation of First and Second Tiers, alas, may fall prey to the same criticism, since it may suggest ordinality.

The designation and elaboration of tiers helps organize understanding of the contemporary system. It allows us to focus on the very real differences between and among states of the two tiers, how the tiers interact among themselves (intratier relations), how those intratier relations are different within the two tiers, how the two tiers interact with one another, and what consequences each of these distinctions has on international relations.

The First Tier

The First Tier is roughly the equivalent of what was called the First World in the Cold War international system. Its core is the so-called Group of Seven (G–7) leading economic powers—the United States, Germany, Japan, France, Great Britain, Italy, and Canada—which have become a policy-formulating and -influencing bloc as their series of "economic summits" has become institutionalized. The membership of the First Tier currently extends to the membership of the European Economic Area (the European Community and the European Free Trade Association) and to Australia and New Zealand. The membership list is somewhat arbitrary and is subject to change as other states qualify for inclusion. A number of states of the Pacific Rim, notably the "Four Tigers" (South Korea, Singapore, Hong Kong, and Taiwan), are prime candidates, although the status of the latter two will be affected by projected or possible levels of association with China. It is conceivable that states could slip from First to Second Tier status by renouncing democracy or falling into economic disarray, but such a reversion is unlikely.

The list is also notable for those not included. It conspicuously excludes all the states of the former Second World. Almost all those states fail to meet both criteria, although some are making strides toward both democratization and market economies (Poland, Hungary, and the Czech Republic, for instance, which may use the EC as a mechanism for inclusion). China's continued adherence to authoritarianism excludes the world's fastest-growing economy, although economic prosperity and freedom are likely to erode authoritarian rule over time. The successor states of the Soviet Union, with the possible exception of the Baltic states, face dim prospects on either criterion, although the First Tier has security motivations to assist the largest and potentially most powerful successor states (notably Russia, Ukraine, Byelarus, and Kazakhstan).

The countries of the First Tier share several common characteristics that define and dominate the evolving international system. The first and foremost characteristic is a *shared commitment to political democracy and market-based economy*. This combination is hardly coincidental. Political democracy and market economies are essentially the political and economic expressions of freedom; given the freedom to choose one, most people will choose both.[28] Moreover, the two reinforce one another: politically free people are more likely to be happy and productive than are repressed people, and economic prosperity usually breeds the demand for political freedom (a dynamic the Chinese leadership will soon have to confront). Thus, "the inseparable nature of political and economic change as well as the politics of economics"[29] has a synergistic effect.

This commonality of values has great consequence for relations among First Tier states. It means that the most important relations between them—political and economic—start from a fundamentally similar base and that their similarities far outweigh their differences. Although they differ in areas such as history, culture, and religion, their commonalities overbalance their differences. They share a common worldview and set of preferences about how the world should be ordered.

Second, the First Tier *contains the most important, core powers of the contemporary world.* In the evolving international order, a major criterion for effective power is economic preeminence driven by technological proficiency. Being at the forefront of high technology is one of the defining differences between the tiers, because it is the basis for economic strength. The First Tier states lead the global economy, and their leadership is demonstrated militarily as well, as demonstrated by the technologies employed in the Persian Gulf War.

This distinction does not mean there are no consequential states outside the First Tier. Russia's sheer size and possession of nuclear weapons makes it important and explains the First Tier's nurturing of Russian change. As the world's largest potential market with the most vibrant rate of economic growth, China is of consequence, and an India whose population may exceed China's in the twenty-first century cannot be ignored. While each of these states is important for some purpose, what defines the First Tier is its comprehensive centrality to the system. The distinction also means that the most important states share a commonality of outlook and values unprecedented since the eighteenth century.

This commonality leads to a third characteristic: *the absence of conflict with military potential that could lead to war between First Tier states.* The reason derives from the shared value of political democracies: free peoples do not initiate wars with other free peoples, and their common values mean they have little to fight about. This does not mean that states of the First Tier will not fight wars; it means they will not fight among themselves. The absence of universal democracy guarantees that war will continue, but, as Huntington puts it, "If democracy continues to spread, wars should become less frequent."[30]

This characteristic defines a tremendously important—possibly the most important—difference between the Cold War system and the future. Because all the most consequential members of the state system belong to the peaceful First Tier, there is no military confrontation in the world that threatens the integrity of the system itself. This is an enormous improvement in world affairs. During the Cold War, the possibility of a thermonuclear confrontation between the superpowers threatened the world system; deterring such a conflict was quite rightly the central systemic concern.

That concern has all but evaporated. It is still physically possible for war to break out between Russia and the West if, for instance, Russia went to revert to expansionist authoritarianism. Short of that (or even if that were the case), it is hard to imagine the motivations for such a war. More to the point, it strains credulity to the breaking point to conjure *any* war between members of the First Tier, much less war that would threaten the integrity of the system.[31]

Moreover, the predominant role of the United States as the remaining superpower (the only power with global economic *and* military reach) provides a generally stabilizing influence.[32]

A growing interdependence among First Tier economies provides a fourth characteristic and stabilizing force. The idea of interdependence can be traced back to the 1960s and 1970s, as the multinational corporations began to penetrate foreign borders and hopes arose for a more cooperative, peaceful environment. In the contemporary scene (discussed more fully in chapter 3), the First Tier is largely defined as the core of a truly global economy where national borders are of modest economic consequence and where business operates routinely across those borders. A common economic philosophy and set of values combine with modern technology to facilitate this interchange. Competition between firms and between countries on economic issues continue in arenas such as the General Agreement on Tariffs and Trade (GATT) and may even temporarily be increased if regional economic arrangements such as NAFTA increase. The likelihood that relationships could seriously deteriorate is vitiated by the growing intertwining of economies. Economic commonality contributes much more to First Tier tranquility than economic disagreements roil those relationships.

The role of military power in the First Tier forms a fifth characteristic: *the principal limitation on applying military force will be public opinion, not military capability*. Because of technological factors, the First Tier has an enormous and widening military capability advantage over the countries of the Second Tier; smaller but more sophisticated First Tier armed forces will, for the foreseeable future, be capable of defeating larger but more primitive Second Tier military forces. One of the lessons of Operation Desert Storm, for instance, is that the United States–led coalition could have defeated Iraq with far fewer forces than were actually sent. The military imbalance present in that war is the one way in which the Persian Gulf War can be said to have been the harbinger of the future.

Public opinion will, however, dictate when and where the First Tier uses its forces. Because of the tranquillity within the First Tier, there will be few if any occasions to use force within the First Tier, where interests are most important and where force could thus be most easily justified. Rather, most opportunities will arise in areas of the Second Tier that are basically unfamiliar to most publics and where important interests are not apparent. In those circumstances, it is difficult to predict when public support will and will not be forthcoming. More specifically, the preeminent role of the United States means that *American* public opinion will have a disproportionate voice in where the First Tier employs force. The "battleground" for much of this debate will likely be the Security Council of the United Nations, where public opinion could reactivate the veto power (these dynamics are discussed more fully in chapter 8). First Tier indifference to the carnage in Rwanda in spring 1994 suggests the limits public opinion can place on activism.

A general preference for global peace and stability constitutes the sixth shared characteristic of the First Tier. The motivation is both economic and political. Expanding the ring of market democracies increases the markets for First Tier goods and services, and the promotion of political democracy would expand the list of countries unlikely to go to war with one another. There will always be selective exceptions to this preference: instability in Iraq that resulted in the overthrow of Saddam Hussein would currently represent one such exception; greater destabilization of Cuba eventuating in the fall of Fidel Castro from power would be another.

The major question is the extent to which the First Tier can and will act to promote the spread of peace and stability. Currently, there are two lightning rods of this concern. One concerns the successor states of the Soviet Union, notably Russia, and the question is not whether we should promote democratization and the development of market economies, but rather the extent to which it is possible to do so. The other lightning rod is United Nations activism in the Second Tier with regard to imposing and enforcing the peace. This matter affects both the extent to which the major powers are willing to incur the sacrifices necessary and the plausibility of succeeding in specific missions.

A shared preference to organize the peace around the principle of collective security is the seventh characteristic of the First Tier. Regardless of the extent of involvement in attempting to tranquilize the Second Tier, it is clear that all First Tier states see spreading the task around—burden sharing—as desirable. This is particularly the case for the United States, which will be asked to carry a large amount of the load but which has a public generally aversive to foreign adventures with dubious outcomes. The obvious venue for this activity is, once again, the Security Council of the United Nations, possibly enlarged to include other First Tier members (Germany and Japan are the most often cited candidates) as permanent members. The major potential problem of using the Security Council is that either of the Russian and Chinese vetoes could become obstructionist (for instance, Russia objecting to a multilateral effort in one of the successor states).

The Second Tier

The countries of the Second Tier are more difficult to describe. They lack the commonality and shared values of the countries of the First World. Most (but not all) are noticeably poorer than the First Tier; only a few are political democracies. Most of the world's misery and problems reside in the Second Tier, although those conditions are not evenly distributed. Their deprivation is longstanding and was the source of manipulation within the context of the Cold War geopolitical competition. If we are more aware of the Second Tier's problems, it is because we are no longer focused on Cold War problems.

It is misleading even to think about a single Second Tier. Rather, one can divide those countries into six categories, from those most proximate to First Tier status to those least like the First Tier. At the top are the *structurally developed and stable states*. Generally speaking, these countries have well-developed economies with little structural debt but lack well-established democratic traditions. The Four Tigers are examples. Second, there are the *structurally developed but unstable countries*. The distinction between these states and those in the first category is the existence of large external debt that poses a barrier to further development and has destabilizing political ramifications. Brazil and Mexico are examples.

Third are the *resource-rich but politically underdeveloped countries*, those nations that have high standards of living from resource exploitation but lack what Singer and Wildavsky call "quality economies" (countries with "a highly productive citizenry operating a complex information-intensive economy"[33]) and democratic political traditions. The oil-rich states of the Persian Gulf littoral are obvious examples. Fourth are the *partially developed countries*, those states that have made some progress in both economic and political development but that lag behind the more advanced states. India is a prime example. Fifth are the *potentially developable countries*, those states with some unrealized potential for development. Much of sub-Saharan Africa falls in this category. Last, there are the *undevelopable countries*, those states that lack the human and material wherewithal ever to develop. Formerly designated the Fourth World, Mali, Bangladesh, and Somalia come rapidly to mind.

Despite this diversity, it is possible to discuss the Second Tier using the same set of categories as was applied to the First Tier. One must remember, however, that diversity means a lack of uniformity on any dimension and that each characteristic is just the opposite of its First Tier counterpart.

The absence of common economic and political values is the first characteristic of the Second Tier. Political systems in the Second Tier vary from the last vestiges of communism, to virtually archaic monarchies in parts of the Middle East, to nascent, fragile democracies. There are no real ideological rivals to political democracy in the Second Tier other than the limited appeal of fundamentalist Islam; authoritarianism and even thuggery are practiced, but they are not openly advocated (except, as noted, by the Chinese to avoid a Soviet-style disintegration). As the typology presented above indicates, there is great economic diversity as well, ranging from economies that rival those of some First Tier countries to others that are hopelessly mired in traditional agrarian forms. Moreover, the combinations of political and economic systems create a wide variety of permutations. The result is an absolute absence of political and economic common ground from which to deal with the First Tier, thereby almost encouraging a piecemeal approach toward the Second Tier.

A second characteristic is that *virtually all Second Tier states are peripheral to the overall international system*. This does not mean that all Second Tier states are unimportant or inconsequential. What it does mean, however, is that no Second Tier states are in a true position to engage in actions that threaten either the integrity or the existence of the system. A senseless Russian nuclear attack against the major First Tier countries remains the signal exception to this broad statement, but such an attack is unlikely enough to be reduced to a footnote.

The peripheral nature of the Second Tier *does* mean that none of the wars that might break out within or between Second Tier states pose a direct threat to system integrity. None would automatically draw a sizable number of First Tier states into the fighting, especially on opposite sides, and the regional escalatory prospect for most is slight. Some, notably a new India–Pakistan war over Kashmir, could be quite bloody and could even conceivably escalate to nuclear exchange, but that would not necessarily either threaten the system or result in First Tier involvement. The only place that would inevitably draw in the First Tier would be a renewed threat to Persian Gulf oil. In that case, the First Tier would act in unison, ensuring success. When combined with the general absence of military threat between First Tier states, this means the system has the respite of the absence of system-threatening wars.

The third characteristic of the Second Tier is that it is *the primary locus of violence and instability in the international system.* This is manifested both in internal violence and in regional conflicts or their potential. Internal wars of secession, chaos in the failed and failing states, and struggles for political power are the dominant forms, increasingly expressed in intercommunal and ethnic violence that has been the visible objective of U.N. activities in places such as Somalia and Bosnia. What, if anything, the First Tier can or should do about this problem will be a major issue within the First Tier in the years to come.

Economic dysjunction is a fourth characteristic that contrasts with the growing interdependence of the First Tier. Second Tier states are not only very unlike one another in levels of economic development, they have little if any economic common ground. Beyond the effect this has on forging a common approach to the First Tier for things like developmental assistance, it often places countries of the Second Tier in competition with one another in ways that only increase their marginality within the overall system.

Second Tier states are *limited in their use of military force primarily by military capability*, the fifth characteristic of the area. Second Tier areas such as the Middle East have traditionally devoted greater proportions of their national wealth to military matters than has the First Tier, and the cutback on military spending attending the end of the

Cold War accentuates that trend. The result is not, however, a military capability on a par with the First Tier; arsenals and those who employ them are still uniformly less sophisticated than their First Tier counterparts. This gap between the tiers also means that even the bloodiest conflicts, like that in Bosnia, will be fought largely with hand-held weapons and relatively primitive forms of artillery and armor.

A lesser commitment to peace and stability in the Second Tier represents the sixth characteristic. War and violence as instruments of power are viewed as a viable alternative for solving many internal and some international conflicts in ways utterly absent in the First Tier, where the viability of violence is limited to criminal activity. In much of the Second Tier, the settlement of old grudges remains high on the agenda. The sights of marauding Somali teenagers on machine-gun festooned jeeps (the so-called technicals) or bodies floating in the Rusomo River separating Tanzania from Rwanda are not likely to disappear soon.

In some real sense, the First Tier bears some responsibility for this. European colonialism suppressed but apparently did not remove the vestiges of intergroup hatred where it existed, and Communist authoritarianism left smoldering ethnic and other hatreds, not the "Soviet man" extolled a generation ago. Removing the veil of Cold War competition similarly removes what constraints the superpowers could wield over their clients.

The seventh and final characteristic is *a general, if implicit, preference for collective defense rather than collective security.* This is a preference that many in the Second Tier would certainly deny, but it is likely to emerge if the First Tier adopts an aggressive stance of collective security, especially through the United Nations. It will not take Second Tier countries long to realize that they will be not so much a *part* of the collective security system as the *object* of that system. Within the United Nations, this will likely be manifested in the effective transference of the center of gravity from the Second Tier–dominated General Assembly (where they are in the majority) to the Security Council, where the veto insures First Tier domination.

Conclusion: International Politics in the World of Tiers

The foregoing analysis suggests an altered sense of focus in the way international relations will occur in the future. The Cold War system represented a hierarchical organization based around management of the central military confrontation, and most other concerns—including those with the Second Tier—flowed from the central relationship.

The world of tiers will be dominated by three relatively independent foci. The first will be on the relations within the First Tier. Their content, devoid of military overtones, will be overwhelmingly economic and political, dealing with ongoing relationships between them, how to deal with the increasing intertwining of the global economy, and how to take care of rising phenomena such as the role of regional trading arrangements within a movement toward the GATT goal of free and unfettered commerce.

The second focus will be within the Second Tier. Its content will include an economic component largely expressed in developmental terms, such as progression through the categories of performance (or subtiers) described earlier. These relations will also have a prominent military component, as emerging nations struggle to establish viable polities and to sort out the ethnic and other animosities within and among them. Dealing with the problem of NBC weapons and ballistic missiles in regional conflicts will also be a concern.

The third, and perhaps both most interesting and problematical, focus occurs at the intersection of the tiers: how does the First Tier relate to the Second and vice versa? This is an area where the superior resources by all measures of the First Tier will dominate the agenda: how the First Tier treats the Second will be more important than the other way around.

The First Tier's agenda will likely be debated along two lines. The first is the degree to which the First Tier can and should assist the Second Tier to achieve First Tier status. How much effort can and should be devoted to widening the ring of market democracies? The second is the degree to which the First Tier becomes involved in moderating violence in the Second Tier. The choice is between a more or less selective collective security system that intervenes sometimes but not others (and has yet to decide on the criteria for doing so) and a collective hegemony that attempts to enforce the peace universally. President Clinton threw down the gauntlet of this debate in his 1993 speech at the United Nations, where he said, to paraphrase, that for the United States to participate (say yes) to U.N. peace operations, the United Nations would have to learn to be selective (learn to say no).

The Second Tier lacks the leverage to affect this debate greatly for the next decade or so. The First Tier is largely insulated from the Second except in isolated ways such as occasional terrorism, the prospect of nuclear blackmail, environmental concerns such as burning rain forests, illegal immigration from the Second Tier to the First, and drugs and other criminal activity.

How this new configuration will evolve is our concern in the pages that follow. To understand how we got to where we are requires looking first at the forces that ended the Cold War and also at the dynamics they unleashed. This will permit us to look at the central dynamics of the current situation with some sense of perspective.

Notes

1. The seminal works on systems change remain Morton Kaplan, *System and Process in International Politics* (New York: Wiley, 1957); and Richard Rosecrance, *Action and Reaction in World Politics: International Systems in Perspective* (Boston: Little Brown, 1963).

2. See Donald M. Snow and Eugene Brown, *World Politics Transformed? A World of Tiers* (New York: St. Martin's Press, forthcoming), especially chapter 3.

3. Stanley Hoffmann, "What Should We Do in the World?" *Atlantic Monthly, 264,* 4 (October 1989): 84.

4. Sergei A. Karaganov, "The Year of Europe: A Soviet View," *Survival, 32,* 2 (March–April 1990): 123.

5. John Lewis Gaddis, "Coping with Victory," *Atlantic Monthly, 265,* 5 (May 1990): 49.

6. Mikhail S. Gorbachev, *Perestroika: New Thinking for Our Country and the World* (New York: Harper and Row, 1987).

7. See Donald M. Snow, *The Necessary Peace: Nuclear Weapons and Superpower Relations* (Lexington, MA: Lexington Books, 1987).

8. James Schlesinger, "The Impact of Nuclear Weapons on History," *Washington Quarterly, 16,* 4 (Autumn 1993): 5–16.

9. Edward N. Luttwak, "The Shape of Things to Come," *Commentary, 81,* 6 (June 1990): 22.

10. Steven R. Bowers, "East Europe: Why the Cheering Stopped," *Journal of Social, Political and Economic Studies, 15,* 1 (Spring 1990): 28–29.

11. Daniel Bell, "The World and the United States in 2013," *Daedalus, 116,* 3 (Summer 1987): 11.

12. Harald B. Malmgren, "Technological Challenges to National Economic Policies in the West," *Washington Quarterly, 10,* 2 (Spring 1987): 27.

13. B.R. Inman and Daniel F. Burton, Jr., "Technology and Competitiveness: The New Policy Frontier," *Foreign Affairs, 69,* 2 (Spring 1990): 116. See also Donald M. Snow, *National Security: Defense Policy for a New International Order,* 3d ed. (New York: St. Martin's Press, 1994), chapter 9.

14. Karaganov, "The Year of Europe," 124.

15. Mikhail S. Gorbachev, "Our Ideal Is a Humane, Democratic Socialism," *Vital Speeches of the Day, 56,* 11 (March 15, 1990): 324.

16. Hoffmann, "What We Should Do in the World," makes this point.

17. Malmgren, "Technological Challenges in National Economic Policies of the West," 30.

18. Gaddis, "Coping with Victory," 60.

19. Samuel P. Huntington, *The Third Wave: Democratization in the Late Twentieth Century* (Norman: University of Oklahoma Press, 1991).

20. Amitai Etzioni, "The Evils of Self-Determination," *Foreign Policy, 89* (Winter 1992–93): 21–35.

21. For example, see Joseph S. Nye Jr., "What New World Order?" *Foreign Affairs, 71,* 2 (Spring 1992): 83–96. More recently, see Robert G. Neumann, "The Next Disorderly Half Century: Some Proposed Remedies," *Washington Quarterly, 16,* 1 (Winter 1993): 33–50.

22. Max Singer and Aaron Wildavsky, *The Real World Order: Zones of Peace, Zones of Turmoil* (Chatham, NJ: Chatham House, 1993).

23. Franz Schurmann, "After Desert Storm: Interest, Ideology, and History in American Foreign Policy," in Meredith Woo-Cumings and Michael Loriaux (eds.), *Past as Prelude: History in the Making of the New World Order* (Boulder, CO: Westview, 1993), 205.

24. Richard Rosecrance, "A New Concert of Powers," *Foreign Affairs, 71,* 2 (Spring 1992): 64–82.

25. Samuel P. Huntington, "Clash of Civilization?" *Foreign Affairs, 72,* 3 (Summer 1993): 22–49.

26. Ali E. Hillal Dessouki, "Globalization and the Two Spheres of Security," *Washington Quarterly, 16,* 4 (Autumn 1993): 112.

27. Singer and Wildavsky, *The Real World Order*, 3.

28. See Tony Smith, "Making the World Safe for Democracy," *Washington Quarterly, 16,* 4 (Autumn 1993): 197–218, for a good literature review.

29. John D. Sullivan, "Democracy and Global Economic Growth," *Washington Quarterly, 15,* 2 (Spring 1992): 175–76.

30. Samuel P. Huntington, "No Exit: The Errors of Endism," *The National Interest, 17* (Fall 1989): 6.

31. Singer and Wildavsky make this point forcefully in *The Real World Order.*

32. W.Y. Smith, "U.S. National Security after the Cold War." *Washington Quarterly, 15,* 4 (Autumn 1992): 21–34.

33. Singer and Wildavsky, *The Real World Order*, 14.

——— 2 ———

Necessary Peace: The Changing
Role of Military Force

The Cold War system that has crumbled under the combined forces of democratic revolution and economic and technological international- ization was the product of the end of World War II and the sweeping changes in the balance of power attendant to the war's end. The United States and the Soviet Union were the only major nations to survive the war with significant residual power. Of the other prewar powers, the other nominal victors, Great Britain and France, lay exhausted, their economies shattered, while the losers, notably Germany and Japan, were occupied and prostrate.

The war had been a devastating affair. Unlike its predecessor, it had been a truly global conflict, with combat occurring at some levels on all the world's major land masses. Huge numbers of people had partic- ipated in the war as combatants (an estimated 80 million in uniform, although that is just a guess), and upwards of 40 million combatants and civilians had perished in the process. Of these, conventional ac- counts suggest that almost 20 million were Soviet, although recent anti-Stalinist revisionists in the Soviet Union have upped that figure to more than 30 million if Soviet citizens killed by the Soviets are in- cluded. Moreover, the war's end was punctuated by the atomic bomb attacks on Hiroshima and Nagasaki, making nuclear weapons a perma- nent part of the future landscape of military affairs. World War II was the quintessential war of total purpose and total means: the total re- sources of societies were harnessed to the goal of the total capitulation of defeated enemies.

From this maelstrom, the United States and the Soviet Union emerged as the only states with residual power to address the problem of organizing the peace. It was not, however, a contest between equals. The Soviet Union had lost vast numbers of citizens in the war, and its countryside and industrial plant lay in shambles from the German on-slaught. What the Soviet Union retained was a very large land army of over 12 million, which it did not demobilize after the war and which was largely deployed in the occupation of the central and east European lands it had "liberated."

By contrast, the United States had actually been strengthened by the war. American casualties, around 300,000, were among the lightest of any of the major combatants. By devoting the American industrial plant to producing the "arsenal of democracy," American industry escaped the depression and was brought to peak capacity. It was the only truly functioning economy among the major powers, giving the United States an economic sway and advantage that we can only look back upon nostalgically today. Although the United States rapidly demobilized its army (as it had done after every major war in United States history), its monopoly on atomic weapons provided the United States with a military mystique that somehow substituted for its lack of men under arms.

It is in this context that the Cold War international system evolved. Understanding its evolution requires first looking at how and why the system became what it was, and then looking at what has eroded the system. This requires examining sequentially the impact of nuclear weapons on the military balance, the declining relevance of military solutions arising from nuclear stalemate, other sources of superpower decline, and finally, as the great precipitating cause of overall change, the general decline of the Soviet Union that forced it to cancel the old competition.

The Cold War System

As the war's end approached, the question engaging the winning policy makers was about the shape of the postwar peace. In some large ways, it was a matter of avoiding the mistakes of 1919, which had allowed the slide from one great conflagration to another. All were in agreement that this time the United States would have to be a major player. The real question was whether the wartime United States–USSR collaboration could be continued.

Although there was not great optimism about postwar cooperation, there was at least hope. The United Nations system was proposed to provide a vehicle for organizing a postwar peace based on big power accord. It was not born of utopian expectations but from the conviction that the new organization could stabilize the peace only if peacetime unity prevailed among the major wartime allies. Success was not assumed among the Big Five (the United States, the Soviet Union, Britain, France, and China), only the realization that the United Nations plan would work "if—and only if—they did."[1] To realize this arrangement, the Security Council was to be given sweeping military powers, and a Military Staff Committee composed of the highest military commanders of the five powers was to coordinate military action and essentially police the affairs of an otherwise disarmed world.

The collective security provisions of the U.N. Charter (see the appendix) may have seemed hopelessly naive prior to the U.N. action in the Persian Gulf War in 1990–91. The U.N. system as designed was never employed before 1990, because, before Saddam Hussein, the United States and the Soviet Union had never actively participated on the same side in an action sanctioned by the United Nations. The collective action taken in Kuwait, in fact, only partially conformed to charter provisions in that permanent U.N. forces were neither available nor employed. The perception of charter naivete, however, is mistaken. What the framers were saying is, if you can cooperate, here is a system that will organize the peace. If not, you will have to find another way. To make provision for the other way, the framers included one article nearly totally at odds with the rest of the document: Article 51 allows for individual and collective self-defense, meaning defensive alliances; this formed the institutional basis for the Cold War. Because the precondition to continued collaboration was agreement on the shape of the postwar order, the absence of such agreement doomed the implementation of the U.N. system and paved the way for the Cold War. Clearly, a common vision was necessary if both the United States and the Soviet Union were to defend it.

Unfortunately, the two sides had very different world views. The Soviets were, understandably, obsessed with their physical security and demanded a buffer zone, a *cordon sanitaire*, around the Soviet Union that would guarantee a future attack could be stopped short of Soviet soil. At the same time, the Soviets were messianic, anxious to export the brutal Stalinist form of Marxism-Leninism to the world. By contrast, Americans characteristically saw the war as a triumph for the democratic ideal, which they sought equally fervently to spread abroad. Stalinism gradually emerged as the threat to that vision.

The Cold War evolved gradually during the remainder of the 1940s from these diametrically opposed views. Following the Iran crisis of 1946, the major flash points were in the center of Europe, where the Soviet Union gradually turned its combined visions of security and messianic communism into a series of Communist puppet regimes in Eastern and Central Europe. These actions violated what the United States believed to be guarantees for self-determination. The response was a series of bold policy initiatives, the Truman Doctrine, the Marshall Plan, and the North Atlantic Treaty Organization, which defined the policy of containment of Soviet communism. By the time containment was first called to question militarily with the North Korean attack on South Korea in 1950, the Cold War was joined.

The Cold War international system had at least six salient characteristics. First, it was at its height a *tight bipolar system* in which the two major powers, the United States and the Soviet Union, maintained control over their individual spheres of influence. For the Soviets, this meant military domination of Eastern Europe, since military power was the basis of Soviet power and influence. For the United States, it initially meant economic power arising from the fact that the United States had the only healthy economy in the world. However, the tightness of control gradually weakened, in the West because revived economies no longer needed American economic help so much and could thus afford to say no, and in the East because the brutality of military repression, as in Hungary and Czechoslovakia, did more harm than good.

A second characteristic was that *East–West confrontation was the dominant theme of international relations* and was the measure by which international activity was gauged. The extension of the containment line into Asia (against which containment's father, George F. Kennan, argued vigorously) by a series of bilateral and multilateral treaties made East–West differences universal and meant that difficulties everywhere would be considered in East–West terms. The worldwide battle between communism and anticommunism was the overarching force in the world.

Third, *power was measured largely in terms of military force.* For the Soviets, of course, this was the only level on which the competition could be played, as the Soviet system, even before its most obvious warts were revealed, never competed on the economic plain. Ultimately, this competition came to be defined in nuclear terms, and the possession of large thermonuclear arsenals capable of societal incineration came to define superpower status.

Fourth, *measuring the competition in military terms provided the notion of the salience of military power* for resolving international differences and led to the maintenance of large military forces at a high degree of readiness as the mark of competitiveness in the system. The most obvious example of this was the forty-year standing confrontation between NATO and (after 1955, when it came into being) the Warsaw Pact across the former inter-German boundary. Another example is the maintenance of contingency forces for elsewhere to implement the Brezhnev Doctrine (giving the Soviets the "right" to come to the aid of beleaguered Socialist states) or the Reagan Doctrine (giving the United States the "right" to beleaguer those Communist states).

Fifth, as a near corollary to the second point, the East–West orientation of the competition meant that *all concerns worldwide were reduced to East–West terms* whether their substance merited the extension or not. This overlay occurred especially in conflictual areas such as the Middle East, South Asia, and parts of Africa, where both sides scrambled for primary influence, attempting to deny influence to the other. That most Third World problems were based on the need for development and did not lend themselves to such interpretation was largely irrelevant.

Sixth, *the protracted and consuming nature of the competition gave rise to the national security state* and the definition of international relations in national security terms. Foreign policy and defense policy increasingly became synonymous, and budgets on both sides of the iron curtain were geared, with damaging economic consequences, to the needs of military security.

The End of Cold War

The revolutions of 1989 punctuated the increasingly hollow shell of the Cold War scenario. As time passed, less and less of the world saw international matters in Soviet–American terms. Moreover, nuclear weapons, the great symbol of the Cold War system, became its curse. As Dmitri Simes states it, "The war which the Soviets do not want, absolutely do not want, is one of major proportions, a nuclear or even a conventional war in which cities are destroyed, millions of innocent people are killed, and the whole country is devastated. *Perhaps even more than most Americans, they do not want such a war"*[2] (emphasis added). Because the Cold War always had as its darkest shadow the prospects of that major war, real security required admitting the culprit (Cold War competition) and moving on to something less threatening.

The other side of this, of course, was the internal malaise of the Soviet Union. This will be the subject of detailed examination later in this chapter. Suffice it to say here that as an ideological competitor, the Marxist-Leninist ideal proved to be bankrupt. The Gorbachev regime was slow to bring itself to admit defeat of the ideal, but it has clearly been rejected explicitly throughout the world. In that sense, we have witnessed the "end of history" (at least for the time being) where, as Francis Fukuyama has argued, liberal society has triumphed for lack of a better alternative and where its detractors "end their ideological pretensions of representing different and higher forms of human society."[3] One sees little queuing up to mount the road to socialism; the ideological debate that remains centers on how pure market capitalism should be and what social obligations best apply. The focus of that debate is likely to be over whether the countries of Eastern Europe hew to pure market democracy or to Western European social democracy models.

As argued in chapter 1, these two forces came together to lead the Soviet leadership to conclude that the Cold War could not be won—indeed it was being lost—and therefore needed to be ended. The extension of necessary peace to encompass the conventional as well as the nuclear relationship left the entire military confrontation an obviously hollow enterprise. The negative economic consequences of military spending made the continuation of the military aspects of the Cold War unacceptable; the Cold War was no longer affordable. Ending it simply made sense.

Once this determination was made, the problem shifted to convincing a West made suspicious by forty years of confrontation that the Soviet leadership was sincere. Pure rhetoric, such as that contained in *Perestroika,*[4] was not enough. Only concrete action would do. Accepting (or orchestrating) the revolutions of 1989 was such an action, effectively destroying the military side of the confrontation beyond the anachronistic continued possession of large thermonuclear arsenals. While nationalist desires continue to inflame the politics of Central Europe, the prospect of the great conventional war that Simes maintains the Soviets so feared has disappeared.

The Soviets also took the rhetorical lead in proposing to dismantle the artifacts of Cold War. While it is no longer as certain as it once was that writings coming out of the Soviet Union have governmental imprimatur, consider a proposal by Henry Trofimenko, long a senior scholar at the U.S.A. and Canada Institute, published in early 1990. To end the Cold War, he proposes the following "determinants": termination of the arms race; demilitarization of Soviet–American relations in the Third World; abandonment of the Brezhnev and Reagan doctrines; demolition of the Berlin Wall (already done); progress toward European unity through institutional cooperation; cessation of the ideological competition; cooperation within the United Nations; defused U.S.–Soviet naval competition in the Pacific Ocean; and worldwide acceptance of peaceful coexistence.[5] All of these things have, of course, occurred.

Necessary Peace

One of the truly revolutionary differences between the world since 1945 and the world before was the advent of nuclear weapons. From 1945 to 1949, the United States had a monopoly on the possession of these awesome weapons of mass destruction. Until the Soviet Union successfully tested the first intercontinental ballistic missile (ICBM) shortly before launching *Sputnik* in 1958, the United States also had a monopoly on the ability to deliver nuclear warheads to the opponent's soil. (The Soviets did not develop a strategic bomber capability after World War II.)

The difference nuclear weapons make was a matter of some conjecture after the war. In light of the strategic bombing campaigns against Axis population centers during the war, some of the old inhibitions against attacking noncombatants had effectively disappeared. The international legality of that activity was never tested against war crimes standards, since the bombardiers won. From one vantage point, nuclear munitions were simply the perfect explosive for strategic bombardment, because one nuclear sortie could accomplish what had heretofore taken scores or hundreds of attacks. Moreover, though the effects of nuclear attacks were certainly grisly, fewer people were killed in the nuclear attacks on Hiroshima and Nagasaki than in the fire bombings of Tokyo and Dresden. Were nuclear weapons really all that special?

At least a few people clearly thought so. When the Truman administration commissioned Bernard Brodie in 1946 to look at the question, it was implicitly taking thinking and theorizing out of the hands of the U.S. military, some of whom were openly muttering about exploiting the nuclear advantage and dealing with the Soviets once and for all. (General George S. Patton was a particularly vocal advocate of this position.) At the same time, many in the U.S. government felt that nuclear weapons were an ideal counterweight to the huge Red Army in Europe.[6] Against this position, Brodie intoned that in the future, nuclear weapons meant that the sole purpose of military forces was to deter war.[7]

Before the Soviets developed the capability to attack the United States with nuclear weapons, deterrence was solely a Soviet problem. For the United States, the avoidance of nuclear war was a simple matter of self-restraint. Ballistic missiles changed all that in two fundamental ways.

First, ballistic missiles made American soil vulnerable to direct attack. The most basic interest of any state, the physical survival of its territory and people, was brought into question for the first time since the birth of the nation. As the arsenals of thermonuclear weapons grew into thousands on both sides, the ability of the Soviets to decimate the United States became unquestionable. Second, there was not at the time, nor is there still, any proven way to defend territory against a nuclear rocket attack, to use Soviet language. The long-term outcomes of schemes such as the Strategic Defense Initiative (SDI) notwithstanding, ballistic missile defense against a large, concentrated attack remains an elusive goal abandoned in 1993 with the formal demise of the SDI effort.

Under these circumstances, the only way to avoid being destroyed in a nuclear war is to avoid having such a war. Amidst the Cold War animosities of the late 1950s, a fatalism about nuclear war developed; for example, "the question is not whether we will have a nuclear war, it is *when* we have one" was a popular conception at the end of the 1950s. Anyone who lived during that period can only look back with bemusement at things such as school air raid drills where students put their heads beneath their desk tops to be "shielded" from atomic bomb effects.

In this highly unsettling period, Brodie's ideas from 1946 were dusted off, and a large body of literature was developed on how to deter a nuclear war and hence its consequences. During this "golden age" of deterrence debates, nuclear arsenals on both sides were expanding and being placed on diverse and highly invulnerable launch platforms that guaranteed that these weapons, if not the populations they sought to protect, would survive a preemptive attack by either side on the other. By 1970, U.S. and Soviet arsenal sizes were about equal, and they continued to grow through the 1970s and 1980s. Prior to the Strategic Arms Reduction Treaty (START) I, strategic arsenals (those targeted on one another's territory) stood at something over 12,000 apiece; START limits reduced that number to between 7,000 and 8,000 bombs each, hardly enough to reduce how many times the rubble bounces, to paraphrase Sir Winston Churchill. The START II limits would further reduce the arsenals to about 3,000 warheads each for the United States and Russia (once the other possessing successor states—Ukraine, Kazakhstan, and Byelarus—have physically surrendered missiles based on their soil).

The situation that evolved was one of *mutual societal vulnerability*, where each of the superpowers remains totally vulnerable to an attack that is not unleashed because the other side would retain sufficient residual power to counterattack and destroy the attacker's society. One does not have to make the explicit threat to decimate the enemy to appreciate that the result *could* be devastating to both if the arsenals were used. Quite apart from strategic intent, this effect "exists as a fact, irrespective of policy."[8] The result is a necessary peace between the two sides, in which each side effectively deters itself. This condition of realistic self-deterrence is born not of comity but of the need to survive.[9]

The starkness of this mutual power to destroy was first brought home at the time of the Cuban Missile Crisis, when both countries went to the brink of war and were forced to confront the very real prospect of nuclear exchange. Since then, leaders on both sides have consistently argued vehemently that nuclear war must be avoided at all costs. Gorbachev repeatedly harped on this theme, especially after the Chernobyl nuclear energy plant disaster brought home fully what a nuclear event can cause. Gorbachev's predecessor, the late Konstantin Chernenko, stated with particular clarity: "In a nuclear war, there can be no victors and no political aims can be achieved by means of it. Any attempt to use nuclear weapons would inevitably lead to a disaster that could endanger the very existence of life on Earth."[10]

The Gorbachev regime was very consistent about the necessity of avoiding nuclear war. It was an explicit part of the "new political thinking" that underlay the Soviet leader's approach to international relations[11] and was the basis of his various arms reduction and disarmament proposals. Because differences cannot be solved with nuclear weapons, they must be solved politically. The late Marshall Sergei F. Akhromeyev, former chief of the general staff and close military advisor to Gorbachev, states a common theme when he says that in the "nuclear and space age the guaranteeing of security appears to be even more a political problem. It can never be guaranteed solely by military-technical means."[12]

This is not an altogether bad state of affairs. At the minimum, nuclear-induced fear arguably made war between the superpowers much less likely than it otherwise would have been, especially at the height of the Cold War. At the same time, the mutual perception of a common interest in self-preservation created a positive dialogue between the two superpowers when, in the early 1960s, there was very little if anything they felt they had in common. In this sense, nuclear might was the father of detente and a powerful incentive toward improved relations in the late 1980s that eventuated in the end of the Cold War.

Large, unusable nuclear arsenals have another, more systemic influence on the emerging world order: *their possession and the inhibitions they produce depreciate military force among those who possess them.* This is certainly true in the relations between the superpowers, and also of those states related closely to the nuclear superstates (those under the nuclear umbrella). The very unusability of the weapons means the threat to use them against anybody, except in the limited case of retaliating after a nuclear attack, is hollow and ineffective as a means to gain compliance.[13] The implications of this phenomenon clearly extend to nonnuclear military relations as well.

The Changing Relevance of Military Force

Predictions that the international system will evolve into a more benign, less militaristic entity are so common in the literature of international relations that one is, or should be, suspicious of anyone extolling the transition to a more peaceful world. This transition has been the professed goal of leaders and observers of every generation since 1914, and the development of nuclear and other weapons of mass destruction creates a perceived urgency to transform world politics so warfare will be abolished. David Fromkin explains that this predilection lies in the nature of those who study international relations: a group intent on doing away with war because "it is a peculiarity of this academic field that those who study it dislike the facts that are its subject matter."[14] Leading the list of the disagreeable facts, of course, are war and violence.

The clear contribution of nuclear weapons to ending the Cold War makes some examination of their contribution to military relations, at least among possessing states, valuable. What, if anything, was so different about nuclear weapons that they made a fundamental change in the way nations, or at least those nations possessing nuclear weapons or associated with weapons possessors, view force? The late Bernard Brodie thought there was a real base for what I call necessary peace. Writing over thirty years ago, he argued that the real difference nuclear weapons make is in the ability to calculate victory in war. In all previous contemplations of starting war, one side or the other, or both, could calculate (or miscalculate) the prospect of victory. In thinking about starting a nuclear war, by contrast, everyone knows that the outcome will be disaster for all sides, with no side being able to calculate postwar advantage. Everyone, in other words, loses, and everybody knows that in advance.[15]

That it took such a long time for Brodie's simple point to attain something like universal acceptance was largely the result of the Cold War. The mutual suspicion between the superpowers was such that it was difficult for observers and policy makers to believe the Soviets *really* accepted mutual deterrence (just as the Soviets questioned Americans' adherence to the concept). Soviet political leaders had long argued the disaster that nuclear war would be, but at the same time, Soviet military leaders devised elaborate war-fighting scenarios employing nuclear weapons should war occur. This nuclear sabre rattling seemed a darker side of Soviet thinking that was captured most dramatically in 1977 by Richard Pipes in his stern warning that the Soviets planned to fight, win, and survive a nuclear war.[16]

Hardly anyone believes today that the former Soviet Union wanted nuclear war any more than the United States, and certainly no one suspects contemporary Russia has such desires. Because the threat of nuclear war was the ultimate symbol of the Cold War competition, the competition could survive in the old sense without the threat. The continued presence of nuclear weapons means nuclear war remains always a possibility. Nuclear weapons undoubtedly have the necessary sobering influence of keeping our minds focused on the dire possibility of peace failing, especially in the event a less hospitable regime comes to power in Russia. Those weapons did, however, make us change the nature of the East–West relationship, and we shall always be beholden to them for doing that.

Our perception of the nuclear relationship with the Soviets changed under Gorbachev because, when he said the same things his predecessors had said, we believed him. Why did we believe in 1990 what we resisted five or ten years before? I would suggest at least three reasons. The first was Gorbachev himself and the process of change he unleashed. Gorbachev was a different kind of leader; he was at once more Western, more cosmopolitan, and more apparently trustworthy than all the Soviet leaders who preceded him. Although one could question aspects of his motivations, his sheer presence and aura disarmed those who harbored significant suspicions about the Soviets.

I think the second reason has to do with Americans. Because the idea of plotting nuclear war as a rational exercise seems so patently absurd to most Americans, it was always hard to imagine that this could seem sensible to anyone else, including dour Soviet generals. In light of the Soviet self-assessment caused by the disaster at Chernobyl and Gorbachev's open anguish over that event, it was more and more difficult to imagine that their attitudes are much different from ours. Gorbachev, in this sense, "normalized" the Soviets as rational thinkers rather than as faceless, mindless monsters.

The third reason is that the calls for normalization occurred simultaneously with the very public internal crisis in the Soviet Union. The crisis, and especially its economic aspects, made deemphasis of the military confrontation sensible regardless of the sincerity of Gorbachev's calls for a peaceful relationship. The House Armed Services Committee as early as 1988 made this point, concluding "the equation is simple: in order for his economic reforms to succeed, Gorbachev must shift resources from the defense sector to civilian use."[17] Thus, goodwill disappeared from the necessary assumptions about Gorbachev's motivations. Rather, it became a part of the geopolitical equation: "Gorbachev must secure peace abroad if the country is to advance at home."[18]

Because we believed Gorbachev, we were increasingly willing to think that his stewardship of the Soviet Union could have ended his country's status as a "rogue" out to destroy the system; this goodwill has extended to Gorbachev's Russian successor, Boris Yeltsin. What changed was Western acceptance of Gorbachev's attitudes; that, in turn, was a major force in the evolving international system. No one, for instance, paid much attention to Gorbachev, then the number two man, when he said in Moscow on December 10, 1984, "Only an intensive, highly developed economy can guarantee a consolidation of our country's position in the international arena and permit it to enter the next millennium as a great, flourishing state."[19] In 1994, the question is how much assistance can and should we provide to try to assist that transition to market democracies in Russia and the other successor states.

Nuclear weapons were the cause and effect here. They are the cause because avoiding nuclear war was what made the whole process appealing in the first place. They are also effect. As Henry Kissinger has pointed out, political normalization will make security concerns less dominant. In this circumstance, nuclear weapons—the special advantage of the superpowers—will become less and less relevant to the political issues.[20] In the conclusion of his controversial treatise on great-power decline, Paul Kennedy makes the similar observation that the salience of military bipolarity defined in nuclear terms is gradually losing its importance.[21] The demise of the former Soviet Union completes that process.

What all this means is that nuclear weapons states and their associates are much more restrained in how and where they can use military force among themselves. All the major powers have, implicitly or explicitly, recognized that the use of force among them that could conceivably escalate to nuclear war is now unacceptable, and thus necessary peace is a dominating part of the landscape of the new international system, especially within the First Tier.

The Extent of Change

Have the military dynamics created by necessary peace contributed to a general lowering of the level of violence within the new international order? The answer requires that we place the discussion back into the world of tiers. Within the First Tier, the general contribution is positive, adding to the general peace and tranquillity among First Tier states. Within the Second Tier, nuclear weapons do not currently contribute to stabilization, because they are present in few Second Tier states. Thus, their contribution is basically in the future; and most observers feel that, by contrast, their introduction will be generally destabilizing, yet another example of how the tiers differ from one another. The impact of nuclear weapons on intertier relations is also a subject of disagreement and controversy.

Within the First Tier, there are no major conflicts that could escalate to war between members of the tier. Nuclear weapons—the old nuclear umbrella of the Cold War days—bound members, almost all of which were united through defense arrangements, together. The sense of necessary peace between the United States and the Soviet Union extended to American allies in Europe, Japan, and elsewhere. There was always some conjecture, especially by the French, about whether the nuclear pledge would have been honored if the need arose: would the United States *really* risk its own annihilation in the defense of France? That argument, happily, has proven moot.

The principal First Tier concern with necessary peace continues to focus on Russia and the other nuclear-possessor successor states (Ukraine, Byelarus, and Kazakhstan have agreed to surrender their nuclear-tipped missiles in return for economic developmental assistance and security guarantees). The size of the former Soviet/Russian arsenal makes this a special case regardless of whether Russia falls into the First Tier or the Second.

The nuclear balance continues to have a positive influence on American–Russian and hence First Tier–Russian relations, particularly during the difficult process of change and, hopefully, normalization of the Russian state. What nuclear balance essentially does is to provide a baseline, or a floor, for Russia's relations with the rest of the world beyond which those relations cannot be allowed to deteriorate.

This benefit is most obvious in terms of leadership uncertainty, and especially the horror scenario of the return to power of an authoritarian regime of either the left or right that is xenophobically Russian and expansionist, a prospect currently associated with Vladimir Zhirinovsky. No matter how anti-American or anti–First Tier such a regime may be, it would still be constrained in its behavior by its possession of the huge nuclear arsenal and the knowledge that war between itself and the First Tier is potentially a nuclear war. The fear that an irresponsible, even maniacal, leader who was not sufficiently chastened by the nuclear responsibility to honor these limits is realistic and cannot be entirely dismissed. The dynamics of necessary peace *did* restrain the former Communist leadership, however, and it is difficult to imagine an alternate leadership coming to power in Russia that we would distrust any more than we did the Soviet hierarchy.

This does not mean that competition in Europe is over, that history has ended. Among history's constants are its inconstancy and the arrival of new and unforeseen forces. Right now, there is significant volatility in the center of Europe in regard to rationalizing boundaries throughout the region, especially the artificial boundaries drawn in Eastern Europe, at the fringes of the old Soviet state, and over minorities in several countries. The ability—or inability—to settle differences and to adjust boundaries peacefully will determine the tranquility of the European continent, as will the evolution of former Communist states toward First Tier status.

For the time being, however, the locus of recourse to military force has instead moved to the peripheries of the traditional Euro-centered system, to those areas where it is still "safe" to wage war, because fighting does not run the risk of escalating to the nuclear inferno. Certainly the reasons for violence, both within and between nations of the Second Tier, continue to exist. The real question, which once again will determine much of the shape of the new international order, is how the First Tier will respond.

The role of nuclear weapons in the Second Tier is another matter. With the exception of China, there are no Second Tier states with sizable nuclear arsenals or the capacity to develop a nuclear capability on a scale even remotely resembling the old nuclear superpowers. This has two immediate consequences. First, the small size of any arsenals that are developed will not produce a capability to destroy utterly states under its shadow the way the U.S.–Soviet confrontation did; hence, the basic realistic self-deterrence phenomenon that underlies necessary peace is not necessarily triggered. Second, it further means that for the foreseeable future no Second Tier states will likely be able to menace the First Tier, except for the limited possibility of something like a terrorist attack with a single weapon.

There is a fear within the First Tier that states of the Second Tier cannot be expected to act as responsibly with nuclear weapons as First Tier states have. Cloaked often in pompous terms of differences in culture and the like (some cultures do not have the same respect for individual life as we do in the West), these charges are basically ethnocentric, even racist, and have little empirical evidence to support them.

The track record of Second Tier nations employing nuclear weapons in anger is, after all, identical to the record of the First Tier.

Still, we worry. Nuclear weapons have not been used in intra–First World relations because there are not the animosities and hatreds between the democratic nations to justify even thinking about them. In the Second Tier, however, there are numerous rivalries and hatreds of a depth and desperation that could more conceivably result in a nuclear decision. Would the Indians and Pakistanis, for instance, use their arsenals in a desperate struggle over Kashmir? The historical hatred is there, and neither nation has large enough arsenals to threaten societal devastation. Are the rules different in such a case?

As another example, Iraq's Saddam Hussein showed no reluctance about using other outlawed weapons, notably chemical weapons, against Iran during the Iran–Iraq War and against his own Kurdish minority in 1987, and he may have used them against coalition forces during the Persian Gulf War. What if his nuclear program had borne fruit and provided an alternative against Iran and the Kurds, neither of whom had any earthly way to defend themselves or to retaliate? He might have been restrained from attacking the coalition by the probability of retaliation, but even that is no more than conjecture.

The list of highly unstable circumstances in the Second Tier creates the basis for First Tier–Second Tier interactions regarding nuclear weapons. That basis is to prevent the proliferation of NBC, notably nuclear, weapons capability to any more Second Tier states, to get those pursuing weapons programs to cease doing so, and to influence those in possession to destroy their stockpiles. The United States-led effort through the United Nations to persuade North Korea to abandon its nuclear pretensions has provided a particularly vivid example in 1993 and 1994.

The structure of conflict and violence in the Second Tier is extensive, manifested in internal wars and regional conflicts. The nasty stain of ethnic intolerance and racial hatred spilling over into internal atrocities is one of the most notable manifestations of the new international order. While regional conflicts have been enlivened by NBC prospects, internal wars are likely to remain the major form of conflict for the foreseeable future.

The question that is a central feature of relations between the tiers to which we return periodically is what, if anything, the First Tier wants to do about conflict within the Second Tier. There are, I think, four possibilities. The first is *benign neglect*: leaving the situation essentially alone. For the United States and the rest of the First Tier, this is a tempting solution because it is the cheapest. At a time when all countries face economic problems of varying intensity, military and economic disengagement has it attractions. Rather, the former rivals would benefit by letting others, notably the Germans and the Japanese, and private industry, attack the problems of the periphery—especially those problems with a heavily economic content.

Second, the major powers could engage in *selective activism*, becoming involved only in selected places where there are special interests for one or the other or both. This is the model of United States engagement in Panama, of the coalition response to Saddam Hussein's invasion of Kuwait, and of the United Nations–sponsored intervention in Somalia. This solution shares with benign neglect the improbability of seeing underlying Second Tier problems solved. It also suggests selective passivism, as in Rwanda.

The third possibility is *massive development*—global commitment on a scale akin to what Second Tier nations, under the banner of the New International Economic Order (NIEO), have been demanding for years. Such an approach would involve massive infusions of human and financial resources into the Second Tier to speed economic and political development, presumably transforming the Second Tier into something akin to the developed world. The rationale is that a democratic world would be a more peaceful world; the problem is where one finds the money.

The fourth possibility is overt *major power cooperation*. This could occur at two levels. At the level of military violence, it is possible to imagine the major military powers of the First Tier finding enough mutuality of interest in situations such as the Iraq–Kuwait crisis to band together, based on the collective security provisions of the U.N. Charter, to deal with threats or breaches of the peace. At the level of economic development a similar condominium among the economic superpowers, the United States, the European Community, and Japan, is possible, with these powers acting both through governmental resources and through incentives to private enterprises based in their countries. The Gulf War, of course, is only a partial example in this regard; a number, but not all, of the major powers participated. As argued earlier, the U.S. role as the remaining superpower is critical in providing leadership and resources for collective actions.

The model chosen will, of course, have great salience for the role of force in the Second Tier under the new system. The more interventionist the policy emanating from the North, the more likely the crisis of the South is to subside. Similarly, a passive reaction from the North can only make the problems of the South and their violent manifestations all the more severe.

Broader Sources of Relative Decline

Nuclear stalemate and its limiting effect on military utility have accompanied the relative decline in the power and influence of the superpowers for other reasons. For the United States, the decline has been less severe; the United States has slipped from its position of economic hegemony in the world as Japan and the European Community have emerged as economic competitors. For the Russians, who have never been part of the global economic competition (although they would now like to join the race), the internal crisis in the former Soviet Union has been the source of decline. This has led to the emergence of a revised power pecking order, at least in the eyes of some. It could well be that the economic "Big Three" (the United States, Japan, and Germany) will supplant the "Big Two" as effective powers that will shape much of the twenty-first century.[22]

One may argue with this assertion, at least with the sweep of time it claims to predict. Nonetheless, almost no one would argue with the basic notion that in the near term the economic element of power will become more decisive than it has been in the past. The United States remains a central player in that competition. The former Soviet Union is not, unless the internal political crisis can be reversed and market forces revitalize the economy. Neither is terribly likely in the near term.

This set of problems extends directly to the former Soviet Union's source of influence—military power. Seweryn Bialer argues, for instance, that economic strength, military power, and international status are closely intertwined in the modern era and that this relationship was elevated by the former Soviet leadership to be the central premise of its economic policy.[23] The economic aspect of the crisis makes it more difficult to spend competitively on military power. There are competing demands for almost all resources, including "young, well-educated professionals" currently concentrated in the officer corps.[24]

At the same time, one of the causes of malaise within Russian society is its technological inferiority, at a time when the military competition is turning decidedly high-tech, especially in the areas of electronics and new materials, both areas of Russian weakness.[25] The success of U.S. high-technology weaponry against Soviet equipment in the Gulf War, while not as spectacular as early estimates, reconfirms this problem.

The Russian ability to affect international events thus suffers from what Samuel T. Huntington refers to as a (Walter) Lippman Gap: the difference between Russian commitments and Russian ability to carry out those commitments is wide and growing.[26] The problem is becoming acute to the point that Russian political influence is arguably lower now than "at any time since the mid-eighteenth century."[27] Because that crisis is having such a dramatic impact on the overall structure of the system, it is worth examining.

The International Crisis of the Former Soviet Union

The pervasive crisis centered in Russia but extending to the other successor states has at its heart the implosion of the old economic and political systems, which are in a state of disarray and fluidity unprecedented in recent history. The problem of increasingly assertive nationalisms in the successor republics adds to this volatile mix. Reforms in one area, such as political rights of self-expression, lead to problems elsewhere, such as secessionist demands, increasingly candid criticisms of economic performance, and movements for ethnonationalist purification. The ultimate irony of Gorbachev's liberalization was to set in motion dynamics that would both destroy the Soviet state and remove Gorbachev from power.

At the core of the crisis is the performance of the economic system. The dimensions of this problem include stagnation marked by inefficient agriculture, an inadequate supply of consumer goods, and a substantial technological gap with the West. All of this adds up to a weak infrastructure, poor quality of life, lower productivity, and less creativity. The economy continues to worsen, particularly in its ability to satisfy consumers, whose legendary patience is being put to the test.[28] The crisis is exacerbated by the fact that it accumulated during a time of unprecedented growth in the West, accentuated by rapid gains in the areas of high technology,[29] where the Soviets hardly compete at all, except in weapons systems (which generally do not employ state-of-the-art technologies anyway).

Such a crisis did not occur overnight. The Soviets themselves admitted that it went back at least to the Brezhnev days of the early 1970s, when the "period of stagnation" began: the Soviet economy failed to grow and change while other economies did. As Gorbachev himself put it, "A country that was once quickly closing on the world's advanced nations began to lose one position after another."[30] He maintained that the full scale of the problem was not apparent at first, that "the magnitude of many domestic problems—political, economic, social and moral—was not evident at once but revealed itself as the process moved on."[31]

Although the evidence is sketchy, it appears that there was a cadre of intellectuals in the Soviet Union who recognized the outline of the problem early on and even published articles in technical journals that somehow evaded censorship (presumably because they were too technical for the censors to read). In a fascinating interview, Dr. Eugenii Novikov, former senior official of the International Department of the CPSU Central Committee, indicated such an underground community. He gives large credit for what has become Gorbachev's "new thinking" to this group, many of whom were able to gain perspective as staff at the Institute of Social Studies of the Central Committee, whose job of training non-Soviets in the workings of the Soviet system exposed them to ideas from the outside. Moreover, he maintained that Raisa Gorbachev, a professor at Moscow State University before her husband's rise to power, was instrumental as a conduit between this group and her husband. The criticism of ongoing practices was incorporated into Gorbachev's thinking, and many of these intellectuals, apparently at her suggestion, became "new assistants and new consultants."[32]

There is some fragmentary evidence that critics were gathering for a decade or more. For instance, in a speech given on June 11, 1985, Gorbachev hinted that "one cannot help noting from the early 1970s certain difficulties began to be felt in economic development."[33] Another author, without attribution, also makes indirect allusion to this intellectual group, asserting that "certain Soviet analysts, many of whom now occupy influential positions in Gorbachev's administration, have attempted systematically to assimilate the meaning of international developments."[34] From this vantage point, the major contribution of Gorbachev himself was to serve as a sponsor for the reformists, letting them out of the closet. Unfortunately, this group proved more adept at identifying problems than at proposing and implementing solutions. As conditions continued to worsen economically in most of the successor states after 1991, there was a backlash against the reformers. The strongest expression of that discontent was seen in the distant second-place finish of the major reformist party in the December 1993 Russian parliamentary elections.

The identified villain in all this was the Stalinist economic and political system. Politically, Stalinism produced the repression and atrocities that are now acknowledged by the new Soviet revisionist thought and, according to Gorbachev, "proved incapable of protecting us from the growth of stagnation phenomena in economic and social life in the latter decades."[35] At the economic level, the problem was the Stalinist command economic system based on centralized planning and forced mobilization of the population to meet centrally determined goals.

Blaming dead leaders for the country's ills, if not unique to the Soviet Union, certainly is a Russian art form. In this case, Stalin, a character tailormade to be vilified, was identified as the fall guy. The system he created was indeed hideous and inhumane, easy to criticize, but it could not have existed without support. As Walter Laqueur suggests, "It is unlikely (to put it cautiously) that an outlandish system, which was alien to Russian mentality and tradition and totally opposed to the Bolshevik doctrine and practice, would have generated so much enthusiasm, lasted for so long, and would have found supporters even decades after the demise of its founder."[36] Such a rejoinder has particularly chilling relevance in light of the resurgence of a strand of ultra-Russian nationalist and pro-authoritarian sentiment centering around Vladimir Zhirinovsky and his electoral success in the December 1993 elections. It is too early to assess the seriousness of his challenge; that it is in tune with historical Russian tendencies cannot be ignored.

The rejoinder is important in a more general sense. If Stalinism is both the problem and a part of the Russian psyche, then the structural monster must be exorcised from the body politic, no easy task and undoubtedly part of the backlash against the new system obvious in Russia today. Still, Aganbegyan is undoubtedly correct when he asserts that "the existing system of economic management, based on the command system, represses democracy, initiative, and the creativity of workers and does not encourage the potential for work or social activity."[37]

The problem is that the system was also uniquely Russian, which is why the magic wands of rhetoric and reform have not proven instantly successful. As an example, the first thrust of reform, *uskeronie*, or acceleration, was aimed at getting people to work harder (getting them to drink less was part of this); it has basically failed. An irony of Stalinist life was that the average worker did not toil very hard and was neither rewarded nor punished based on his or her productivity. The new system hopes to ask workers to increase their output for the good of the system, which, when it improves, will lead to reward. The problem is that Russian workers are refusing to improve their work performance before the system produces something concrete to improve their lives and thus justify the hard work—a sort of Catch-22.

This is, of course, a bleak tale. Nine years after the reforms began, the system—now fifteen successor state systems—remains more chaotic than before. An authoritarian order has devolved into disorder and chaos in Russia, and the Russian people are increasingly questioning whether this is an improvement. Crime—from drug dealing to bank robbery to murder—has become epidemic, a *nouveau riche* class has emerged to accentuate the economic gap that socialism was supposed to close, and the overall economy remains in shambles. It is not hard to see why average Russians would question the value of change.

Conclusions

The central argument put forward in the preceding pages is that the role of military force in conducting international relations has been restricted, and that the restriction is likely to continue and to be a major limiting factor in the international system that postdates the Cold War period, at least within the First Tier. The driving factor in this changed status is thermonuclear weaponry, which endows the possessor with both awesome power and even more awesome responsibility for the management of that power.

The necessary peace created by nuclear weaponry is not, of course, a product of 1989. Nuclear weapons were one of the defining characteristics of the Cold War system, because they provided the operational definition of what it took to be a superpower. In the "simpler" days of that period, the possession of nuclear weapons was thought to provide the possessors with special power that could be translated into usable influence in the international system. Certainly the United States nuclear umbrella, for instance, was believed to provide the protection for Western Europe against a Soviet invasion that probably could not have been deterred by the conventional forces available to the NATO alliance at most times.

The evolution of the nuclear balance stands as clear testimony to what happens when one gets too much of a good thing. As nuclear arsenals proliferated into the thousands of invulnerable warheads capable, even after absorbing an initial attack, of decimating the opponent's territory, they lost their utility beyond deterrence. There has been from the beginning a debate about whether nuclear weapons had any utility beyond deterrence. Leaders faced with the responsibility for these weapons have answered the question: there is no other utility for nuclear weapons. Brodie was right.

There are two broad systemic effects of necessary peace. First, it affects the utility of armed force as an instrument of national power. In the Cold War system, superpower status enhanced the ability of its members to get others to do what they would not otherwise do (the definition of power). In the contemporary world, that is no longer true. We have come to recognize that nuclear weapons inhibit, rather than enhance, the usable military options available to those who possess them. A nuclear weapons state contemplating the potential use of military force has an extra question to ask of itself: Will my action raise the prospect of escalation to nuclear exchange that might lead to the destruction of *my* country? One hopes, as noted earlier, that this dynamic will come to extend to the Second Tier as well.

Any conflict directly involving nuclear powers and their close allies clearly has escalatory potential. Recognizing that, especially as it applies to the center of Europe, both sides moved rapidly after 1989 to dismantle the threatening structures that could have led to the failure of deterrence. As a consequence of nuclear weapons, general war in Europe has become unthinkable. Given the violent history of Europe, that is quite an accomplishment. Those who would dismantle nuclear arsenals have the burden of demonstrating how they would do better. One of the major tasks that will be faced in the post–Cold War international system will be how to deal with the continuing reality of nuclear weapons that are unlikely to be dismantled. There will be powerful pressures for nuclear disarmament arising from nuclear allergy; while understandable, one only hopes that the disarmament urge is dealt with soberly. Disarmament, appealing on the surface, contains the prospect of rearmament —possibly clandestinely—that could destabilize the system.

The second effect of necessary peace has been to change the pattern of military usage. Nuclear powers may be inhibited by their own capabilities, but those "blessed" by nonpossession are not. As violence wanes from the agenda of the First Tier, it remains a viable part of the operational environment for many Second Tier nations.

This reality is disturbing for at least two reasons. First, Second Tier conflict is increasingly lethal. The proliferation of sophisticated weaponry, from chemical munitions to ballistic delivery vehicles, has made such warfare extraordinarily earnest and deadly. The toll of fighting in Afghanistan and the Iran–Iraq war rivals some of the largest conflicts between the so-called civilized powers now insulated by necessary peace. There are simmering disputes worldwide, with the continuing prospect of ignition.

Second, Second Tier conflicts could involve the major powers. If the analysis to this point has been cogent, the powers of the First Tier will increasingly find stability in their best interests and may work to bring about peaceful resolutions to Second Tier conflicts, up to and possibly including the commitment of their own forces to end such conflicts as in Operation Desert Storm.

This change in the locus of violence should affect the way the superpowers and others arm themselves. To date, the response has been disappointing. A recent "definitive" statement, former Secretary of Defense Aspin's "bottom-up review" released in September 1993, reads depressingly like old Cold War constructs.[38] Falling back into the comfortable rhetoric of a Cold War that is gone, the rationale is that new "bad old days" could return. That is conceivable in the sense that anything one can think of, regardless of its plausibility, is by definition conceivable. In confronting the new international system, we need a fundamental reorientation of attitude on employing military force that recognizes the changed utility that force has for those who possess the most of it.

Notes

1. Inis L. Claude, Jr., *Swords into Plowshares: The Problems and Progress of International Organization*, 4th ed. (New York: Random House, 1971), 76.

2. Dmitri K. Simes, "Soviet Foreign Policy under Gorbachev: Goals and Expectations," in Arthur B. Gunlicks and John D. Treadway (eds.), *The Soviet Union under Gorbachev: Assessing the First Year* (New York: Praeger, 1987), 57.

3. Francis Fukuyama, "The End of History?" *The National Interest, 16* (Summer 1989): 13.

4. Mikhail S. Gorbachev, *Perestroika: New Thinking for Our Country and the World* (New York: Harper and Row, 1987).

5. Henry Trofimenko, "Ending the Cold War, No History," *The Washington Quarterly, 13,* 2 (Spring 1990): 28.

6. Donald M. Snow, *The Necessary Peace: Nuclear Weapons and Superpower Relations* (Lexington, MA: Lexington Books, 1987), 8.

7. Bernard Brodie (ed.), *The Absolute Weapon: Atomic Power and World Order* (New York: Harcourt, Brace, 1946).

8. Robert Jervis, *The Illogic of American Nuclear Strategy* (New York: Cornell University Press, 1984), 34, 146.

9. This idea is developed at length in Snow, *Necessary Peace, passim.*

10. Quoted in *Whence the Threat to Peace*, 3d ed. (Moscow: Military Publishing House, 1984), 14.

11. Margot Light, *The Soviet Theory of International Relations* (Brighton, Sussex, UK: Wheatsheaf Books, 1988), 310.

12. Quoted in Sergei Zamascikov, *Gorbachev and the Soviet Military*, Rand Library Collection Papers p–7410 (Santa Monica, CA: RAND Corp., January 1988), 20.

13. Thomas H. Naylor, *The Gorbachev Strategy: Opening the Closed Society* (Lexington, MA: Lexington Books, 1988), ix; and William C. Hyland, "Setting Global Priorities," *Foreign Policy, 73* (Winter 1988–89): 26.

14. David Fromkin, *The Independence of Nations* (New York: Praeger Special Studies, 1981), 35.

15. Bernard Brodie, *Strategy in the Missile Age* (Princeton, NJ: Princeton University Press, 1959).

16. Richard Pipes, "Why the Soviet Union Thinks It Could Fight and Win a Nuclear War," *Commentary, 64,* 1 (July 1977): 21–34.

17. Defense Policy Panel, "General Secretary Mikhail Gorbachev and the Soviet Military: Assessing His Impact and the Potential for Future Changes," Committee on Armed Services, U.S. House of Representatives (100th Congress, 2d Session), September 23, 1988, 3.

18. Christian Schmidt-Hauer, *Gorbachev: The Path to Power* (London: I.B. Tauris, 1986), 3.

19. Quoted in ibid., 12–13.

20. Henry A. Kissinger, "A Plan for Europe," *Newsweek* (June 18, 1990), 23.

21. Paul Kennedy, *The Rise and Fall of the Great Powers: Economic Change and Military Conflict From 1500 to 2000* (New York: Random House, 1987), 538.

22. Fred Bergsten, "The World Economy after the Cold War," *Foreign Affairs, 69,* 3 (Summer 1990): 96.

23. Seweryn Bialer, "Gorbachev's Program of Change: Sources, Significance, Prospects," *Political Science Quarterly, 103,* 3 (Fall 1988): 411.

24. Defense Policy Panel, "Mikhail Gorbachev and the Soviet Military," 4.

25. Dmitry Mikheyev, *The Soviet Perspective on the Strategic Defense Initiative* (Washington, DC: Pergamon-Brassey's, 1987), 58. See also Central Intelligence Agency, *The Soviet Weapons Industry: An Overview* (Washington, DC: Central Intelligence Agency Document DI 86–10016, September 1986), 40.

26. Samuel P. Huntington, "Coping with the Lippman Gap," *Foreign Affairs, 66,* 3 (1987–88): 453.

27. Allen Lynch, "Does Gorbachev Matter Anymore?" *Foreign Affairs, 69,* 3 (Summer 1990): 19.

28. See, for example, Naylor, *The Gorbachev Strategy*, viii; Mikheyev, *The Soviet Perspective*, 65; and Ed A. Hewett, *Reforming the Soviet Economy: Equality vs. Efficiency* (Washington, DC: Brookings Institution, 1988), 85, 78–79.

29. Seweryn Bialer, "New Thinking and Soviet Foreign Policy," *Survival, 30,* 4 (July–August 1988): 292. He makes much the same point in "Gorbachev's Program of Change," 412.

30. Gorbachev, *Perestroika*, 46.

31. Mikhail S. Gorbachev, "The Progress of *Perestroika*," *World Today, 45,* 6 (June 1989): 94.

32. Henry Hamman, "Soviet Defector on Origins of 'New Thinking,' " *Report on the USSR, 1,* 42 (October 20, 1989): 14–16.

33. Mikhail S. Gorbachev, *The Coming Century of Peace* (New York: Richardson and Stierman, 1986), 206.

34. Lynch, "Does Gorbachev Matter Anymore?" 23.

35. Mikhail S. Gorbachev, "Key Sections of Gorbachev Speech Given to Party Conference," *New York Times* (June 29, 1988), 8.

36. Walter Laqueur, "Why Stalin? A National Debate," *Society, 27,* 3 (March–April 1990): 26.

37. Abel Aganbegyan, *The Economic Challenge of Perestroika* (Bloomington: Indiana University Press, 1988), 20.

38. Secretary of Defense Les Aspin, *The Bottom-Up Review: Forces for a New Era* (Washington, DC: U.S. Department of Defense, September 1, 1993).

3

The Rising Importance
of Economic Factors

Just as the limiting aspects of necessary peace have transformed the utility of military force for nuclear weapons states, so has the international economic system gradually changed. Beginning in the early 1970s with the dual traumas of renunciation of the international gold standard and the oil price shocks, the major phenomenon has been the loss of economic hegemony by the United States. In this process, the economies of Japan and Western Europe (especially Germany) have burgeoned. Fertilized liberally by United States dollars in the early postwar period, these countries have become the principal economic competitors of the United States in an extraordinarily vibrant and prosperous evolving world economic order that remains in a state of rapid change.

Not everyone has shared equally in the largess. Those prospering at this point are North America (the United States and Canada), the countries of the European Community (EC), and the nation-states of the Pacific Rim, prominently Japan (the First Tier) but also including the Four Tigers (Republic of Korea, Taiwan, Hong Kong, Singapore), and the Association of South East Asian Nations (ASEAN) states (Thailand, Malaysia, Singapore, Indonesia, Brunei, and the Philippines), the near–First Tier states. As the global economies grow by leaps and bounds, those on the outside—notably the former Soviet Union, Eastern Europe, and the rest of the Second Tier —clamor for a piece of the action. In addition, the emergence of supranational intergovernmental economic organizations of varying formality, the North American Free Trade Area (NAFTA) and the Asia- Pacific Economic Cooperation (APEC), in addition to the existing European Community (or Union), portend additional changes.

The success of the international market economic system, in the sense of creating envy and a desire to join the game, contributed to the revolutionary events of 1989. While Western economies soared, Marxist economic systems soured, and the gap in standards of living and productivity between the two systems widened. The telecommunications revolution that is part and parcel of the economic revolution has meant that televised images worldwide deprived governments, notably in the Communist world, of the ability to hide their comparative failure.

It is impossible to measure the degree to which the desire to emulate the success of the West influenced the overthrow of Communist regimes in 1989, but that desire was certainly there. The simple fact is that Socialist economics in the form practiced by the Communist and former Communist world failed miserably. The triumphant model combines political and economic freedom to make decisions and works best in the seedbed of political democracy. In this sense, economics and politics have combined to create a powerful force that has transformed the international system into one of two tiers where the combination of political and economic freedom forms the entrance criterion for First Tier status.

This is a relatively recent phenomenon, and our understanding of how the system is evolving and where its problems lie is less than clear. Superimposing the capitalist model onto the world system is bound to be a difficult chore, especially since there are no international regulatory authorities to rein in the more carnivorous practices of international corporations. Capitalism as it has evolved in the United States and elsewhere has always featured a love–hate relationship of promotion and regulation between business and government. It is not clear who will provide the counterbalance to control the international Ivan Boesky figures in the new system.

In this chapter, we will begin to look at this new international economic phenomenon and its implications for understanding the new international political system. We will begin with how the system has evolved in the last decade or so, particularly the relative rise of economic "power." One of the results of the expanding international economic system is a growing interdependence between the major players, which has strong—and often negative—consequences for individual states and their ability to regulate international activity. At the base of much of the new international economic phenomenon is the so-called High Technology or Third Industrial Revolution that is transforming the world productive system. It will be argued that the road to international economic competitiveness and success begins with mastery of high technology, currently symbolized by the electronic superhighway concept. A particularly important component of the high-technology phenomenon with obvious geopolitical ramifications is the telecommunications revolution, which is rapidly expanding global knowledge transfer and communication. We will look at the dismal performance of the former Soviet Union in the new economic competition and at why joining the race was the bottom line of Gorbachev's reform program. Finally, the place of the Second Tier, as participant or outsider, will be examined.

The Evolving Order

In the quarter century following World War II, Americans did not concern themselves terribly about international economic matters. As the only country whose economy was physically strengthened by the war and whose industrial plant escaped strategic bombardment, the United States was the economic envy of the world: American goods were the global standard; the American dollar was the world's currency, *the* hard currency; and American hegemony meant you played by the American rules in international economics or you did not play at all.

That has all changed. The recovery and expansion of European and Asian economies has meant that there are alternatives to American goods and services, in many cases better and cheaper. Renouncing the gold standard and allowing the value of the dollar to "float" and be determined in relation to other currencies meant the end of the dollar's absolute monopoly on hard currency status. (A currency is deemed "hard" if it is acceptable as payment in international trade.)

In this new environment, the key basic concept is *competitiveness.* As defined by the Young Commission, which was formed by President Reagan to investigate the American competitive position, competitiveness is "the degree to which a nation can, under free and fair market conditions, produce goods and services that meet the test of international markets while simultaneously maintaining or expanding the real incomes of its citizens."[1] The key concepts in this definition are the notions of fairness and marketability of goods and services. The notion of fairness is generally pegged on the absence of artificial barriers to trade, which make one nation's goods and services more or less attractive because of government actions such as tariffs, quotas, or subsidies (such as dumping). A primary source of major disagreement between the United States and Japan is Japanese restrictions on importing American goods. The removal of barriers to fairness is a major goal of the General Agreement on Tariffs and Trade (GATT) process, notably the conclusion of the Uruguay round of negotiations in December 1993. Even the ability of states to regulate activity, however, is further restricted by the increased internationalization of economic activities by individuals and corporations. Using capital as an example, Daniel Bell argues that *"the internationalization of capital . . . means that few countries, if any, are able to control their own currency. There is a loss of one of the main levers of power and influence"*[2] (emphasis in original).

The international attractiveness of products and services is increasingly tied to the mastery of high technology that allows firms and nations to be on the cutting edge of production. This is a relatively new phenomenon in the international system, and one understood imperfectly by policy elites until the election of President Clinton. The competition is about the production of new knowledge and, more important, the translation of that knowledge into products and services that people want and will pay for. The resulting technology race is an increasingly complex, fast-moving, and internationally competitive enterprise.[3]

The United States entered the technology race with a clear lead, but almost all observers agree that the relative position of the United States eroded during the 1980s. The Young Commission, for instance, reported a comparative world market share loss for the United States in seven of ten "sunrise industries" that are associated with high technology.[4] Writing in 1989, one observer saw this decline continuing, with strong implications for U.S. foreign and national security policy. He perceived a growing dependence on economic and technological policy "not seen since the advent of nuclear weapons."[5] Tom Forester, one of the major chroniclers of the high-technology phenomenon, went so far as to argue that American failure to compete economically and technologically could relegate the United States to second-rate economic status.[6]

Very few observers would go that far in describing either the problem or its consequences. At the other end of the scale are observers such as Joseph S. Nye, Jr., who dispute the entire "declinist" thesis, arguing that the relative decline of American predominance from the early postwar world creates an artificial benchmark for measurement, since the early postwar American position was inflated by the war's outcome. Rather, Nye and others maintain that the distribution of relative strength settled down in the middle 1970s, and that the U.S. position has remained about the same since then.[7] Spurred by the resurgence of the American effort in high-definition television (HDTV) and elsewhere, United States economic health has taken an upturn in the early 1990s.

There may be disagreement about the nature and consequences of the new economic competition, but there is little disagreement that it exists, beginning as a three-sided competition between the United States, Japan, and the European Community in the 1970s and 1980s and apparently moving in the general direction of regional blocs and GATT-led trade barrier reductions in the 1990s. If there is general agreement on who the Big Three will be, there is less agreement about how the relationships among the First Tier powers will evolve. We are clearly in transition from a period of U.S. hegemony toward something else. The political and economic homogenization of the First Tier suggests that rivalry will be conducted within a general framework of agreement on basic values and that conflict will occur in marginal areas that do not seriously threaten basic relationships. An example of such peripheral conflict is French insistence on limiting the access of American motion pictures into the French market on ostensibly cultural grounds.

However, the world has never experienced anything quite like the economic realities and changes we now observe. Chief among these are the unparalleled prosperity of growing parts of the globe (despite the global recession of the latter 1980s) and the massive economic cross-penetration that have "unleashed new competitors and opened national borders."[8] The loss of hegemony may place us in uncharted waters, but the question of whether the system will produce "conflict over economic issues or a healthy combination of competition and cooperation"[9] seems to be tilting toward the latter.

Each of the major players enters the competition with advantages and disadvantages. The United States has the largest economy of the three and the most productive basic research and development infrastructure. At the same time, the lead the United States has enjoyed is gradually eroding, particularly in the translation of scientific and engineering advances into commercial enterprises (products and services). Moreover, the United States lagged behind Japan and the European Community (now technically the European Union) in the most important areas during the 1980s: surplus capital combined with national self-discipline, advanced technology, and superior education.[10] During that period, there was virtual unanimity about relative American slippage, especially at the cutting edge of technology; there was also agreement that appropriate, if severe and painful, remedial actions discussed below can either restore American preeminence or at least stop the slide and stabilize the United States' place in the economic order. There are now clear signs of American relative recovery, as leaner U.S. corporations are increasingly challenging Japanese and European competitors in high-technology electronics and even in automobiles.

The Japanese economic miracle is at least temporarily on hold. Japan also enters the competition with advantages and disadvantages. The peculiar genius of the Japanese has been in translating technologies into products faster and better than anyone else. The most obvious examples have been in electronics and the application of microelectronics (notably computer chips) to a whole range of consumer products from watches to on-board automotive computers. Combined with very high domestic savings rates and consciously suppressed standards of individual living, Japan has also become the world's, and notably the United States', creditor. Conspicuous Japanese investment in the United States, such as the purchase of Rockefeller Center in New York, has created much suspicion and resentment among Americans. This is not aided by published Japanese polls in which the Japanese describe Americans as lazy and self-indulgent, among other things.

The peak of the curve may have been reached by the Japanese, however, for at least four reasons. First, Japan is the smallest of the competitors, with a population of only about 123 million. Unlike the United States, Japan cannot, for lack of space, and will not, because of cultural and racial beliefs, augment that population through immigration. Second, the Japanese population is aging more rapidly than those of the other economic superpowers. This means the Japanese will have a larger nonproductive population segment than the others, translating into higher social costs and labor shortages. Third, the Japanese face increasing competition, notably from other Asian nations such as South Korea, in market areas where Japan predominates. Korean automobiles and consumer electronic products nip at Japanese market shares but have very little effect on American and European industries. (For example, one might choose between a Hyundai and a Toyota but probably not between a Hyundai and a Mercedes or a Hyundai and a Pontiac.) Fourth, a certain amount of self-doubt began to emerge within Japan during 1993 about both government direction of the private sector and possible Japanese complacency. None of these factors suggest that the Japanese are in for a fall, only that the growth curve cannot rise indefinitely.

Particularly in light of the revolutions of 1989, the most interesting and uncertain member of the competition is Western Europe. Because of historic rivalries based in national divisions, Europe has lagged a bit behind, especially in the crucial areas of high technology. The prospects of economic union even before 1989 contained a European Community with a population larger than that of the United States and a gross national product (GNP) nearly equal. Those projections were based on, among other things, a divided Germany that no longer exists.

The breakdown of the Cold War system in Europe changes the EC 1992 scenario and probably will cause the scheduled union (the Maastricht Treaty) to be implemented cautiously. There are two key elements and uncertainties. The first is the reunified German state. Germany is having to devote considerable resources to the "economic development" of the former German Democratic Republic, and the integration of former East Germans into the highly competitive West German economy and society has proven to be more difficult than most assumed in 1989. The eventual outcome may prove to be a dominating German state. How that state will fit inside the institutional bounds of the European Community without obviously overwhelming everyone else is still unclear.

The second part of the equation is Eastern Europe, now referred to as Central Europe and the Balkans. Freed of the bonds of Soviet overlordship, the less developed states of this area are clamoring to partake progressively of the benefits of the West. Although the stigma of communism is gradually lifting, the Eastern European states still face considerable barriers: the need to develop democratic political systems and market economic practices that will make them "like" the West; the need for considerable infrastructure—including environmental—upgrading to make their economies competitive; and the peaceful resolution of long-simmering ethnic and national problems suppressed for forty years by the Russian boot. In other words, East Europe must meet the "entrance requirements" for First Tier membership through the European Community: stable political democracies and prosperous market economies.

None of these problems will be solved easily. Certainly the EC countries have incentives to help. A peaceful transition to democracy in Eastern Europe and the former Soviet Union would resolve the security dilemma that hung over the continent in the form of a mushroom cloud between 1945 and the end of the Cold War.

Much of this continues to depend on the course Germany takes. The German economy is the strongest in Europe, making its leadership and participation in the European Community (possibly eventually expanded eastward) vital to continental prosperity and competitiveness with the United States/NAFTA and Japan. At the same time, the more prosperous Germany becomes, the more powerful it becomes, which makes many of Germany's neighbors, mindful of past actions, nervous.

Economic Intertwining

One of the major driving factors in the new international economic order is the enormous interpenetration of economies by foreign concerns. It is not quite the "complex interdependence" extolled twenty years ago as the vehicle to peace. Rather, it is the intertwining of economic activity across national boundaries that is producing a more and more global economy in which national political borders are decreasingly relevant. This phenomenon is occurring mainly within the First Tier of states and is a primary defining characteristic of the First Tier. Gaining access to this globalizing system is the economic task of aspiring states.

Two examples may help capture some of the essence of what is going on. First, there is the emergence of the "true" multinational corporation (MNC). In its earlier form, we thought of the MNC as a company owned by people in one country who operated in several others, either through agencies or by buying subsidiaries overseas. A major characteristic of those MNCs was that they were nationally identifiable; and even if the "home" government had some difficulty controlling the actions of foreign subsidiaries of its MNCs, at least it could identify the parent by national origin.

The new MNC transcends this model because it adds to the characteristic of operation in multiple countries multinational ownership of the firm, either by individuals or by corporations, as well as an international management and work force and products made of components from several countries. Thus, Japanese and American automotive firms own considerable stock in one another's corporations, and when Kabota Tractor of Japan decided to get into the home computer business, its first act was to purchase interests in a number of small American electronics firms as a way to gain access to American technology. The MNCs are the prototypes of the so-called stateless corporations, companies so thoroughly internationalized in ownership and operation that it is difficult to identify them with any single state. The result is to lower the traditional barriers to economic activity created by national borders. This trend, according to Yasuhiro Nakasone, has been particularly stimulated by the electronics revolution that has facilitated global communications.[11]

A second example is the internationalization of production: relatively speaking, products of any complexity at all are rarely made of components produced exclusively in one country. More typically, there is some specialization of subcomponents, whereby one corporation in one country will control a particular component common to a given finished product line. In the process of producing finished products, however, there is considerable international commingling to the point that, for instance, "it is virtually impossible to separate Japanese from American technology; almost any advanced machine includes so much of both that it is fruitless to determine a machine's origin."[12] An example has been Mazda–Ford and Toyota–General Motors automobile collaboration. Using parts from all over the world, the Mitsubishi Eclipse, Plymouth Laser, and Eagle Talon have rolled off the same Bloomington, Illinois, assembly line, their only difference being their identifying logos. The Chevrolet-marketed Geo Prizm and the Toyota Corolla are similarly produced in the same factory in Fremont, California.

The increasing intertwining of economies is influenced by the high-technology phenomenon. The science that underlies technology is fundamentally international and will by nature flow across borders. The value of science is the accumulation of knowledge, which lends itself to a great deal of interaction among scientists, for whom boundaries are only hindrances to the ultimate goal.[13]

Scientific interchange is facilitated among like-minded First Tier capitalist democracies that do not try to shackle the flow of information across those boundaries. It is not coincidental that the three repositories of high technology and leadership in the new international economic order, the United States, Japan, and the European Community, share a common economic and political system and that the root of their commonality is the freedom of action in which science and technology also thrive. Indeed, intellectual entrepreneurial freedom is one of the defining characteristics of the First Tier.

The sharing of technologies adds to the international intertwining of the world economy and is a key element in prosperity. It has been argued, for instance, that technology transfer underpins economic growth and that accelerated transfer of modern technology creates a common dependence on science and technology for the maintenance of standards of living and economic progress.[14] This suggests that the internationalization of economies may be a positive-sum game in which all can benefit from cooperation and all who do not cooperate could lose. The Clinton administration seized these trends in its advocacy of NAFTA, APEC, and GATT (all discussed below).

A further element that both derives from and contributes to the dynamism of high technology is the revolution in knowledge generation and transmission. The exponentially increasing rate at which scientific knowledge is being expanded is the result of great strides in microelectronics, notably, smaller but more effective microchips capable of processing more information faster. At the same time, advances in photonics, notably the use of laser beams to send information through fiber-optic networks,[15] allow much more information to be transmitted over longer distances much faster than was ever before the case. This applies both to digitized computer interfaces across national boundaries and to fax transmission. The ability of scientists or corporations to communicate large bodies of knowledge that lead to the attainment of even greater advances is on the very near horizon—the well-publicized information superhighway.

The problem for the new international order is how to organize and accommodate this phenomenon in such a way as to maximize the benefits to all and thus avoid conflict. Particularly in the case of communications-based technologies, sovereign nation-states are decreasingly able to regulate activity. The advent of communications satellites and portable satellite dishes (the suitcase-sized dish that costs only a few hundred dollars is not far away) makes it virtually impossible, for instance, to keep television transmission out of a country. Video camcorders record almost any event that takes place, and Ted Turner's Cable News Network (CNN) and the British-based Independent Television Network (ITN) guarantee that it is broadcast.

One danger in this new system is the rise of something like intellectual protectionism, a call for which is occasionally heard in the United States for the purpose of protecting American technology from Japanese exploitation. If, indeed, the intertwining of technologically based international economies can produce a higher benefit for all through cooperation, then it will be necessary to create formal and informal structures and regimes to facilitate the interaction. Technology itself, however, is likely to transcend any efforts to shackle the flow of knowledge.

For better or worse, one victim of this phenomenon is likely to be effective national sovereignty. As corporations become progressively stateless,[16] they will fall further beyond the detailed control of individual states. Among other things, this places a limit on the usefulness of the economic element of national power in a system where the effective locus of economic activity transcends national bounds.

The High-Technology Motor

The driving force behind both the vast competition in the economic realm and the progressive internationalization of the world economic system is the complex of scientific breakthroughs collectively known as high technology, or the Third Industrial Revolution. What are these high technologies? Writing in 1989, Bobby Inman refers to telecommunications, microelectronics, aerospace, new materials, and biotechnology as areas that "hold promise for major new product opportunities over the next fifteen years."[17] Another analyst expands this list to include computers, communications and information-processing capability, artificial intelligence and robotics, smart weapons and associated technologies, computer-aided design/computer-aided manufacturing (CAD/CAM), and catalysis.[18]

This revolution began in the latter 1950s with the invention of the microprocessing chip, which allowed much larger amounts of information to be stored and manipulated than was previously possible, in the process creating the basis for the microelectronics industry that is at the core of the high-technology industry. Of equal revolutionary importance was the invention of digitization, the ability to reduce information to a two-digit vocabulary for processing purposes. This process allows information to be treated by the computer as a series of ones and zeros that can be added and subtracted so that virtually any kind of information can be converted into those streams of ones and zeros.[19]

Digitization radically increases the magnitude of information that a computer can analyze in a given time frame and makes plausible the transmission of enormous amounts of data instantaneously over great distances. The digitization of HDTV signal transmission by American firms allowed the United States to recoup world leadership in this vital link in the information superhighway. The key element in this aspect of the high-technology revolution is the use of fiber-optic communications networks, which are tiny glass cables that transmit blasts of digitized laser beams at incredible speeds. A *Scientific American* article recently reported that fiber-optic cables have been reported to carry as many as one *trillion* bits of information per second. In the past decade, the rates achieved by optical fibers increased by one hundred times, while the cost of fibers fell from three dollars to fifteen cents per meter.[20]

This combination of burgeoning capability and falling cost is also true of the microelectronics industry in general. We are just beginning to grasp the dimensions of this revolution and what it portends. Robert D. Hormats, for instance, attributes three major characteristics to the phenomenon: high dependence on advances in knowledge and information rather than on fixed investment, simultaneous spectacular rates of growth in a variety of areas touched by technology, and an important international component that transcends borders.[21] Some believe that within twenty years, information processing will be the industrialized world's largest economic activity.[22]

The high-technology phenomenon has come upon us so suddenly that observers and policy makers do not fully comprehend it. As Walter Wriston suggests, "Policymakers are discovering that many of the events that are altering the world come not in response to their actions, but are driven by technologies which they may only dimly understand."[23]

This is a serious concern for at least three reasons. First, preeminence in high technology will increasingly define economic developmental status. In the next century, superpower status may be defined in largely economic terms, but the basis of economic strength will be the ability to produce and commercialize the fruits of high-technology endeavors. Second, preeminence in high technology will belong largely to those countries and companies that are best able to nurture and develop the high-technology sectors of their overall economies. Clearly, understanding the phenomenon is a prerequisite to exploiting it. Third, the very dynamism of the process means that those who are ahead will tend to stay ahead or increase their leads, while those who fail to compete will be progressively disadvantaged.

High technology as an economic phenomenon can best be portrayed as the culmination of a two-step operation conducted by three different groups of people. The steps in the process are knowledge generation and knowledge application; the sets of actors are scientists and engineers (most congregated in research universities and institutes), government, and private industry. Each group is prominent at a different stage, and the quality of the outcome is largely the result of the quality of the interaction among the various groups along the way.

How and whether the relationships between these actors should be nourished continues to be controversial. In the 1980s, the Japanese approach involved forced collaboration among firms by the government through the Ministry of Industry and Trade (MITI), which received much credit for Japanese international economic success. Partially because it pushed the wrong technologies for HDTV, MITI is being forced to accept some of the blame for Japan's current economic downturn. By contrast, the Reagan and Bush administrations eschewed federal intervention in the economy as philosophically undesirable and economically counterproductive. Efforts to use government to stimulate collaboration is a cornerstone of President Clinton's economic and industrial policy.

Knowledge Generation

The first and most basic building block in the process toward high-technology status is scientific research and discovery, in other words, *knowledge generation.* Theoretical science is normally conducted by scientists in an academic setting and is carried out for the sake of the advancement of knowledge. Scientists do not generally seek to unlock the secrets of the universe with an eye on how discovery can be converted into something people will buy. Moreover, since the purpose of science is the most efficient production of knowledge possible, the free dissemination of knowledge within the international scientific community is a basic value of science.

Both the generation and the dissemination of knowledge benefit from the science that helps foster them. After all, scientists invented computers that are the tools for creating ever more capable generations of computers. Scientific exchange is now often based on the long-range interaction between scientists' computers exchanging digitized information by fiber-optic transmission or facsimile transmission. (Emerging generations of fax machines will produce greatly enhanced images, thanks to the conversion of telecommunications networks from copper wire to fiber-optic cables.) The effect is progressively to merge the computer and telecommunications revolutions into a unified phenomenon.

The unresolved questions about research are sponsorship and ownership. Scientific research is expensive, its outcomes are uncertain, and scientists want to publicize and share their results. All three of these characteristics make the sponsorship of research unattractive to most private enterprises. Since it is difficult to translate investments in science directly into profits and losses, many firms find it impossible to justify large research budgets to investors. Moreover, when corporations do sponsor research, they do not want it shared widely, because "the future of any high technology business lies in its accumulated intellectual property, including patents, copyrights, trade secrets, and know-how."[24] This latter friction is really over ownership of science, and places scientists and businessmen at direct odds, making collaboration difficult, at least in the United States.

This relationship between the scholarly and business communities brings out a contrast between the United States and Japan that has been a source of American historical disadvantage. American corporations are notoriously reluctant to invest in basic research, and most American firms do not do so in any sizable amounts. Because basic research requires a long-term investment, this reluctance reinforces a bias toward looking only at the short run of quarterly profits. In turn, "for technology-based industry, an obsession with the short term can be devastating. Science and technology, including manufacturing excellence, are inherently long-term propositions."[25]

Given the reluctance of American firms to cough up research dollars, the vast bulk of research monies comes from government, mainly the federal government and specifically the Department of Defense

(DOD), justified in national security terms. One investigator notes that in 1988 the DOD accounted for 17 percent of all federal spending for university research, up from 12 percent in 1980.[26] The major cause for this upsurge since 1983 has been former President Reagan's Strategic Defense Initiative, which was the nation's single most highly funded research project during the 1980s.

The situation has created some competitive disadvantages for the United States. On the one hand, sponsorship by the government, and especially the DOD, means there is very little coordination of overall effort, especially in the direction of aiding and guiding the application of knowledge to commercial advantage. Even the suggestion that research funding might be tied to commercialism creates great furor at both ends of the spectrum: in the liberal community, it is "welfare for the rich"; in the conservative business community, it is restrictive, regulatory "industrial policy." On the other hand, quite predictable cuts in overall defense spending will almost certainly hit research funding first. Given that the government has been slow to fund nondefense research historically, those funds could largely dry up. Recognizing that potential problem and committed to industrial policy, the Clinton administration reverted the major DOD research-sponsoring agency—the Defense Advanced Research Projects Agency (DARPA)—to its original designation by dropping the *D* from its name and moving it administratively.

The Japanese experience is different. The Japanese government is very active in aiding and directing industry. In one instance, four major Japanese electronic firms were forced to pool their resources for funding and developing HDTV. The government's reasoning and argument in that case, as well as other precedents, was that there would be plenty of profit for all once this technology was mastered, and that it was the country that got HDTV first that would win. Unfortunately for the Japanese, they rejected digitization as the means for transmitting images, opting instead for more traditional means. The result has been a tremendous boost for American technology—and especially electronics—that is helping to reverse the negative technological trends of the 1980s.

Despite the more difficult relationship among the three constituent groups in the United States over basic research, basic research remains the great source of American advantage. American universities, especially those with graduate programs that train scientists, remain the envy of the world by any measure, such as the number of Nobel laureates working in American universities. Unfortunately, those programs are increasingly made up of foreign students, raising the concern that "although high technology is growing, it will meet severe competition down the road because foreign students in U.S. universities are returning to their countries after graduation."[27] Many of those students are staying here as well, but if they ever decide to go back to their native countries in massive proportions, there will be a "reverse brain drain" that would constitute a national emergency.

Knowledge Application

The second part of high technology is *knowledge application*, translating basic scientific discoveries into goods and services that can be marketed successfully. In essence, this is a two-step process. First, one must see what applications are possible from a given technology, and these are normally not obvious. When the laser was first discovered, no one thought of it as a way to make telephone lines sound clearer or as a way to enhance the quality of musical recordings. Second, one must have the marketing skills to determine whether a market exists for an application to be created. When the transistor was first devised as an alternative to vacuum tubes, one of the first applications devised by its American inventors was in small, portable radios. American firms determined that the quality of sound from such a device would be so vastly inferior to large stereo systems then appearing on the market that they abandoned the idea. Sony picked it up, and the success of the Walkman is history.

Almost all observers agree that commercialization of technology has been the area of the most glaring Japanese advantage in the new international economic competition. Japan's strength has been in commercializing ideas from elsewhere into high-quality products. A particularly glaring example is consumer electronics: most of the basic scientific breakthroughs underlying that industry occurred in the United States; the profits, so important in balance-of-trade terms, have been reaped in Japan.

There is some indication that this is still occurring, but American successes like HDTV may narrow the gap. Robotics and its associated technologies, for example, are critical to the automation of assembly, to quality control on the assembly line, to the CAD/CAM process, and to the "flexible manufacturing plant" concept most agree will be crucial to future competitiveness. (This term refers to production facilities capable of rapid changes in production and products to meet changes in demand.) Yet the Young Commission found in 1985 that the United States had failed to apply its own technologies to manufacturing, and that robotics, automation, and statistical quality control, all developed in the United States, have been more effectively applied elsewhere.[28]

This is an important problem because it will help define competitiveness in the future. As former Secretary of Defense Harold Brown describes it, "The application of advanced microelectronics and robotics to the functioning and production of other manufactured goods will be critical to productivity and marketing. If Japan takes a decisive lead in that application, American manufacturers will fall irretrievably behind in competitive markets."[29]

The opportunities and potential problems that high technology creates will likely multiply with time and contribute greatly to the new international economic caste system that divides the First and Second Tiers. At the top will be those who have mastered both the basic and the applied aspects of the process; they will have the expertise and products that everyone else wants. In the Second Tier will be those countries benefiting indirectly from the process; for instance, the countries in which high-technology leaders invest and build their automated production facilities. At the lowest rung of the Second Tier will be those left entirely outside the process. The gap between the top and the bottom will almost surely widen, creating an envy that may prove too great to control. Moreover, the communications revolution that accompanies and is an integral part of the entire high-technology movement will make it painfully clear to all who are the "haves" and who are the "have-nots."

The Teleommunications Revolution

At one level, the revolution in global communication is simply one part of the broader technology phenomenon, permitting instantaneous exchange of information among scientists and researchers. As we have seen, this role itself is significant because it creates the ability to accelerate the process of scientific interchange.

But the telecommunications revolution is more than that. It is also one of the core components of the international economic phenomenon. The discovery and commercialization of telecommunications advances constitite one of the key high technologies that define success in the high-technology competition. At the same time, breakthroughs in telecommunications have facilitated the internationalization of economic activity. The diverse, complex international interchange on which the stateless corporations are based would have been quite impossible to undertake with the communications instruments available ten or fifteen years ago. Also the "worldwide, twenty-four-hour-a-day" stock market —in which traders all over the world can conduct transactions all the time in New York, Tokyo, or London—has added to the increasingly international character of the global economy.

The Impact of Global Television

The revolutionary changes associated with modern telecommunications have, by and large, occurred outside the realm of public awareness. Clearly within the public eye, however, is another phenomenon with equally dramatic effect: the emergence of global television. The cumulative impact of satellite transmission of television images, small video camcorders, and satellite dishes has been to transform "the content of television news broadcast by making news from around the world available almost immediately, certainly on the same day."[30]

Global television news organizations have combined these technologies, providing a common news base to essentially everybody in the world. Cable News Network (CNN), although basically an American television company broadcasting globally rather than a truly global company, is available around the world, as is ITN. Moreover, anyone in the world can become a "stringer" for CNN by sending camcorder film of events to Ted Turner's Atlanta headquarters. One dramatic instance of this was in 1989 when the People's Republic of China used troops to suppress a nationalist uprising in Tibet. The Chinese thought they were conducting the exercise in seclusion and must have been chagrined to see same-day coverage on CNN, courtesy of a tourist's video taken on the scene.

The effects of global television are, one suspects, greater than its inventors had dreamed. At the simplest level, events from all over the world come into one's home virtually as they are happening, as was so obvious during Operation Desert Storm. Moreover, governments are discovering that it is futile to try to stop this flow of information (a few places such as the People's Republic of China and Cuba are slow learners in this regard), because "the satellite knows no national boundaries."[31] With a common and very broad base of information available to just about everyone, the globe has to shrink conceptually, and there has to be a lessening of distortion about what is going on in the world. Moreover, we have some reason to believe that this common reference point represented by CNN may prove to have been the prerequisite to some common base of knowledge and attitude for the emergence of the "global village." By way of example, CNN no longer allows its employees to use the word "foreign" on the air.

Modern, worldwide television has an increasingly strong impact on the way in which governments do business and on the business that they do. Although many public figures find an omnipresent network of reporters and television cameras an annoyance and an intrusion, for the most part this influence has been for the good, if democratizing domestic and international politics is a praiseworthy endeavor.

Among the qualities that "borderless television" brings to the public is the decreasing ability of public figures to lie, although the effects may be doubled-edged. Governments will be less able to separate their audiences, telling one thing to their domestic public and another to foreigners. This was evident during the early stages of Operation Desert Shield, when George Bush's warnings to Saddam Hussein mostly frightened Americans. On the other hand, in addition to less duplicity, there will be more ambiguity in government positions as these are diluted for multiple audiences.[32] This means, of course, that internal and external positions will have to be consistent with one another, imposing a standard of honesty that has not hitherto been evident in some societies.

One can argue that a main effect of the telecommunications revolution is to restrict governmental actions: "Governments were freer to do whatever they wanted—good or bad—before TV. So be it. Television is here to stay and getting more proficient every day at seeing everything anywhere."[33] If this is true, as at least arguably it is, the impact of modern telecommunications is in line with the general phenomenon of democratization begun by the revolutions of 1989.

Consider two ways in which modern telecommunications may have influenced change in Eastern Europe and even the Soviet Union during the crucial months of 1989. First and fundamentally, the transmission of West European, and especially West German, television into the Eastern bloc was clearly part of the reason that change was desired. No amount of government propaganda could erase the clear demonstration of a fundamental, and growing, disparity in economic performance and living standards in the two regions. Of the various East European leaders, Nikolai Ceausescu of Romania tried most seriously to lie to his people about the success of communism in his country, and his "reward" from his people was most severe (he and his wife were brutally executed).

A second effect was the contagion of events. When the first movements toward real democratization began to occur, people throughout the Warsaw Pact countries could see their success. Most important, they could see the absence of Soviet military suppression. Gorbachev's renunciation of the Brezhnev Doctrine was sincere; with no Soviet tanks acting as props for the regimes, fear disappeared and the regimes fell with breathtaking speed.

Modern telecommunications also strongly affect the way international relations and foreign policy are conducted. Diplomacy, traditionally the stuff of top hats and closed doors, is increasingly tailored as a media event, where positions and offers are stated before cameras and where negotiating sessions end with televised news conferences. In this regard, it is remarkable—and shows considerable inventiveness— that the Oslo negotiations between Israel and the Palestine Liberation Organization (PLO) escaped television exposure. At the same time, the way crises are handled is increasingly influenced by the fact that almost all potential crises are subject to the unrelenting glow of the cameras from the virtual moment of inception.

The diplomatic victims of modern telecommunications are those involved in operating the embassy system. Prior to the advent of almost instantaneous global communication, the embassy system was the hub of international relations. The embassy was a government's major source of information (intelligence) about a foreign country, and the slowness of communications allowed an ambassador considerable discretion in solving problems. The ambassador was the critical link in the chain.

He or she no longer is, because governments no longer need ambassadors to do the things they used to do. In terms of information, policy makers turn to CNN when events are occurring in a country; no policy maker in Washington, for instance, could function without access to

CNN. World leaders are avid watchers. The intelligence role of the embassy is thus restricted to providing more in-depth material or to "covering" things not newsworthy enough for the news networks.

At the same time, ambassadors no longer need to make important decisions. Worldwide telecommunications have made ambassadors conduits, errand boys between governments. When an important matter comes up, the ambassador is called into the foreign office, where a problem is handed to him. He then returns to the embassy, calls his own foreign office, and waits for the officials there to decide what to do. Once they have done so, he relays the decision back.

Often, the embassy is bypassed altogether. Governments today increasingly communicate with each other through the media, with the public as the major spectator. In the extreme, "The result of public diplomacy resembles that of air warfare—the target and non-target populations become subject to the same battery of fire."[34] It was reported shortly before the June 1990 summit that the Soviet government wanted to relate a significant change in position to the U.S. government. However, the Soviets did not go to the U.S. embassy to expedite the announcement; instead they called the CNN Moscow bureau chief.

One area in which the media can most dramatically influence international affairs, potentially with very salutary effects, is that of crisis management. The media can use several different approaches: publicizing potential crises before they become major problems, clarifying positions and even acting as go-betweens and mediators, and helping to influence public opinion. Each approach can contribute to the amelioration of a conflict situation.

Crises tend to thrive in environments of maximum mistrust, lack of information, and misunderstanding among parties. Differing versions of events can have a major influence on how the sides view an incident and whether it will expand. Accurate reportage thus becomes a tool for ensuring that all involved at least understand something like the same reality in a potential crisis situation.

Communication between parties involved in a conflict is also a very difficult matter that can add to distortion of issues. Here, modern communications operatives can be of assistance because of their "ability to cut through bureaucracy and reach governmental leaders directly with information about the world situation, through their capacity to affect official priorities, and through their power to mobilize public opinion, which decision-makers must take into account."[35] The fact that the media possess an increasing ability to publicize events makes public participation through mass media an increasingly important factor in managing international conflicts.[36] The image that instantly comes to mind is one in which the leaders of both sides of a blooming crisis appear simultaneously on Ted Koppel's *Nightline* on the day an incident occurs. During the Iraq–Kuwait crisis, Saddam Hussein and George Bush communicated regularly, if indirectly, by issuing statements, proposals, and positions in the daily news.

It is hard to imagine some of history's tragedies occurring in a world of modern mediation. The series of misunderstandings between Kaiser Wilhelm and Czar Nicholas that contributed to the slide to World War I would probably not have occurred had there been the kind of mediation we have today. At the same time, the Japanese attack on Pearl Harbor would have been impossible to disguise from the watchful eyes of satellite cameras and television cameras.

As a pillar of democratic society, the expansion of modern telecommunications can act to promote the democratization of the globe, which is one of the hopeful consequences of the end of the Cold War. At a minimum, modern media capabilities make it increasingly difficult to run an old-fashioned repressive government, one of whose bases of power is a monopoly on information and thus the ability to deceive its own population. In addition, the exposure of most of the world's population to a uniform pool of information about what is happening globally is bound to have a homogenizing effect on perceptions around the world. In the process, we may be able to test the old conundrum of whether familiarity produces comity or breeds contempt.

Emerging Trends: Signs of Economic Globalization

Technological progress and the telecommunications revolution have not only increased the amount of scientific and economic interchange, they have also allowed interaction across national boundaries, which, in addition to stimulating interchange and interaction by private firms, is resulting in increased interactions among countries and regions as well.

If there were any previous doubts about the extent to which the world's economy—especially but not exclusively within the First Tier —was becoming global, three occurrences in 1993 should have laid those doubts to rest. The events were the highly publicized Seattle meeting of APEC, the ratification of NAFTA by the member governments, and the successful completion of the Uruguay round of the GATT. All three have histories that precede 1993: APEC was initiated by then-Australian Prime Minister Keating in 1989; NAFTA was originally negotiated by the Bush administration; and the Uruguay round started seven years before its completion. All three arose in the public consciousness during the second half of 1993 as symbols of economic internationalization coming on the heels of EC ratification of the Treaty of Maastricht.

The European Community

The European Community, especially as it moves toward full economic union under the terms of the Maastricht Treaty (whose provisions extend to political and security concerns but whose heart is economic), will also contribute to the emerging pattern. The economic union will not only eliminate all internal trade barriers, barriers on movements and people, and common tariffs for goods coming from the outside. In addition, it is scheduled to create a monetary union and common currency to eliminate remaining barriers to trade among the twelve members. When it is fully implemented, the European Community will represent an economic and trading bloc that would rival the United States prior to its association with NAFTA (which, of course, was part of the lure of the arrangement).

All the other forms of economic association are less developed than the European Community, which, after all, dates back to the implementation of the Treaty of Rome, which created the then–European Economic Community. Thus, the European Community has a thirty-five-year headstart on the others.

The North American Free Trade Area

The NAFTA agreement, which survived bitter ratification struggles and considerable opposition in all three countries, the United States, Canada and Mexico, will lead to a free trade area among its original members and will likely extend more broadly through the hemisphere. The purpose of the union, which will be implemented gradually over a period of fifteen years through a complicated schedule of action, is to remove all tariff and other trade restrictions among the three members. When NAFTA is fully implemented, goods and services will flow freely across the member borders, subject to no restrictions.

The balance within NAFTA is asymmetrical. The United States represents something like 85 percent of the market measured in GNP terms, and thus will likely dominate. This leads some within Mexico and Canada to fear the arrangement as a form of American private economic imperialism that may overwhelm indigenous enterprises. The U.S. opposition, symbolized by the mercurial H. Ross Perot, fears that American jobs will be lost as firms move their operations to Mexico to exploit cheaper labor costs there (Perot described this as the "great sucking sound" of American jobs moving south of the border).

Although it did not negotiate the NAFTA agreement, the Clinton administration embraced the concept and forcefully lobbied its ratification. The arguments used were similar to observations made in the preceding pages about the internationalization of the world economy. Clinton argued that rejection of the pact would mark a retreat from trends in the world economy and could trigger a dangerous return to protectionism that also would buck emerging trends. NAFTA is likely to spread to other countries of the hemisphere. Chile and Argentina have already applied for membership, and others will undoubtedly follow suit if the association is a success. It is not inconceivable that NAFTA will become a hemispherewide organization. Alternatively, Brazil has recently promoted a parallel South American Free Trade Area.

Asian-Pacific Economic Cooperation

APEC is a fairly recent, more amorphous phenomenon. It first convened in 1989 as a forum for countries along the Pacific Rim to discuss economic issues of mutual interest—a kind of G-7 for the countries lapping the Pacific Ocean. It has met as a moving conference ever since, although most Americans were barely aware of it until it met in Seattle and was made a major media event by the personal and highly visible appearances of, among others, President Clinton and China's Deng Xiao-ping.

APEC currently has eighteen members. From the Western Hemisphere, the members are the United States, Canada, Mexico, and Chile. The Asian members include Australia, Brunei, China, Hong Kong,

Japan, Korea (South), Malaysia, Indonesia, New Zealand, Papua–New Guinea, the Phillippines, Singapore, Taiwan, and Thailand. It is the most inclusive organization in the region, by virtue of the participation of both the United States and China (the major competitor organization, the East Asian Economic Council, excludes the United States). The inclusion of China creates a means of continuing an economic dialogue between the world's fastest-growing economy and the rest of Asia and the United States. (President Clinton used the Seattle meeting to pressure Deng on Chinese human rights violations.) Moreover, the organization also includes several First Tier and the major near–First Tier states, notably the ASEAN states and Korea.

The future evolution of APEC is uncertain. Currently, it is no more than a series of conferences where states meet to discuss their differences. That, of course, was how the Group of Seven began, and its activities have expanded. All G-7 members, however, are firmly entrenched First Tier states; the membership of APEC is more politically and economically diverse. At the same time, American participation creates an important link between the United States and the dynamic economies of this part of the world.

The General Agreement on Tariffs and Trade

GATT is the oldest international organization devoted entirely to the lowering of international trade barriers. It was the result of negotiations held in 1947 to create an International Trade Organization (ITO) as part of the United Nations system of specialized agencies. When it became clear that the United States Senate would not ratify the treaty creating the ITO, the GATT was negotiated as a less formalized organization under an executive agreement. When it began operations in 1948, GATT had twenty-three member states (called contracting parties to suggest something other than member states); at the signing of the Uruguay round in December 1993, the GATT had 116 participating states. Most of the nonparticipating states are poorer Second Tier nations that have historically viewed the GATT as a "rich man's club."

The purpose of GATT throughout its existence has been to negotiate reductions in trade barriers such as tariffs and quotas. It accomplishes this through annual business meetings among the contracting parties that attempt to broaden the list of items on which trade barriers are removed or substantially reduced. To this end, tariff barriers on manufactured goods have fallen from about 40 percent in the latter 1940s to about 5 percent today through GATT agreements among the contracting parties.

The Uruguay round got its name because it was initiated at the 1986 GATT meeting in Puenta del Este, Uruguay. It covers a number of items, including reductions of tariffs on such things as agricultural products (a sticking point between the United States and the European Community over restrictions to protect European, especially French, agriculture) and pharmaceuticals, protections of intellectual property (such as patents and copyrights), and the creation of a new, and more powerful, international trade organization (a provision opposed by the Clinton administration). Industries expected to be affected by implementation include agriculture, automobiles, financial services, steel, textiles, and entertainment (motion pictures, television programs, and musical recordings). The Organization of Economic Cooperation and Development (OECD) estimates that the agreement could stimulate more than $270 billion in annual worldwide trade by the year 2002.

The progress in GATT is part of the broader impact of economic globalization. If the goal is to create a global free market that facilitates increased trade across national boundaries, then regional associations like the European Community and NAFTA may be interim solutions, broadening trade bases somewhat but not universally. The same could be said of a formalized APEC. On the other hand, the global success of the GATT process could eventually make regional associations less necessary by knocking down trade barriers more widely. Any or all could also act as conduits, bringing Second Tier states into the First Tier.

The Second Tier and the Global Economic Revolution

Most of the exciting change in the international economic order is occurring in the First Tier—the old First World of the Cold War days —and in those principally Asian states that are near-members. Currently left out are the countries of the old Second or Socialist World and the traditional Third World states, which collectively comprise the Second Tier. The outcome of change is problematical in the old Second World, where a few states have legitimate medium-term aspirations to First Tier status but where the majority, including most of the former Soviet Union, are likely to wallow somewhere down the ladder of Second Tier status.

Understanding where these states stand in the evolving order is of consequence. The states most traumatized by change were those of the former Soviet Union; of those, the Russian Republic, which encompasses 75 percent of the landmass and half the population of the old Soviet Union, is by far the most consequential. Since Russia retains the Soviet Union's nuclear arsenal and has begun to display neonationalist signs (like the emergence of Vladimir Zhirinovsky), the prospects for Russian economic success are important geopolitically. Given that it is the locus of considerable political and military instability, the rest of the Second Tier is also of interest.

Russia and the Global Economy

The momentous events that overtook and ultimately destroyed the Soviet Union can only be fully understood in terms of the revolutionary events in the global economy, and especially the progressive disadvantage the Soviets accumulated in the critical high-technology areas. The situation was stark: the cause of Soviet decline was a failed economy that could not compete with the West and that had lost its appeal as an economic or political model both within and outside the Communist world. Gorbachev and his reformers understood their position, especially the central importance of joining the First Tier of international economics to retain major power status into the next century. Yeltsin's reformers seem to understand this as well.

In order to enter the technology race, the Russians must do in essence two things. First, they must encourage the kind of entrepreneurial behavior that underlies high technology in the West. In the West, progress has been most closely associated with the ability to benefit greatly on the material level. The old Soviet system, which was consciously structured to level wealth, will have to be turned on its head to create such a situation. Given that many Russians still see the egalitarian bias of Marxism-Leninism as its principal strength, this will not be easy.[37] Moreover, for material incentives to become meaningful, the system has to start producing. The early experience with restructuring is clear evidence that the initial effects of reform may stimulate the disruptive effects of reorganization, impeding the application of quality control and the introduction of new technologies.[38]

Creating an internal environment compatible with the dictates of modern technological and economic development must clearly be a major goal of reform. The difficulty of making the transition can be ameliorated to some degree by doing the second necessary thing—getting Russian scientists plugged into the international network of high-technology development. Traditionally, the Russians have excluded themselves from the world economy as a way to buffer their system from the exigencies of international economics, and have been excluded from scientific exchange on national security grounds, as most technological breakthroughs are "dual use" (they have both civilian and military applications). To gain access, the Russians have introduced the new political thinking as a way to appear less threatening and have unleashed a broad interpersonal dialogue between Russian and Western scientists. It is unmistakable that a major benefit of ending the Cold War for the Russians is gaining entrance into the world scientific community. It is really their only chance, "an enabling precondition,"[39] of joining the First Tier. Pooling resources with the Americans on building the space station is a good first step toward scientific collaboration.

The failure to compete technologically is not simply a matter of where the Russians will be ranked among the future world economic powers, although that is certainly an important aspect. Technological inferiority will also affect the competitiveness of the Soviet military. Recognition that the "scientific-technical component has become the most dynamic factor in military comparison" was a recurrent theme of Soviet military writing for most of the 1980s.[40] Recognition of the dual-use nature of military technology apparently convinced the Soviet military of the need to reform the civilian sector to provide a firmer scientific base for military innovation,[41] although some erosion in that support was evident in the 1993 Russian election, where 25 to 50 percent of the Russian military apparently voted for Zhirinovsky. The performance of U.S. military technology against Iraqi-operated Soviet equipment in the Kuwaiti desert must have reinforced this perception.

The Old Third World and the Global Economy

If the position of Russia in the new international economic order is problematic, that of most of the rest of the Second Tier is even more bleak. Russia has at least gone through the so-called First Industrial Revolution of heavy industrialization and has some of the basic human intellectual and material infrastructure in place to have some prospect of eventual competitiveness. For most of the Second Tier, the gap between the poor South and the rich North is simply widening to the proportions of an unbridgeable chasm.

One of the major difficulties in talking about the Second Tier is that there is no single Second Tier that serves as the basis for comparisons, as noted in chapter 1. When we speak of the Second Tier, we are generally talking about the countries of Africa, Asia, and Latin America. Particularly in economic terms, they are an exceedingly diverse lot that can be viewed in the six sequential categories of wealth and possibility already noted.

At the top of the list are the structurally developed and stable states, those that are on the threshold of joining the First Tier. Concentrated largely on the Pacific Rim, these are the newly industrialized countries—the NICs—such as the members of ASEAN and the Four Tigers. Most of these countries have not gone through the traditional period of First Industrial Revolution development. Rather, they have made themselves appealing to firms in the most advanced countries by providing an attractive climate for private investment in such ways as tax structures and legal systems tempting to foreign investors, and developing infrastructure and good educational systems to provide a quality work force. From that base, these countries have developed the capital and expertise to engage in development on their own. The Republic of Korea is a prime example. The NIC success story may provide a model for countries in the other subtiers, notably the second.

The next category of Second Tier states are those that are developed structurally but have unstable political systems. Generally speaking, countries in this category have achieved reasonable economic development but have political democracies that either are in their infancies or are nonexistent. Usually, the tenuousness of the systems results from the accumulation of a large external debt that simultaneously constricts the funds available both for further development and for the provision of social services that would bring popularity and stability to political systems.

Thus, for many Second Tier states, the most important single barrier to the development of Third World countries in directions that would facilitate their entry into the new economic order is accumulated debt and the enormous privations that come from the simple servicing (paying the interest on the debt without retiring the principal) of that debt.

Most Third World external debt is a product of loaning practices by governments and private lending institutions during the 1960s and 1970s based on the notion that such lending would allow countries to "take off" and develop rapidly enough so that they could retire their debts from earnings. Unfortunately, this did not occur. Instead, debt was simply allowed to accumulate, eating progressively into the ability of governments to deal with it. To get some idea of the magnitude of the problem, seventy-nine cents of each new dollar borrowed by Latin American nations has historically been used solely to pay interest on past loans. Two-thirds of Latin America's export earnings were being consumed by debt payments. Moreover, in every year since 1986, at least $43 billion in net financial resources has been transferred from the South to the North, making the total external debt of the Third World a crushing $1.2 trillion.[42] Moreover, not only is the gulf between rich and poor nations widening, the gap within these societies is increasing as well, meaning "the hopeless masses of the periphery will witness the spectacle of the wealth of others."[43] A prime example is Mexico, whose prospects for escaping the cycle have been enhanced by membership in NAFTA. Chile, Argentina, and a number of others may also eventually share in this prospect.

Apart from the future of the resource-rich but politically underdeveloped countries (the third subtier), whose prosperity is guaranteed by an unremitting First Tier addiction to petroleum energy, the prospects for the rest of the Second Tier are not so good. The fourth subtier comprises partially developed states, those countries that have undergone some development, usually in selected areas of the economy, but which remain underdeveloped in others. Their prospects for progress are probably tied to sharing in the success of the regions in which they find themselves. Thus, India—or some of the successor states to an India whose disintegration is not entirely unlikely—may be enhanced by being part of the greater success of Asia, and places in South America like Peru or Bolivia may share in the growing prosperity of the NAFTA region (should that succeed).

The prospects are most grim for the potentially developable and undevelopable countries (the fifth and sixth subtiers). In an era when there is unlikely to be an expanding supply of publicly available development assistance, these countries must devise strategies to attract private investment. By definition, they lack the infrastructural items (roads, power sources, educated populations, and the like) to be attractive, and political instability and physical isolation only add to their problems. Of all the parts of the world, much of Africa falls into this dim set of prospects.

One question is how long the peoples of the Second Tier will put up with this situation. Clearly, the countries of the Second Tier are too diverse and too poor to rise up in unison and take things away from the rich of the North. They can, however, attack people of privilege in their own societies, which is a major continuing source of internal violence in the Second Tier. At the same time, they may increasingly follow the lead of many in Central America and vote with their feet by simply migrating to the North.

The alternative to this unsatisfactory situation is to provide opportunities for Second Tier countries to join the action. Although these countries cannot soon, if ever, attain the status of the economic superpowers, they can, under the right circumstances, derive the prosperity of the advanced countries through collusion. This means emulating the strategy of the Four Tigers for breaking out of the cycle of underdevelopment. This requires breaking out of the cycle of low-wage activities common to the Second Tier that provide very little opportunity for growth. It often requires "external interventions" to improve the quality of resources through better education and health, all matters of infrastructure development. Once this has occurred, Second Tier countries can become attractive to private investors. The advantage to industry is lower labor costs once commercialization has been routinized, because technologies are standardized and skills are embodied in the equipment.

There is, of course, nothing new about such arguments, which have their roots in the 1950s and 1960s. The new emerging international order changes the context of the transfer of technology and jobs to the South. First, the internationalization of economics makes firms more receptive to investing in the South. Internationalization is more accepted by today's industrial leaders; they are more comfortable working in international environments. At the same time, the telecommunications revolution makes it possible to run global enterprises in a way that was simply impossible earlier. Second, the model of the NICs suggests that inclusion of the Second Tier can be a positive-sum game. From the vantage point of the most developed countries, transferring highly developed technologies to the South, where wages are lower, results in cheaper products. From the vantage point of the South, such investment means jobs and prosperity and, with enterprise, the progressive ability to compete with the North. The technological revolution, in other words, contains the potential—admittedly unrealized—to narrow the gap between North and South.

The secret to success, clearly, is the kind of development that will make individual Second Tier countries as attractive in the future as places such as South Korea and Taiwan have been in the past. The question is, where are the resources going to come from to facilitate the necessary infrastructure development? If debt service eats up most of the earnings that can be invested in the future, then the answer may be to find a nonruinous way to forgive that debt and lift the monkey from Second Tier backs. At the same time, countries such as Japan, with its great accumulation of capital, can aid in the process through the provision of what Zbigniew Brzezinski calls "strategic international economic aid—the deliberate allocation of economic aid to Central America and countries as varied as the Philippines, Thailand, Pakistan, Afghanistan, Egypt, and Poland."[44] Clearly his concept contains both economic and geopolitical criteria, but nonetheless, promoting political stability through economic prosperity is not an altogether discredited idea.

This is not, unfortunately, a comprehensive solution to the problem of Second Tier position in the new order. There is yet a sixth category of Second Tier countries—those countries that are underdeveloped and that, through lack of human and natural resources, have little if any realistic prospect of joining the world's developed states. These poorest of countries, at the bottom rungs of the Second Tier's subtiers, offer only anguish.

Conclusions

It is absolutely clear that a greatly changed economic environment will play a major role in how the post–Cold War international system is structured. Economic concerns will be more important in the highly competitive economic environment that will mark the twenty-first century. Three preliminary conclusions can be stated about that influence.

First, the international economic system is in a state of massive transition. The dynamism and magnitude of change that the structure of international economic activity has undergone, noted extensively in purely economic terms to date, has received only scant attention in political, and especially geopolitical, terms; that examination is long overdue.

The examination of the economic transformation and where it will lead is made more complicated by the dynamism of the high-technology motor that has made the transformation possible and continues to drive the system. Technology has made change possible by allowing an unprecedented amount and quality of communication. At the same time, continued preeminence in technological proficiency marks success or failure in the economic competition of the new international order. Once again, our understanding of the geopolitical impacts of high technology is currently deficient. Not only are we seeking a good handle on how to legislate an atmosphere domestically that will enhance high technological prospects; we have hardly looked at the problem in an international political perspective.

A second conclusion is that the new economic order will be internationalized to an extent never before imaginable. Economic activity will become increasingly international in all its aspects: ownership, management, labor, and production. The 1960s and 1970s image of the multinational corporation as a giant company owned and operated out of one country and doing business in several countries is inadequate for current and future understanding. The model for the future may well be the stateless corporation—a company whose ownership is multinational —that does business in many states, with management and labor forces internationally defined. What we do not know is how the stateless corporation fits into the new order: "Are all industrial nations part of one big happy global economy where nationality doesn't matter? Or are they merely entering a new stage of intensified economic competition?"[45] The internationalizing roles of regional arrangements such as NAFTA and APEC offer tantalizing prospects for change within varying levels of organizational formalization.

The answer to this question remains to be seen, but one thing that comprises the third conclusion is clear. As economic activities and institutions become increasingly international, they will move progressively away from the effective control of individual nation-states. We may be witnessing the progressive "privatization" of international politics. If so, this has three important implications for the shape of the future international system.

One implication is that, although we will undoubtedly continue to rank countries on the basis of economic power, the rankings will not mean as much as they once did. In the Cold War system, power ranking was equated with military prowess, and until that power became excessive to any application, it could be used to compel other states to act in accordance with national interest. In a system where economic rank means the strength of the component companies that operate in a country, and where those companies are owned and operated internationally to the point where national origin is blurred, it is more difficult to see how meaningful national threats can be fashioned to employ the economic element of power.

A second implication is in the area of national political control and influence over economic activity. The nature of emerging business is such that "as cross-border trade and investment flows reach new heights, big global companies are effectively making decisions with little regard to national boundaries."[46] One of the legitimate reasons national governments want to maintain some control over economic activity is to guarantee that the nation's defense needs can be met by national resources. When the means of production are no longer in national hands, some reasonable question has to be raised about the state of a country's national security.

A third and related implication has to do with state sovereignty. The possession of supreme authority is and has been the cornerstone of the international system of nation-states since its birth. The state, however, is in danger of simply becoming irrelevant to effective sovereign control over its economic health, due to interpenetration and internationalization of economic activity. Clearly, state sovereignty has been the cause of much misery and grief through the years, notably as a major justification for going to war. As a result, some applaud any dilution of sovereignty. At the same time, sovereignty has provided an organizational basis and rationale for the international system; a world in which the basis of sovereignty is weakened will have a different, and less predictable, organizational base as well.

Notes

1. John A. Young, *Global Competition: The New Reality* (Washington, DC: The Report of the President's Commission on Industrial Competitiveness, January 1985), 6.

2. Daniel Bell, "The World and the United States in 2013," *Daedalus, 116,* 3 (Summer 1987): 9.

3. Robert D. Hormats, "Introduction," in Andrew J. Pierre (ed.), *A High Tech-*

nology Gap? Europe, America and Japan (New York: New York University Press, 1987), 4.

4. Young, *Global Competition*, 13.

5. Charles H. Ferguson, "America's High-Tech Decline," *Foreign Policy, 74* (Spring 1989): 124.

6. Tom Forester, *High-Tech Society: The Story of the Information Technology Revolution* (Oxford: Basil Blackwell, 1987), 273.

7. Nye's argument, particularly in contravention to Paul Kennedy's declinist thesis, is found in *Bound to Lead: The Changing Nature of American Power* (New York: Basic Books, 1990). See also Nye's summary article, "The Misleading Metaphor of Decline," *Atlantic Monthly, 265,* 3 (March 1990): 86–94.

8. Daniel F. Burton, Jr., "Economic Realities and Strategic Choices," in Daniel F. Burton, Jr., Victor Gotbaum, and Felix G. Rohatyn (eds.), *Vision for the 1990s: U.S. Strategy and the Global Economy* (Cambridge, MA: Ballinger, 1989), 3.

9. Fred Bergsten, "The World Economy after the Cold War," *Foreign Affairs, 69,* 3 (Summer 1990): 97.

10. Felix Rohatyn, "America's Economic Dependence," *Foreign Affairs, 68,* 1 (1988–89): 59.

11. Yasuhiro Nakasone, "Toward a New International Community," *Survival, 30,* 6 (November–December 1988): 498.

12. David E. Sanger, "U.S. Parts, Japanese Computers," *New York Times* (September 7, 1988): 28.

13. Leichi Oshima, "The High Technology Gap: A View from Japan," in Pierre (ed.), *A High Technology Gap?* 110.

14. Frank Press, "Technological Competition in the Western Alliance," in Pierre (ed.), *A High Technology Gap?* 37–38, 43.

15. Ian M. Ross, "Information Technology and U.S. Technological Leadership in the 1990s," in Burton, Gotbaum, and Rohatyn (eds.), *Vision for the 1990s,* 52.

16. For an overview, see William J. Holstein, "The Stateless Corporation," *Business Week, 3159,* (May 14, 1990): 98–105.

17. Bobby R. Inman, "U.S. Technology in an International Context," in Burton, Gotbaum, and Rohatyn (eds.), *Vision for the 1990s,* 46.

18. Press, "Technological Competition in the Western Alliance," 14.

19. G. A. Keyworth, II, "Goodby, Central," *Vital Speeches of the Day, 56,* 12 (April 1, 1990): 359.

20. Karen Wright, "The Road to the Global Village," *Scientific American, 262,* 3 (March 1990): 92.

21. Hormats, "Introduction," 1–2.

22. Ferguson, "America's High-Tech Decline," 130.

23. Walter B. Wriston, "Technology and Sovereignty," *Foreign Affairs, 67,* 2 (Winter 1988–89): 63. The same point is made by Seweryn Bialer, "The Soviet Union in a Changing World," in Kinya Niiseki (ed.), *The Soviet Union in Transition* (Boulder, CO: Westview Press, 1987), 4.

24. William Reichert and Harry Sello, "Whole-Earth Technology," *High Technology Business, 9,* 7 (July–August 1989): 18.

25. Ross, "Information Technology and U.S. Technological Leadership in the 1990s," 61, 62. See also Burton, "Economic Realities and Strategic Choices," 10.

26. Rosy Nimroody, *Star Wars: The Economic Impact* (Cambridge, MA: Ballinger, 1988), 78.

27. Thomas A. Vanderslice, "Technology and Economic Transition," in Burton, Gotbaum, and Rohatyn (eds.), *Vision for the 1990s*, 66–67.

28. Young, *Global Competition*, 20.

29. Harold Brown, "The United States and Japan: High Tech Is Foreign Policy," *SAIS Review, 9,* 2 (Summer–Fall 1989): 5.

30. Derrick Mercer, Geoff Mungham, and Kevin Williams, *The Fog of War: The Media and the Battlefield* (London: Heinemann, 1987), 9.

31. Herbert S. Dordick, "New Communications Technology and Media Power," in Andrew Arno and Winral Dissanayake (eds.), *The News Media in National and International Conflict* (Boulder, CO: Westview Press, 1984), 38.

32. Richard N. Cooper and Ann L. Hollick, "International Relations in a Technologically Advanced Future," in Ann G. Keatley (ed.), *Technological Frontier and Foreign Relations* (Washington, DC: National Academy Press, 1985), 240.

33. Richard M. Clurman, "Should TV Be Barred? Only Tyrannies Say Yes," *New York Times* (national ed.) (March 28, 1988): 21.

34. Patricia A. Karl, "Media Diplomacy," in Gerald Benjamin (ed.), *The Communications Revolution in Politics* (New York: The Academy of Political Science, 1982), 149, 150.

35. W. Phillips Davison, *Communications and Conflict Resolution: The Role of the Information Media in the Advancement of International Understanding* (New York: Praeger, 1974), 6.

36. Andrew Arno, "Communication, Conflict and Storylines: The News Media as Actors in a Cultural Context," in Arno and Dissanayake (eds.), *The News Media in National and International Conflict*, 11.

37. Trevor Buck and John Cole, *Modern Soviet Economic Performance* (Oxford: Basil Blackwell, 1987), 135–36. The same point is made in Central Intelligence Agency, *The Soviet Weapons Industry: An Overview* (Washington, DC: Central Intelligence Agency Document DI 86–10016, September 1986), 16; and by S. Frederick Starr, "Soviet Union: A Civil Society," *Foreign Policy, 70* (Spring 1988): 27.

38. Marshall D. Shulman, "The Superpowers: Dance of the Dinosaurs," *Foreign Affairs, 66,* 3 (1987–88): 496. See also Stephen Sestanovitch, "Gorbachev's Foreign Policy: A Diplomacy of Decline," *Problems of Communism, 37* (January–February 1988): 4.

39. Graham T. Allison, Jr., "Testing Gorbachev," *Foreign Affairs, 67,* 1 (Fall 1988): 21. This argument is elaborated in Donald M. Snow, "Soviet Reform and the High-Technology Imperative," *Parameters: U.S. Army War College Quarterly, 20,* 1 (March 1990): 76–87.

40. Sergei Zamascikov, "Gorbachev and the Soviet Military," Rand Library Collection Papers P–7410 (Santa Monica, CA: RAND Corporation, January 1988), 3.

41. F. Stephen Larrabee, "Gorbachev and the Soviet Military," *Foreign Affairs, 66,* 5 (Summer 1988): 1018. See also Condoleeza Rice, "Defence and Security," in Martin McCauley (ed.), *The Soviet Union under Gorbachev* (London: Macmillan, 1987), 196.

42. Kathy McAfee, "Why the Third World Goes Hungry: Selling Cheap and Buying Dear," *Commonweal, 117,* 12 (June 15, 1990): 382, 386.

43. Jacques Attali, "Lines on the Horizon: A New Order in the Making," *New Perspectives Quarterly, 7,* 2 (Spring 1990): 5.

44. Zbigniew Brzezinski, "Europe and Amerippon: Pillars of the New World Order," *New Perspectives Quarterly, 7,* 2 (Spring 1990): 19.

45. William G. Holstein, "The Stateless Corporation," *Business Week, 3159,* (May 14, 1990): 104.

46. Ibid., 98.

4

The Collapse of the Soviet Union

Nowhere in the world has change been more dramatic and consequential for the entire international system than in the fifteen states that used to constitute the Soviet Union. The changes began with the ascension to power of Mikhail S. Gorbachev in 1985 as the culmination of a succession process triggered by the death of Leonid Brezhnev. Concerned with the lack of growth in the Soviet economy, Gorbachev and his reform-minded colleagues instituted a series of reform measures intended to fine-tune the socialist economy in which he believed.

The process clearly got out of hand and beyond the control of the architects of change. When initial attempts to stimulate the economy failed, the response was to broaden the reforms until, at length, the entire structure came under attack. Similarly, political reform under the name of *glasnost* (criticism or openness) turned increasingly into open criticism of the system and the regime.

The results, now so offhandedly familiar, were shocking then, culminating in the physical breakup of the entire Soviet Union into fifteen independent states that were once "soviet socialist republics" of the USSR. Of the successor states, Russia, with roughly three-fourths of the land mass and 150 million citizens, is clearly of the greatest consequence and concern.

The dynamics begun under Gorabachev continue. The Soviet economic crisis is now Russia's economic crisis. Soviet political reform is now the teetering democratization of Russia. Formerly internal politics of ethnicity have become the "nationalities problem" that wracks several successor states and energizes Russian military preparations. From this cauldron of change will come Russia's place in the new international order.

The process began mildly, or at least so it seems in retrospect, and it took a while before the West paid particular heed. The original *perestroika* (restructuring), under the banner of *uskeronie* (acceleration), was an entreaty and "program" to make more efficient a Soviet economy that was lagging behind that of the West (although it is hard to find Western analyses from the early 1980s that recognized the problem). The caricature of this early phase was the famous antialcoholism campaign aimed at reducing monumental Soviet vodka consumption in the hopes of reducing worker absenteeism and producing a work force that actually showed up for work sober. Accompanying acceleration was a limited form of freedom to criticize (*glasnost*), designed to provide workers with an avenue to criticize the top-heavy, sluggish, party-based management system that had evolved under Stalin and became embedded under Brezhnev. If this *nomenklatura* could be rejuvenated or replaced, things would improve.

This original program was nothing like it evolved to be. Did Gorbachev begin modestly, fully intending to cause radical, revolutionary changes in the Soviet system, even its dismantling? He has not said and may never do so.

Regardless of Gorbachev's original intent, the process he set in motion and over which he presided until the end of the Soviet Union has resulted in a radical change from the Stalinist dictatorship it superseded. There is indeed reasonable freedom of speech and expression in Russia today; multiple parties compete for power, and regional parties splinter off from the main body. Boris Yeltsin has succeeded Gorbachev as the elected president of Russia; a new, formal constitution has been adopted by referendum; the military has been relegated to a lesser status than it formerly had; and forms of capitalism, including the active wooing of investment by private Western corporations, have become commonplace. Over the past several years, the announcement of changes has become such a daily event that we no longer seem surprised by any new initiative emanating from Moscow. The dark side is rising discontent over economic performance, the dilution of a cradle-to-grave welfare system that provided a modest but universal social net, and a wave of crime that leaves Moscow streets unsafe and Russia the center of organized crime efforts in areas such as drugs.

The changes in foreign policy begun by Gorbachev are no less dramatic. As part of the "new political thinking" in his book *Perestroika,*[1] Gorbachev formally renounced the Brezhnev Doctrine by which the Soviets asserted the "right" to intervene on the behalf of beleaguered fellow Socialist states. Those few who took notice at all assumed the renunciation was no more than a subterfuge to justify extrication from a "losing" effort in Afghanistan that was having many of the social effects in Russia that the Vietnam War had in the United States. On the heels of that pronouncement, Gorbachev proposed total nuclear disarmament and opened his society to large-scale communication with Westerners, including active two-way exchanges between the Soviet and American militaries such as the initial Admiral Crowe–Marshall Akhromeyev visits and the not-so-publicized visits between staffs of the U.S. Army War College and its Russian equivalent, the Voroshilov Academy. Gorbachev allowed relatively open emigration from the Soviet Union, notably to Israel; permitted, even encouraged, the overthrow of Communist governments in Eastern Europe; backed away noticeably from Second Tier commitments in places as diverse as Nicaragua and Angola; and allowed Soviet students to study in the West. This embrace of the West, so necessary if Russia was to become a "normal" state with legitimate aspirations to join the First Tier, has been continued—even expanded—by Yeltsin.

And yet, during the forty-plus years of the active Cold War, *none of these things could have occurred*. None of the changes we now take for granted were even conceivable. If you pick up almost anything written as recently as 1985 in the West, you will find nothing that even generally suggests we would be where we are now.

In a perspective considerably aided by several years of observation, what Gorbachev, wittingly or not, engaged in was nothing less than a total transformation of the Soviet system. The historical Soviet/Russian system has always been characterized by a strong state superimposed on a weak society. This means that the social bonds within the society have traditionally been weak. In the diverse, multinational political entity that was the USSR, there was very little sense of cohesion among the people to make them willing and active participants in the system. In the absence of strong societal bonds, order was imposed by a strong state coercive mechanism controlled for a long time by the czars and more recently by the Communist party and instruments such as the Committee on State Security (KGB). In a multinational empire made up of centrifugal forces uninterested in becoming part of the distinctly Russian culture and society that the czars and commissars sought to impose, there was relatively little choice for the various leaderships. The disintegration of authority in many of the successor states, including bitter ethnic warfare in several states, is testimony to the society's weakness.

Gorbachev was committed to changing all that. He tried to create a strong society that could exist with a weak state, a state mechanism that would rely on the willing association of its members rather than on raw coercion. The old Soviet state simply would have crushed the independence movements, with the KGB jailing dissidents and the army rolling in if that failed. Instead, Gorbachev, although threatening at times, attempted to bargain and cajole, in effect saying to the Lithuanians and others, "Stick around, things are going to get better. And when they do, you will regret it if you have left." The foundation of a strong Soviet society, in other words, was to be a vibrant economy based on a participatory state that no longer needed coercion.

It was a gamble, and it failed. Democratization, the political side of *glasnost*, has not taken hold firmly anywhere in the former republics, many of which operate as they did before—with the same people in charge but lacking the formal Communist imprimatur. Moreover, there is no certainty that it will work. The Achilles heel is the restructuring of the economy, which was the centerpiece of *perestroika*. The economy has not improved; by all accounts, things have gotten materially worse, not better. That there would be temporary dislocations as structural changes began to occur was predictable; that things have not turned around casts an increasingly ominous shadow over the long-term success of the experiment. The gamble was that successful *perestroika* would create the base for a strong society (presumably with suitable homage for its creator). That failed, and the result was the system disintegrating as natural societies reasserted themselves.

The disintegration of the Soviet Union and its corollary, the end of the Cold War, has produced in Russia the tentative beginning of a "normal" state, one that progressively accepts the mores of the rest of the system and seeks to adapt itself to that system rather than trying to force the system to adapt. Partially, of course, this is the result of the spectacular success of the Western economic model and the equally spectacular failure of the Marxist-Leninist-Stalinist model. In this circumstance, the West has won by default; Fukuyama's "end of history"[2] means that for the time being, at least, there are no ideological competitors to the Western system. It is hard to find a believing Marxist anymore other than in isolated places like Cuba, Vietnam, or North Korea.

This transformation, more than anything else, undermined the Cold War international system. For that system to operate, there had to be fundamental ideological disagreement among the major antagonists that translated into a political and military rivalry over whose system would shape the globe. With that disagreement resolved, there is no reason for Cold War or for the enormous baggage it entailed. The rivalry between the United States and the former Soviet Union, and all the resources poured into it, is now no more than the relationship between any two large powers.

In that sense, everyone has won the Cold War, which is a happy prospect and one that portends well for the future. If it is true, as Michael Mandelbaum argues, that the toughest task in reconstructing a postwar security order is finding an acceptable place for all states, notably the losers,[3] then the success of Russian reform is desirable and raises the prospect of a structure with which no one is so dissatisfied that they will seek to transform it, particularly by recourse to violence —the extension of First Tier status to Russia.

As noted, the outcome of change in Russia and the other successor states is fundamental to the shape of the future system, but it is not preordained. To get some kind of idea about what may unfold in the former Soviet Union during the balance of the millennium, we must start by looking at how the crisis that gave birth to the change occurred. With that as a base, we can begin to look at the prospects and consequences of that change.

The Causes of and Need for Change

The underlying and pervasive need for increasingly radical reform in the former Soviet Union can be traced to the massive failure of the Stalinist command economic system—a failure that became obvious to parts of the Soviet intelligentsia in the 1970s and to the West in the early to middle 1980s. The rot was pervasive, and it manifested itself in several ways. The evident inability of the system to produce satisfactory amounts or quality of consumer goods was only the tip of the iceberg. Of far more fundamental importance was the fact that the Soviet Union had fallen dangerously behind the West in the critical areas of science that comprise high technology. This deficiency, in turn, had internal, international, and military significance. Internally, it threatened the production and consumption system and the ability of the Soviet government to satisfy its citizens. Internationally, failure in high technology meant relegation to the category of has-beens in a world order where status and economic power are becoming closely related. Militarily, the emergence of dual-use technologies that meant a technologically inferior Soviet Union ran the risk of being progressively disadvantaged on the technological battlefield of the future.

It is against this backdrop that Gorbachev, supported by the underground intelligentsia and primed through his wife Raisa, rose to power and began the process of change. On his arrival at center stage on the world scene, little was known about Gorbachev, nor was the program he would sponsor evident. In retrospect, however, a Gorbachev figure, if not necessarily Gorbachev himself, may have been inevitable. As one analyst argued, "Almost any Soviet leadership confronting the same set of internal and external dilemmas would have favored a reorientation of energies toward domestic affairs and a dramatic amelioration of tensions with the West."[4] Alexander Dallin believed that a good bit of the intellectual underpinnings came from the detente period of relatively high contact during the 1970s between the Soviets and the rest of the world, when many Soviet intellectuals were first introduced to Western thought.[5] To some extent, the movement of which Gorbachev would become the stalking-horse was simply the revival of the Khrushchev-era dissident movement of which the late Andrei Sakharov (who was, of course, rehabilitated by Gorbachev) was the champion.

The culprit was the Stalinist command economic system, which had so successfully (if at enormous human costs still being accounted) brought the Soviets through the period of heavy industrialization during the 1930s. That system was based on the forced mobilization of labor within a few mammoth industries organized and controlled centrally by a party-dominated planning bureaucracy. Its trademark, in addition to political authoritarianism, was the Five-Year Plan, which produced quantitative production quotas and the guarantee of employment regardless of productivity: "from each according to his abilities, to each according to his needs" was the shibboleth.

The system had many flaws, three of which are illustrative. First, it destroyed the individual incentive to excel. Reward was divorced from productivity when the absolute right to employment at equal wages was the basic value. The victims were both quantitative and qualitative productivity, a large reason why Soviet products were both scarce and generally shoddy. Second, the system divorced supply and demand. Supply was set by individual planning bureaucracies, and demand was not a factor in determining that supply. Moreover, the Soviets never developed any of the accoutrements on which a market economy thrives: market analysis of demand, efficient production of quality products, or a transportation system to get products to consumers efficiently. Third, the system of central control was inefficient and overly bureaucratic. The *nomenklatura* who made decisions became a faceless mass divorced from the workers and the consumers and progressively rewarded by one another rather than by satisfying societal needs. This massive structure, with its reward system based and dependent upon the CPSU, became both self-interested in its own survival and self-rewarding and removed from reality. It is for these reasons that the *nomenklatura* was identified as a chief target for reform, the weapon for which was *glasnost*. Given these deep structural deficiencies and the absence of a framework of commercial law and regulations, it is little wonder that the process of transformation has been as long and its outcomes as uncertain as they continue to be. The old system left the Russians as unprepared for change to a market economy as it is possible to be.

The whole system atrophied beyond resuscitation under Leonid Brezhnev, in the "period of stagnation." Recognition that this was occurring was apparently limited during most of the Brezhnev reign to the small intellectual group that adopted Gorbachev as its standard-bearer, although a 1986 Central Intelligence Agency study believes that realization of the need for change can be dated to the last years of the Brezhnev era.[6]

The difficulty was in recognizing the dimensions of the problem that had to be addressed. From the vantage point of the orthodox Communist establishment, the depth of the crisis and its roots in the nature of the system itself must have been extremely difficult to grasp. Yet the problem was and is fundamental, systemic, and continues to be intractable:

> The Soviet economy and society in its present, modified Stalinist form is a behemoth programmed to move predictably and ponderously in an ordained direction. But the information age demands agility and the ability to change direction quickly. The Soviet leadership appears to recognize its dilemma. Either make the behemoth more agile or lose the game. But can a behemoth lose weight, become agile, and remain a behemoth?[7]

The answer to the rhetorical question is "probably not." Moreover, one can question whether Gorbachev and those around him recognized either the nature of the new economic climate in which they were losing ground or the extent of what would be required to bring about needed change. The pace of change driven by high technology is, after all, so rapid that even those working the problem in the West have some difficulty keeping up. Gorbachev himself was a lawyer, not a scientist, and even the scientists and technologists around him came from a more primitive technological milieu. Moreover, Gorbachev was a professed and practicing Communist who regularly confessed his continuing faith. From his perspective, it was difficult to accept the idea that the system was fundamentally flawed. Rather, his initial instinct was to rejuvenate what orthodoxy could only believe was a basically sound system. His successor, Boris Yeltsin, had much less difficulty eschewing Marxism-Leninism.

Gorbachev's early actions are congruent with such a belief. At the beginning, he sought to "fine-tune" the system by telling people to work harder in the anticipation of future benefits. *Uskeronie* in essence was aimed at exactly that end: if the people could be enticed to work harder and more diligently, things would right themselves.

Moreover, the system was not without its virtues, at least in Marxist eyes. It did produce a certain social security, if at a low level. These virtues are still regarded by much of the population as the Socialist gains that should be preserved, and one of the ongoing traumas of change is undoing the undesirable aspects of the system without doing away with its popular aspects. Nostalgia for the old social net remains high among older Russians who are suffering economically under reform, and they made their discontent known in the 1993 elections.

The difficulty is that those guarantees are part of the problem, because egalitarianism makes the system "loser-proof" in the sense that everyone is "entitled" to a certain minimum standard of living. The same egalitarianism, however, meant there were no real incentives to excel, since leveling created both a ceiling and a floor on living standards. That the Soviets are coming to recognize the dilemma is well illustrated in the reply of Soviet economist Nikolai Shmelev to a question posed by American economist Ed A. Hewett: "I think you understand that the main conflict in our political tradition is the contradiction between economic efficiency and social security. . . . Just now many in the USSR are desperately looking for some distinctive features of that slogan, that word 'socialism' to distinguish it from your social system."[8]

The depth of the problem dawned on the leadership as it peeled away the layers of the malaise, gradually revealing a core that was rotten. As Gorbachev himself put it, "In moving down the path of perestroika, we saw that the crisis that battered the country was immeasurably deeper and more serious than we expected."[9] As gradual, cosmetic reform failed to produce the kinds of improvements that were needed, the process of restructuring, and especially *glasnost*, accelerated to the point that in late 1986 or early 1987, according to Hewett, Gorbachev was driven to plunge ahead into a "full-scale reconsideration" of the roots of Soviet socialism.[10]

Was all that has unfolded part of a careful game plan devised at the beginning, or did it evolve more incrementally? Some believe, for instance, that the process has been gradual and reactionary, accommodating political tendencies that Gorbachev certainly did not intend to countenance at the outset.[11] This is undoubtedly true in that it would have been virtually impossible for anyone, and particularly someone viewing the world through Gorbachev's conceptual lenses, to predict as complex a set of circumstances as those attending the reform movement. At the outset, he certainly did not set out to create forces that would destroy the Communist party, dissolve the Soviet Union, or have him thrown from office. But he did all those things in the end.

The Technological Imperative

If the Soviets were somewhat uncertain about how to reform their system, identifying the underlying cause of the malaise was less difficult. Even arch-conservative Politburo member Yegor Ligachev could identify a lagging Soviet scientific and technological effort as the root, citing a "peculiar socio-economic mechanism" that held back progressive change.[12] If the nub of the problem was deficiency in high technology, then the solution was to create an environment in which scientific inquiry and the production of high-technology outcomes thrive. The difficulty that bedeviled the Gorbachev reform movement and continues to thwart his Russian successors is how to create such an environment in a Socialist context. It is a true dilemma.

The root problem is that scientific inquiry and high technology tend to thrive in a setting marked by individual freedom and the ability of individuals and small groups to work together with reasonable autonomy. Moreover, free access to information and the ability to communicate freely constitute the sine qua non for scientific cross-fertilization and discovery. Further, since scientific and technological endeavor is extremely hard work, those engaged in it must have the reasonable expectation of proportional, even conspicuous, rewards for their efforts.

These conditions, of course, are the virtual opposite of the Stalinist command system. In that system of large, centrally controlled bureaucracy, there was little individual autonomy and freedom. Instead, scientists worked in large government laboratories under the auspices of the Academy of Science, where bureaucratic meddling stifled originality and bred conformity, both necessary attributes for a vibrant scientific community. At the same time, control of information, not its free flow, was the basis for control within the Stalinist system. One of the manifestations of closure was the fact that, until recently, former Soviet laboratories might (or might not) have computers, but they hardly ever had printers: ideas were not to leave the building in someone's briefcase. Finally, an egalitarian economic system with strict ceilings as well as floors on income virtually precludes adequate incentives to excel. Why work as hard as a creative technologist must if your reward is going to be roughly the same as that of a common factory worker?

The entire Gorbachev reform program took on a meaning and coherence it would not otherwise have had when one assumes that its underlying purpose was to create an environment in which technology and science will thrive. Thus, *perestroika* and *glasnost* emerge as vehicles to create such an atmosphere, and the new political thinking emerges as a way for the Soviets to be allowed to join and share in the increasingly international flow of technology development and dissemination.

The Dilemmas of Change

In principle, of course, there is no necessary incompatibility between Marxism and political democracy, since the end state of theoretical Marxism is communism, the political form of which is anarchy, or complete freedom. But here Gorbachev and his followers came upon a conceptually difficult intellectual problem. They were products of the CPSU, and certainly Gorbachev began his odyssey to revive the economic system in the name of the party. The problem, which he came to realize, was that the only way to have any chance at success was to undercut the party. Why? Because the system created to perpetuate the central, exclusive role of the party *was the problem*. The Leninist-Stalinist CPSU was profoundly antidemocratic; the system had become anachronistic and threatened to relegate the Soviet Union to second- or third-class status in the world. This framed Gorbachev's devil's choice: he could keep the behemoth intact and watch as the CPSU presided over the devolution of Soviet power, or he could undercut the party (make the behemoth lean and flexible) and hope for the best. From his vantage point, it was a choice between two evils. The tentative nature of reform under Gorbachev reflected his discomfort with the choices.

By moving his power base out of the party into the Congress of People's Deputies and by presiding over the end of party control (abrogating Article 6 of the constitution, which guaranteed party supremacy), Gorbachev opted for the latter choice. In the process, he gambled not only the party's power but his own as well, and in the end he lost. That those most heavily invested in the party would become restive—as they have and continue to be—is no surprise.

From a Western viewpoint, the decision does not seem so difficult, because democratization offers a clear and preferable choice. What made the Westernizing path more difficult, however, comes from the third requisite for high-technology health—the provision of incentive systems perceived as fair that create adequate reward differentials to overcome the cynical, unproductive environment created by the system of guaranteed job security. This posed practical political and philosophical problems for Gorbachev and his fellow reformers.

An incentive system means that people will be rewarded based upon the excellence of their work, and that means there will be increasing disparity in wages and economic status. In the old system, the social safety net guaranteed a relatively similar slice of the pie for everyone. By contrast, in an open, democratic system, the losers are bound to be unhappy with their new circumstances. To some extent we have already witnessed the resentment that differentiation creates; private entrepreneurs in Russia are regularly accused of gouging by charging market-based prices for their wares (rather than artificially controlled government prices). Differences in status and wealth are greatly resented. A new privileged class of technologists (the party was already a privileged class) is likely to be resented for its higher material status as well.

At the philosophical level, acceptance of an incentive system with differential rewards is tantamount to renouncing socialism. With different levels of compensation, the classlessness that is theoretically at the heart of the Marxist ideal will give way, and the second half of the Communist ideal, "from each according to his ability, to each according to his needs," is stood on its head. Moreover, there is a practical consequence of the entire process that implicitly destroys socialism. One scholar states the dilemma as

> a chimera—if democratic socialism is understood to mean a system that is different in kind and not in degree from democratic capitalism. The problem is not, as some claim, that the two concepts, democracy and socialism, are intrinsically incompatible. The problem is that where the people are sovereign, they never choose socialism . . . they never opt against economic freedom, that is, capitalism.[13]

This left Gorbachev and his associates in a very difficult bind; indeed, Gorbachev found himself increasingly isolated in the new political center of the Soviet Union. To his political left were those who had made their choice between democracy and socialism and had opted to sacrifice communism and the CPSU. Calling for more rapid and radical reform, this political left found a standard-bearer in the person of Boris Yeltsin and a rallying cry in the Shatalin plan. On the political right were the supporters of the old order, the party, the army, and the KGB. For them, maintaining the power of the party is the supreme goal to which all other objectives must ultimately bend. These divisions continue. The right remains in control of a number of the successor states—Ukraine and Kazakhstan, for instance. Within Russia, this distinction formed the battle lines for electing a parliament (the Duma) in 1993; the left associated itself with Yeltsin and the reformers (although Yeltsin did not formally affiliate with or endorse the reformist parties) and the right with its new—and possibly transitory—champion, Zhirinovsky. The debate remains unresolved.

Gorbachev was in the middle. He wanted economic reform and democratization, but within a Socialist context. Although he threw his lot behind the reformers, he remained that practicing Marxist who rose in thoroughly orthodox fashion through the party hierarchy. He wanted the triumph of a reformed system that stood for both democracy and socialism. His dilemma, of course, was that he could not have both; in the end, he achieved neither on his watch.

Reforming Soviet foreign policy to make the USSR a less threatening international force was a conceptually and philosophically easier task. On the one hand, the expansionist tendencies were historically Russian and not Marxist, thereby not violating ideological precepts. On the other hand, it was painfully obvious to Gorbachev and his associates that messianic communism was simply too expensive, especially for the meager returns it brought.

Domestic and international reform went hand in hand, because the need for outside assistance to revitalize the Soviet economy required good relations with the outside world.[14] To accompany domestic reform, the Soviets needed three things from the outside world: increased trade, capital, and the influx of technology. None was likely to be available, especially technology transfer, unless there were "less volatile political relations than those of the past decade [before Gorbachev]."[15]

The technology transfer problem, especially in the area of high-technology items such as computers, illustrated the need for better relations. Historically, computers were on the list of items banned from trade with the Soviet Union on national security grounds. The reason was simple enough: the Soviets were adversaries, and despite their willingness to sign end-use agreements (stating for what ends traded items will be used), there was always the fear that they would use the computers militarily, thereby jeopardizing American national security. As long as the Soviets were viewed as a military threat, there was strong pressure not to deal with them in proscribed areas.

The Soviets, and now the Russians, of course, are in great need of computers. They do not produce competitive machines themselves, and what little they do produce is slower and of inferior quality to Western machines. Moreover, before Gorbachev, there was essentially no market for desktop, personal computers because of restrictive policies on information flow.

In the past, the Soviets, banned from legitimate avenues to obtain computers, resorted to subterfuge, attempting to buy banned items under false pretenses through phony agents, espionage, and even theft. At one point, for instance, the Soviets illegally obtained an IBM 360–50 computer. In order to master the machine, they tore it apart and rebuilt it, so-called reverse designing. However, it took them longer to use the reverse design process to clone the computer than it had taken IBM to design it in the first place, and by the time they completed the process, the 360–50 had been supplanted by more advanced designs. Moreover, Gorbachev pointed out in *Perestroika* that obtaining computer designs in this manner cheated the Soviets of the learning process of how to design computers and was thus to be avoided in the future.

Computers are critical to Russian modernization. First, even as the bloated bureaucracy slims down, computerization offers some means for gaining control over what remains of the centralized economy. Second, things such as CAD/CAM are virtually unknown in Russia and could add measurably to Russian productivity. Third, and most important, the most advanced computers are the major tools of high technology, and anyone who attempts to compete in computing without state-of-the-art equipment is playing with a considerable handicap.

All of this added up to some very real, self-interested reasons for a sincere modification of the basis of Russian foreign policy. The old Cold War competition simply proved too costly and dysfunctional. Rather than watch the world roll by into the twenty-first century of technology-driven power, the Soviets concluded that they would have to join the party. Whether they will succeed in doing so, however, depends to a large degree on whether or how the process of reform works out.

The Continuing Uncertainty of Change

The continuing crisis in the successor states is so pervasive, multifaceted, and deep that any attempt to predict its eventual outcome with some precision is bound to fail. As the reform process unfolds, however, it appears to contain three distinct hurdles: political evolution toward some form of Western-style democracy, economic reform that includes some infusion of market principles, and growing centrifugal forces in the form of secessionary tendencies and ethnic rivalries—the so-called nationalities problem. The prospects for overcoming them varies considerably.

The first two problems center on change in Russia as the major successor state, although they are present in most of the other successor states as well. The nationalities problem, on the other hand, is currently centered in the southern rim of the successor states, where ethnicity and religion intermix with volatile results. Russian interest in this aspect is largely limited to protecting Russian minorities in these areas, a basic concern of the Russian military.

The problems are interactive and paradoxical. Economic and political freedom have created economic disparity, which undercuts political support for further reform and stimulates nostalgia for reversion. In the most volatile successor states, freedom has not meant democracy but instead self-determination expressed as violent "ethnic cleansing."

Also paradoxical is the way in which reform has been attempted. Because of the nature of the Stalinist system and Russian culture, reform has been a top–down exercise, using the strong centralized system as the means to democratize. This creates a paradox in which great centralization is required to decentralize economic control and power. Successful decentralization, however, deprives political leaders of the coercive authority they need in the absence of the legitimacy they seek.[16]

The problems were also interactive in ways that are not always positive. The most notable case in point was *glasnost* and the emergence of a desire for independence in the non-Russian states of the Soviet Union. These desires have existed since many conquered areas from the Baltic states to eastern Asia were part first of the Russian empire and later of the Soviet Union. Gorbachev's unsuccessful gamble was that transforming the Soviet Union into a better, more prosperous place would make it too attractive for states to want to leave. When the desire to break the union apart became inexorable, there was no coercive mechanism with sufficient power to hold it together.

The Political Dimension

Varying progress is being made on the three hurdles. Rather clearly, the greatest advances are political; the freedoms now available to Russian citizens, while arguably not yet comparable to the rights enjoyed in the First Tier, are considerably greater than they were only a few years ago. Russia has, after all, elected a president and a legislature, and it has ratified a constitution, both notable accomplishments for a country utterly lacking a democratic tradition.

Much of the public base for this was laid by Gorbachev. In his opening speech to the CPSU Special Conference on June 28, 1988, he pronounced seven "basic tasks" before the country. They are politically significant and worth repeating:

First, everything must be done to include millions upon millions of people in administering the country in deed, not in word.

Second, the maximum scope must be given to the processes of the self-regulation and self-government of society. . . .

Third, it is necessary to adjust the mechanism of the unhindered formation and expression of the interests and will of all classes and social groups. . . .

Fourth, the conditions must be created for the further free development of every national and nationality. . . .

Fifth, socialist legality, law and order, must be radically strengthened so as to rule out any possibility of power being usurped or abused, so as effectively to counter bureaucracy and formalism, and reliably guarantee the protection of citizens' constitutional rights and freedoms. . . .

Sixth, there must be a strict demarcation of the functions of party and state bodies, in conformity with Lenin's conception of the Communist Party as a political vanguard of society and the role of the Soviet State as an instrument of government by the people.

Finally, seventh, an effective mechanism must be established to assure the timely self-rejuvenation of the political system. . . .[17]

This is an impressive list of changes from an authoritarian to a more open and democratic political system. What is further impressive, over the past years, is the extent to which all or some of these have become part of the political scene.

This movement toward political democratization, toward opening Russia to the world and letting its citizens interact with other peoples, is much more important than many accounts of change would have us believe. It is important for two reasons, one domestic and one international, that are equally valid whether the other aspects of change work out positively or not.

On the domestic side, the broadening of political participation makes the democratization process less and less reversible. People will, on rare occasions arising from extraordinary circumstances, give up their political freedom, as the Germans initially did in 1933, but those occasions are indeed rare. As one watches from afar, the political dimensions of the reforms appear to be making their greatest impact on the younger, better educated members of society—tomorrow's leaders. They are unlikely to forfeit their own freedoms, and it is increasingly difficult to imagine a military cabal arising that would command the support of the troops for any long period of reasserted repression. Politically,

Russia is adopting Western institutions and values, and so are its people.

That could change, of course, especially if the other aspects of reform sour. A complete and utter breakdown of economic reform—which cannot be ruled out—might create the extraordinary circumstances that would convince the Soviet people to make a Faustian bargain with some figure who promises bread for freedom. Or, it is possible that in the ruins of the disintegrated union, rolling Russia back to the shadows of Muscovy could create such a backlash that the citizenry would turn to a modern Ivan the Terrible to restore their glory—which is, of course, the current appeal of Zhirinovsky.

But it is not likely that reversion or repression will occur for a further reason. Thanks to the telecommunications revolution, *glasnost* is now so public that its reversal would be equally public. China has yet to recover fully from the public relations disaster at Tiananmen Square, and the Russians have seen what television coverage can do. Television transmissions of Soviet troops firing on Georgian demonstrators in Tblisi in 1990 brought a wave of internal and international criticism of the kind they would rather avoid in the future. The inability of the Yaneyev-led coup group to manage the press in the summer of 1991 points most dramatically to the perils of trying to seize power illegally in the television age.

The international side of this is that, as the Russians democratize, they may become increasingly like the West. The Cold War competition had as its base, after all, the issue of communism versus political democracy and economic capitalism. At least between the Soviet Union and the United States, there were very few other real sources of conflict; there was, for instance, no history of animosity, no history of wars between them.

A Russian transition to political democracy, with whatever distinctive Russian coloration it adopts, has the potential to complete the transition to a new and more peaceful order among the major powers. Moreover, it raises the distinct prospect that the Russians and the Americans will increasingly see the kind of world they want through the same glasses, making more likely the continued emergence of a sense of international collaboration and condominium between them.

The Economic Dimension

The prognosis for economic reform is nowhere nearly as positive. After almost a decade of reform, the Russians can report hardly any progress in turning around the Soviet economy, and, in fact, visitors report a steady deterioration in the quality of life, even in the large cities such as Moscow. The headlong rush of the individual successor republics to adopt their own economic plans underscores the poverty of leadership and lack of confidence in the citizenry. The openly asked question is how long the status quo can survive in the absence of economic improvement.

This question is important for at least three reasons. First, economic and political reform are intimately intertwined, at least in the sense that political reforms are more likely to take root if they are associated with what Aganbegyan calls "a better way of life" rather than continued economic decline. Second, if there is a real threat to political progress, it is in the prospect of continued economic privation for the Russian masses. Third, improvement in the economic sphere is necessary, along with political freedom, to provide a nurturing environment for the high-technology revolution on which economic progress is based.

Why has economic reform not borne fruit? There are several possible answers, three of which will be raised here. They are an initial failure to understand the depth of the problem and thus to provide adequate remedy, particularly in the short run; pegging reform on a "scientific and technological revolution," which is a long-term remedy unlikely to be of much help in the short term; and first underestimating and then overinflating the value of outside assistance to the process.

Underestimation of the problem and its solution was the first mistake. Gorbachev eventually came to admit that it took time to understand the problems the Soviets faced. In all likelihood, such comprehension was impeded by looking at the world through the eyes of a true Marxist believer who had an initially difficult time accepting the fact that fellow Marxists could mismanage the route to utopia so badly. Moreover, there is no blueprint on how to create a market economy—which Gorbachev struggled not to embrace in toto because it meant abandoning communism—especially for a country the size of the Soviet Union. Russian Yeltsin has not done much better.

Given these limitations, the Russians made mistakes. Some of the early reforms were too timid, such as the alcohol campaign and the introduction of very limited forms of nonstate firms under the Law of State Enterprise.[18] In some cases, such as the simultaneous emphasis on restructuring and economic growth, the advice was simply wrong.

The second error was in basing success on means of change that are unlikely to work in the short run. Thus, Gorbachev said in 1986 that the engines of change in the economy would be "going over to the intensive means of development and by a maximum rise in efficiency."[19] By intensive development Gorbachev and those around him mean high technology, which was also seen as a major means of ensuring greater efficiency.

When one reads Soviet writings on this phenomenon, the impression they leave is one of sincerity, but not necessarily veracity. Aganbegyan summarizes the position:

> In the future it is envisaged that the economy will transfer to intensive development, i.e., development based on increased efficiency and improved quality. Thus the main source of economic growth will be through scientific technical progress.

Having said that, however, he adds:

> A scientific and technical revolution is a complex socio-economic phenomenon. It involves not only a process of integration of science and production . . . but also requires perestroika of the economy and a quite new investment policy.[20]

Something does not ring quite true here. Aganbegyan uses most of the proper words, but it is not clear that he understands their meaning. Does he, for instance, understand what complexities lie ahead? The prescriptions are too neat, too determinant. If we in the West do not fully understand the dynamics of the technology revolution after giving birth to and nurturing it for two decades or more, how possibly can the Soviets, who have not even begun the process, have the answers?

Pegging successful economic transformation on technology may or may not produce a positive outcome in the long run, but it almost certainly will not, beyond the ability to import a few manufacturing improvements, help in the short run. For one thing, the Russians lack the infrastructure in computing and telecommunications to start a scientific revolution, and the nature of science is not such that it can be used as a magic wand to solve all of one's problems.

Moreover, there is a double bind at work here. On the one hand, the science and technology revolution is supposed to fuel economic revival, and in the long run it may. The bind is that improvements in the economy are a necessary prerequisite to the scientific revolution. Material incentives must be available if scientists and technicians are to be convinced to work hard enough to be very productive. But that is the problem in Russia: there is little to buy except at outrageous prices. Giving scientists more rubles when there is little to spend them on is hardly an inducement to long hours and hard work.

Russian flirtation with Western aid and private investment has similarly suffered from fits and starts. From one angle, the idea of opening Russia via the economy is frightening, because it is bound to suffer initial setbacks. As Western goods have been imported, prices have risen to market value, thereby smashing the artificial system of subsidies on things such as food, making the cost of living higher without noticeably improving standards of living. From another angle, many Western businessmen who have dealt with the bureaucracy (the *nomenklatura*) find dealing with it little easier than in the old days. They have thus adopted a cautious stance, waiting for the precedent of a big government–private industry contract in an area of particularly pressing Russian need, such as oil exploration.

From the beginning, most observers have known that long-term improvements in Soviet prospects would come at the expense of short-term economical shortfalls.[21] The problem is that the short term keeps getting longer without visible signs of economic improvement. While a long-term strategy of redeveloping the Russian technological base is undoubtedly the best and only bet the country has of avoiding economic Second Tier status, something has to be done in the interim. Before the Russians can seriously entertain the Third Industrial Revolution, however, they must first enter and complete the Second Industrial Revolution, with its emphasis on consumer goods and services.

Unfortunately, the Russian economy is very poorly structured for this endeavor. As noted, its deficiencies include the absence of any mechanism to identify demand and thus to wed supply and demand, a primitive transportation system that cannot get goods to markets even if it can identify those markets, notoriously shoddy quality of goods, and no identifiable service sector of any kind. When McDonald's first began operations in Moscow, for instance, they found they could not reliably buy potatoes of sufficient quality and quantity for their french fries; thus, they were forced to grow their own.

The solution to these problems is the market, and that means accelerating the process of decentralizing control and embracing and institutionalizing market principles. Yeltsin and those around him plunged forward on this route, abandoning communism in a wink along the way and placing their faith in economic Westernization. Gorbachev was reluctant to go that far. His roots were too deeply grounded in communism to allow him to easily risk throwing the baby out with the bathwater, and this reluctance was nowhere more clear than in his tentative handling of economic matters. In the end, it was probably Gorbachev's personal inability fully to embrace full-scale economic change that doomed his regime and left his mark as that of presider over the demise of the empire. Given the economic travails that have continued to plague Yeltsin, even a thorough embrace might not have been enough.

The Nationalities Dimension

The process of disintegration and change has had yet another largely unanticipated consequence: the emergence of the so-called nationalities problem. It is important in and of itself, because of the turmoil and suffering it has created for countless former Soviet citizens; its broader significance may be that it shares with former Yugoslavia (a country that, not coincidentally, was consciously designed on the Stalinist model at the end of World War II) the chilling prospect of being a harbinger of ethnic violence more generally in the Second Tier in the future.

There are two broad aspects to the problem from the vantage point of those living within the successor states. For Russia and the Russian Republic, the major aspect is the problem of the existence of a large Russian population living in minority status in a number of successor republics over whom the government of Russia has no effective control. From the vantage point of many outside Russia, the problem is the rekindling of ethnic hatreds in the form of resurgent, exclusionary nationalism that has resulted in ethnically based violence as national groups attempt to separate themselves into ethnically "pure" political jurisdictions.

The root of this problem is in the old Stalinist system, which engaged in policies that created both current problems. One policy was to encourage migration of populations within the Soviet Union. Groups such as the Tatars were simply uprooted and forcibly moved from their native lands. Of more current consequence, Stalin encouraged the migration of Russians to the far-flung ends of the empire as a way to encourage russification of non-Russian populations. The other policy was to gerrymander the boundaries of the republics as a matter of political whim or to reward or punish political friends or enemies. The result was highly artificial boundaries that have remained as international boundaries with the breakup of the union but which house fractious population segments. These same problems, one might add tragically, were faithfully replicated by Yugoslavia's Josip Broz Tito, with consequences that are all too familiar.

These problems were manageable under the Stalinist system, which could and did suppress any expressions of opposition through the mechanism of state terror. The loosening of controls, however, also reduced the coercive authority of the state, and, as Alexander Dallin put it in 1990, "Glasnost + [communications] technology + an end to terror makes for an explosive mix."[22] With the breakdown of the Soviet state, the barriers to open and violent expression of differences were cast aside.

The minorities problem as it relates to Russians is that about 65 million former Soviet citizens live outside their native republics. Of these, about 25 million are ethnic Russians, and the great fear of the Russian government is that "they are likely to be the first targets of any hostile outbreaks."[23] To add fuel to these fears, there has been some discriminatory action against Russians outside Russia. In the Baltic states, for instance, laws have been enacted making it virtually impossible for Russians to achieve full citizenship. In 1991, the Republic of Moldova moved to isolate its Russian and Ukrainian populations; only joint threats by the Russian and Ukrainian governments forced Moldova to back down.

The problem of discrimination against Russians outside Russia remains more of a latent than an active problem. The probable reason for this is the highly justified fear that repressing Russians would simply provide a convenient excuse for the Russians to intervene, possibly setting the stage for reconquest. Russian military assistance to the Georgian government of Eduard Shevardnadze against Abkhazian separatists may simply be a foretaste of such possibilities.

There are already indications that this is a problem the Russians take seriously. Recent revisions in Russian military doctrine point clearly to the need to be prepared to react swiftly and effectively in the event of violence against Russians outside Russia but within the confines of the old Soviet Union. Indeed, this emphasis is even extended to the possible preemptive use of nuclear weapons to keep recalcitrant successor states in line. Former Russian discouragement of extending possible associational status in NATO through the Partnership for Peace to former members of the Warsaw Pact reflects a similar focus on Russian sway within the old Communist world. At the same time, much of the appeal of Zhirinovsky is grounded in xenophobic Russian nationalism and thinly veiled threats against anyone who would do harm to ethnic Russians (he has also, in some of his typically loose rhetoric, suggested sending non-Russians back to their native republics).

The problem of resurgent, ethnically purifying nationalism—what might be called *primordial nationalism*—is currently more serious. It is an artifact of freedom from Soviet terror that expresses itself not in terms of inclusionary political democracy but as something quite the opposite—highly exclusionary national self-determination, where the self-determining units are ethnoreligiously defined and seek to separate ethnic groups that have been commingled into separate, purified communities by force.

The current locus of most of this problem is in the southern tier of former Soviet successor states. The major concentration follows a band about three degrees wide along the fortieth parallel north, extending from the Balkans eastward to China (see Map 4.1). Within that region, Islam and Christianity collided, and groups of different ethnic background came into contact. It is also an area that has undergone successive invasions by foreign tyrants across time, of which the Russians and the Soviets were only the most recent.

No one can say definitively why this spate of violence has occurred. Certainly the removal of authoritarian rule made a contribution, probably in two ways. First, the removal of the symbols of authority and political identification left many people adrift, and they reverted to old symbols of identification, notably the ethnicity and religions that divided them. Second, with authority removed and old passions rekindled, there were no formal means by which to suppress violence once it erupted.

The signs of ethnic violence are widespread. The most dramatic ongoing battles have been between Christian Armenia and Muslim Azerbaijan over the Armenian enclave within Azerbaijan known as Nagorno-Karabakh. Separated from their Armenian kinsman by Azeri-controlled territory, Armenia has waged a reasonably successful campaign to create a corridor controlled by Armenia to connect it with

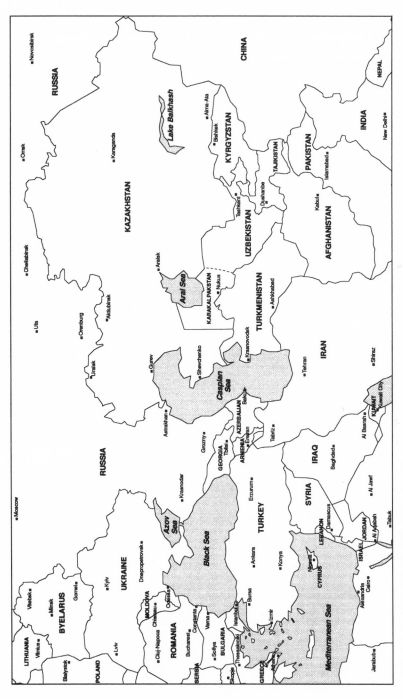

Map 4.1. Locus of Primordial Nationalism

Nagorno, in the process gobbling up large portions of Azerbaijan and creating an Azeri refugee problem that had over a million Azeris fleeing their homes as of late 1993. A smaller reverse problem exists for the Muslim residents of Nakichevan within Armenia.

This problem has escalatory potential within the region. Although Armenia held the advantage at the end of 1993, that country is surrounded by Muslim countries (such as Turkey) that have been its enemies. Should its fortunes become worse, its only hope of assistance comes from Christian Russia, an intervention that would be opposed widely. At the same time, Iranian Azerbaijan borders on successor state Azerbaijan, and it is questionable how long the Iranian Azeris will sit idly by watching the slaughter of their kinsmen.

There are other instances as well. In Georgia, the regime of former Gorbachev Foreign Minister Shevardnadze is under siege by separatists who would like to form an independent Abkhazia. Ethnic violence has occurred within Tajikistan and could easily spread to adjacent republics as well. To the west, there are simmering desires among Moldovans to unite with their ethnic kinsmen in Romania who are troubled by Russian and Ukrainian minorities within Moldova. The desire for ethnic purity (defined largely as the expulsion of Russians) in the Baltic states remains a simmering problem.

The minorities problem is the most important problem within a number of the successor states and is a significant foreign policy problem between Russia and those successors with a significant Russian minority. The ability or inability to deal with the problem of primordial nationalism will thus be a major determinant of First or Second Tier status for a number of those states.

Conclusions

The events that have occurred in the former Soviet Union over the past decade, but especially since 1989, are unprecedented in modern history —the dissolution of a modern major power through a simple act of self-declaration without a shot being fired. It was an event for which one searches in vain for parallels. Its significance is still being absorbed by those who are part of the internal process and by the world at large.

These remarkable events must be seen as part of an ongoing process whose outcome has yet to be determined and is highly unpredictable.

The ongoing process has two distinct, if interrelated, basic aspects. On the one hand is the process of change within the former Soviet Union itself. As argued, the most consequential part of that process is change within Russia as the major successor state, and the dimensions of that process are both economic and political. Elsewhere within the former union, the nationalities problem commands attention. On the other hand is the question of Russia and the other successors as part of the evolving post–Cold War world.

The problem of Russia arises from the growing pains of evolving an authoritarian system centered around a command economy to something like the market democracies of the First Tier. Just as economics and politics were self-reinforcing in the old system (management and control of the economy were a major element in political control, for instance), so too must the two go hand-in-hand in the new system.

Economically, the problem is overcoming the egalitarian bias of socialism and replacing it with an entrepreneurial system from which the majority of the people prosper. The difficulties of making that transition are conceptual (there are no frameworks for guiding the change), structural (the absence of a system of law and regulation to funnel economic activity), cultural (the large-scale absence of an entrepreneurial ethic), and financial (the need for large-scale infusions of capital). Any one of these problems would be daunting; together they are staggering. Given that most of the politicians trying to institute change are amateurs with little political or economic background prior to the fall of the system and the pockets of conspicuous consumption by a few, it is hardly surprising that opposition has arisen and that the prospects remain clouded.

The problem of political transformation in Russia is similar. When Gorbachev began the reform process, he unleashed powerful forces for democratization among the political elite of the country. For the vast majority of the Russian people, however, these reforms meant little. There is, after all, no democratic tradition in a Russia that has known an unbroken string of political despotisms throughout its history (with the possible exception of the brief Kerensky interlude in 1917). If the Russians seem maladroit at the conduct of democratic politics, more emphasis might be placed on their lack of experience than on dark talk of cultural or other failure.

Clearly, economic and political success or failure are closely related to one another. Gorbachev began, probably unwittingly, with political transformation as a means to bring about the goal of democratic socialism. The problem, of course, was that although socialism has its virtues (the social net) and hence bases of support, it also has the considerable liability of being unproductive and uncompetitive. As an economic system, socialism does not compete, a conclusion to which Gorbachev and others have come reluctantly, if at all. Since conversion to the market has not produced instant success, the instinct for nostalgia remains a potent source of political opposition to the regime and its program. The two cannot be disaggregated. In the long run, political and economic freedom is a potent combination; the unanswered question is whether political democracy can survive the process of economic transformation.

If the economic and political fortunes of Russia (and for that matter the other successor states) are cloudy and the evolving process subject to change, the problem of nationalities is even more difficult to predict. Will the current spate play itself out? Or will it spread to other areas adjacent to current outbreaks of violence? The question is lively for the southern successor states and for the Balkans as well. One thing is certain: the Communist interlude may have stifled and frustrated ancient animosities, but it clearly did little to relieve them.

The international consequences of Soviet collapse are more determinant. The implosion of the Soviet state ends the ideological competition and hence the rationale for the Cold War. There is no longer a major ideological schism in the world, which is probably good news for everyone. For the foreseeable future, it is difficult to conjure a new challenge emerging from Russia or elsewhere. Even a reversion of Russia to some authoritarian base would hardly threaten the basic integrity of the system: such a Russia would be isolated and increasingly poor, an angry beggar staring in from the cold but unable to penetrate the system.

Is reversion within Russia and the successor states possible? Making a categorical prediction in 1994 about that prospect is as foolish as predicting events was in 1989. Reversion is, of course, possible; the Faustian bargain could indeed be struck if Russian fortunes remain bleak. Is it likely? The answer is a tentative no: Russia has too much stake in attempting to join the collective prosperity of the First Tier to risk a return to the sullen isolationism of the past. Many Russians strongly desire a return to national glory; most will come to understand that this is only possible by continuing to evolve as a normal state that may become eligible for the widening circle of market democracies.

Notes

1. Mikhail S. Gorbachev, *Perestroika: New Thinking for Our Country and the World* (New York: Harper and Row, 1987).

2. Francis Fukuyama, "The End of History?" *National Interest, 16* (Summer 1989): 3–18.

3. Michael Mandelbaum, *Restructuring the European Security Order* (New York: Council on Foreign Relations, 1990), 24.

4. Allen Lynch, "Does Gorbachev Matter Anymore?" *Foreign Affairs, 69,* 3 (Summer 1990): 25.

5. Alexander Dallin, "Standing Lenin on His Head," *New Leader, 73,* 3, (February 5–19, 1990), 8.

6. Central Intelligence Agency, *The Soviet Weapons Industry: An Overview* (Washington, DC: Central Intelligence Agency, Document DI 86–10016, September 1986), 39.

7. Richard W. Judy, "The Soviet Information Revolution: Some Prospects and Comparisons," in Joint Economic Committee, Congress of the United States (100th Congress, 1st session), *Gorbachev's Economic Plans*, vol. 2 (Washington, DC: U.S. Government Printing Office, November 23, 1987), 173.

8. Nikolai Shmelev and Ed A. Hewett, "A Pragmatist's View on the Soviet Economy: A Conversation between Nikolai Shmelev and Ed A. Hewett," *Brookings Review, 8,* 1 (Winter 1989–90): 31.

9. Mikhail S. Gorbachev, "Our Ideal Is a Humane Democratic Socialism," *Vital Speeches of the Day, 56,* 11 (March 15, 1990): 323.

10. Ed A. Hewett, *Reforming the Soviet Economy: Equality vs. Efficiency* (Washington, DC: Brookings Institution, 1988), 305.

11. Lynch, "Does Gorbachev Matter Anymore?" 19.

12. Yegor Ligachev, "The Revolutionary Essence of Perestroika," *World Marxist Review, 30,* 2 (December 1987): 7.

13. Joshua Muravchik, "Gorbachev's Intellectual Odyssey," *New Republic, 920,* (March 5, 1990): 25.

14. Helmut Sonnenfeldt, "Gorbachev's First Year: An Overview," in Arthur B. Gunlicks and John D. Treadway (eds.), *The Soviet Union under Gorbachev* (New York: Praeger, 1987), 25.

15. J. Martin Ryle, "Gorbachev and the 27th Party Congress of the CPSU," in Gunlicks and Treadway, eds., *The Soviet Union under Gorbachev*, 145–46.

16. See William E. Odom, "How Far Can Soviet Reform Go?" *Problems of Communism, 36,* 6 (November–December 1987): 28.

17. Mikhail S. Gorbachev, "Key Sections of Gorbachev Speech Given to Party Conference," *New York Times* (June 29, 1988): 8.

18. Abel Aganbegyan, *The Economic Challenge of Perestroika* (Bloomington: Indiana University Press, 1988), 28–29, 31, 183–84.

19. Mikhail S. Gorbachev, *The Coming Century of Peace* (New York: Richardson and Steirman, 1986), 194.

20. Aganbegyan, *The Economic Challenge of Perestroika*, 5, 87.

21. Stephen Sestanovitch, "Gorbachev's Foreign Policy: A Diplomacy of Decline," *Problems of Communism, 37,* 1 (January–February 1988): 7.

22. Dallin, "Standing Lenin on His Head," 9.

23. Zbigniew Brzezinski, "Beyond Chaos," *National Interest, 19* (Spring 1990): 6.

5

Europe and the Changing Order

Next to the physical breakup of the former Soviet Union, the most dramatic manifestation of the changes that have occurred in the international system was the series of peaceful revolutions that occurred during the last half of 1989 in Central and Eastern Europe. Beginning with the installation of a noncommunist regime in Poland to which the Soviet Union did not react violently, the phenomenon spread through the former Warsaw Pact nations like wildfire.

The combined forces of Eastern European decommunization, the disbanding of the Warsaw Pact in mid-1991, and the Soviet dissolution at that year's end dismantled the remnants of the old Central Front confrontation at the inter-German border dividing East and West Germany that symbolized the Cold War. As in the former Soviet Union, the result has been to engage a process of change that is ongoing and is altering the geopolitical equation of the European continent.

Change is occurring in two parallel venues. The most dramatic changes have been associated with the countries of Eastern and Central Europe, which have been undergoing political and economic change in a dramatically different environment than before. Now they are much more the masters of their fate than they previously were. Highlighted by the unification of Germany, Western Europe is adapting—albeit more quietly—to a new economic and security circumstance that represents the second venue. The two dynamics come together over the question of how the two halves of Europe will associate with one another.

If one looks back even a year or so before the event, it is remarkable that no one saw the changes in Europe, and especially Eastern Europe, coming. Gorbachev, after all, had stated early in his rule that he would not interfere in the internal affairs of other states—he renounced the Brezhnev Doctrine—but no one took him seriously. It took the Solidarity movement in Poland to test the hypothesis. When it did, and the

Soviets failed to act as they had in the past, the floodgates were opened and the people's passions flowed freely, knocking aside the old regimes as if they were matchsticks in the wind.

The changes are fundamental. By allowing (or encouraging) the breakdown of the old order in Eastern Europe, Gorbachev set in motion the process by which the Cold War international system has disintegrated. The division of Europe that was both cause and effect of Soviet–American postwar disagreement about the world had evolved into an elaborate—and enormously expensive—set of institutions based on the preparation for, or avoidance of, a general war between the systems. That particular relationship had become dysfunctional because the war was made unfightable by necessary peace. Nonetheless, the structure had remained in some ways as a kind of comfortable and predictable vision of how leaders on both sides could view the world.

The most visible symbol of the Cold War system was the Berlin Wall separating the Communist and noncommunist parts of that city and acting as the primary means to separate the two Germanys, a result that had been the major aim of Soviet foreign policy after World War II. Gorbachev was once again an agent of change, first endorsing the massive migration of East Germans out of the GDR via Czechoslovakia, and then benignly overseeing the tearing down of the wall that was the natural consequence of the population transfer.

The results have been startling. The first and most dramatic effect has been to end the Cold War confrontation in Europe. Whether or not this was a clever part of a carefully developed plan on Gorbachev's part is a subject of considerable speculation, but the outcome is not. Half of the Cold War military alliance—the group of Communist states opposing the North Atlantic Treaty Organization (NATO) countries of Western Europe and North America—simply no longer exists, having voted itself out of existence. Indeed, by the end of 1993 Poland and Hungary had both requested formal association with NATO, and more formerly Communist states are sure to follow.

The inevitable consequence of the decommunization of Eastern Europe has been Soviet military withdrawal from what were formerly essentially its colonies, thereby putting to a final end the need for a state of perpetual war readiness on the part of the West. Equally inevitable, the implosion of half of the European security system is pointing toward a new set of institutions that will engulf the old system. The Western alliance no longer has the vital glue that has held it together for over forty years. It must change significantly or disappear, a dynamic that is the subject of considerable ongoing discussion in NATO circles and certainly enlivened formal talks between U.S. President Clinton and his European counterparts during the January 1994 summit.

The other epochal event has been the reunification of Germany. It is an important event for at least two reasons. First, it changes enormously the power map of Europe and hence the configuration of the international political system. Without question, a united Germany has the potential to be the most powerful and influential state in Europe after the process of "developing" the economy of former East Germany is completed. Bringing the economy of the old GDR up to some level commensurate with that of the West is an absolute necessity for the overall health of the reunified German Republic. The process of integration has indeed proven much more difficult than appeared to be the case in the midst of the euphoria surrounding unification. Social differences have been particularly noticeable, as forty years of Communist rule turn out to have produced a much less ambitious and hard-working population in the East. Westerners, for instance, scorn the "easties" for being laconic and lazy; easterners see the "westies" as pushy and overbearing. The gap, if anything, appears to widen with time.

The new Germany makes a vital difference in how Europe is organized and how it sees itself. There was a certain comfort in the old division, because it made Germany manageable; no one had to worry unnecessarily, for instance, about, German resurgence. Even then, West Germany was the most powerful economic entity on the continent, but not by so much that it was overly troubling.

In one sense, increasing the population of Germany from 64 million to 80 million does not make that much difference; it is an order of magnitude change of 20 percent. The symbolism, however, is what counts. A reunited Germany is Germany, after all, and there are areas with German majorities (notably in Poland) that could once again be part of the call for a "greater" Germany. Moreover, one of the primary virtues of the international system in the Cold War years was that it kept tabs on Germany. There is an old saw that says there were three underlying purposes to NATO: to keep the Americans in Europe, to keep the Russians out, and to keep the Germans down. That calculus no longer clearly holds. A Europe with no visible military threat is one where the United States, largely for budgetary reasons, is less likely to continue to station large numbers of forces. Similarly, the Russians have largely removed themselves from the center of Europe, leaving the German question as the remaining part of the equation.

How Europe deals with its new map will be critical to how the post–Cold War international system evolves. A reunified Germany is obviously the key player, and the policies and positions of the German state will affect how Europe organizes itself. The discussions are political, military, and economic. The political agenda is dominated by the question of European relations with the United States, Russia and the other successor states, and the formerly Communist states of Europe. At its heart is the nature of the political map of Europe. Militarily, the question is the relevance of NATO and whether a reconstituted NATO or some other security "architecture" is appropriate, a matter given some urgency by the pitiful impotence of Europe in dealing with the Bosnian crisis. Economically, implementation of the Maastricht Treaty and future directions of the economic union dominate concern.

If the shape of the future in Europe is difficult to predict with precision, one can at least try to understand what has happened already as prelude to what may transpire. To this end, we will begin by looking at the revolutions in Eastern Europe that triggered the whole process, examining particularly what gave rise to them, what made them happen as rapidly as they did, and whether they were the result of the "Gorbachev effect" of unintended consequences[1] or of some greater design. Based on that discussion, we will look at what might favorably or adversely affect the evolution of Eastern European governments toward Westernization and possibly closer affiliation with the West.

Since a key element in changing the power map of Europe is German reunification, we will analyze that. A remarkable aspect of German reunification is how it occurred: once the barriers were down, it was private East German citizens and West German corporations who accomplished the important elements of de facto reunification. In other words, German citizens unified the country and left the formalities to their governments. The "privatization" of international relations that the German reunification process represents (accomplishing international tasks by nongovernmental means) is an important change in how the international system operates, and it deserves special attention. In turn, the process and outcome of German reunification will affect the organization of the evolving international system.

The Eastern European Revolutions

The staccato fashion in which the Communist regimes fell in the last quarter of 1989 caught the world almost totally off guard. If one looks back only as far as early 1989 for prophets, one looks in vain. Only in retrospect can we see the underlying causes and how they bubbled to the surface.

The phenomenon that swept Eastern Europe was part of the greater crisis affecting the Soviet Union, in at least two senses. First, the countries of Eastern Europe were experiencing the same kind of economic decline that was occurring in the Soviet Union. This process was all the more painful because the people of Eastern Europe, by virtue of their proximity to the West and access to the West via television, could see that while they were suffering a "deterioration and retrocession"[2] in their standards of living, the West was booming. Moreover, East Europeans could calculate even greater disparities after the full implementation of the Maastricht Treaty establishes the Western economic union.[3]

Gorbachev's role was absolutely essential. Eastern Europeans could have felt all the frustration in the world over their conditions, but that did not mean anything if the result of voicing their discontent was to be invasion by Soviet tanks. Although the bonds of Soviet overlordship had been loosened somewhat after the invasion of Czechoslovakia in 1968, the Brezhnev Doctrine still dangled delicately over the nations of the Warsaw Pact. Until that threat was lifted, change could not occur.

Gorbachev was the key actor. At one level, it must have appeared anachronistic to the Soviet leader that the very kind of Communists he was trying to remove from his own country were still in power in the rest of the Warsaw Pact countries. *Perestroika* in the Soviet Union without a parallel phenomenon in the rest of the Soviet-influenced Communist world did not make sense to him.

Such a perception was doubtless easier to develop because of the economic situation. This, in turn, was part of the overall loss of momentum of the Socialist world that had caused the relative decline. One observer argues that Gorbachev believed that Socialist ideology lost its intellectual position of preeminence in about 1973, when the oil crisis imposed radical adaptations in capitalist countries that were not matched by the Socialist world.[4] More important, Soviet support for the economies of Eastern Europe, as, for example, through subsidies for oil exported to Eastern Europe from the Soviet Union, was creating a millstone on further Soviet progress. Gorbachev apparently understood that maintaining strict political control in Eastern Europe came at the price of deepening economic stagnation in his own country, a situation he considered unacceptable given the Soviet Union's need for internal reform.

Casting the problem this way makes the decision to allow Eastern European autonomy a matter of Soviet self-interest. Buffeted as Eastern Europe was by economic woes that were not going away, it was clear that a "reformulation of Soviet security interests" was needed.[5] A major conclusion of that assessment was the need to concentrate energies and resources on the faltering Soviet economy rather than on foreign adventures and burdens, including the partial subsidization of the Eastern European economies. Given that the Soviets felt they could no longer afford such assistance, it is plausible to argue that "Gorbachev turned the Brezhnev Doctrine on its head to exert pressure for political and economic change in Eastern Europe."[6]

The problem was how to convey the message in a convincing manner. There had, after all, been other occasions when the Soviets had seemed to loosen their grip, only to tighten it once again, as in the Prague Spring of 1968. Why should Eastern Europeans trust the Soviets now?

Gorbachev acted by traveling to Eastern Europe himself and sending other high Soviet officials such as Foreign Minister Eduard Shevardnadze there during the first half of 1989. They brought with them the message that Gorbachev would not save hard-line regimes in the region with Soviet tanks if those regimes failed "to avert a showdown with their angry populations."[7] In case anyone had failed to hear that message, he made it abundantly clear in a speech before the Council of Europe on July 6, 1989. Gorbachev said,

> European states belong to different social systems. That is a reality. Recognition of this historical fact and respect for the sovereign right freely to choose a social system constitute the major prerequisites for a normal European process. Social and political orders in one or another country have changed in the past and may change in the future. But this change is the exclusive affair of the people of that country and is their choice. *Any interference in domestic affairs and any attempts to restrict the sovereignty of states—friends, allies, or any others—are inadmissible.* [Emphasis added.][8]

The message could hardly have been clearer, although the context may have brought into question Gorbachev's motives and sincerity. The speech quoted is the now-famous "common European home" address in which Gorbachev called for continentwide unity; this was then taken as a code for soliciting Western assistance for the Soviet economy. In that light, appearing to loosen the grip on Eastern Europe could be viewed as a propaganda ploy to open the Western assistance gate.

The Poles, of course, took Gorbachev at his word and installed the first noncommunist government in the Warsaw Pact region, under Prime Minister Tadeusz Mazoweicki. When there was no hostile Soviet response, the revolutions began, and within months the Soviet Union had the only professedly Communist government in the pact.

Although it is a matter of speculation, it seems likely that the telecommunications revolution had something to do with the pace of events. In an earlier time, television images had briefly captured Soviet tanks crushing the Hungarian revolution; in 1989 they captured and transmitted worldwide the absence of Soviet repression. One can only imagine how the people who became the leaders of the cascade of revolutions must have been glued to their television sets during this period, and how intoxicating the stream of successes must have been to them.

The pace of the change process caught everyone off guard, including the Soviets. Soviet academic Valentin Falin suggests, "We were as surprised at the pace of what happened in Eastern Europe as the rest of the world was."[9] Presumably, those surprised included Gorbachev himself, who could hardly have welcomed the extent of ferment that emerged.

One of the most striking features of the revolutionary period was the ease with which Communist governments fell before what were only loosely organized, almost ad hoc movements with no previous opportunities to organize as mass movements. In some measure, the leaders' bewilderment at what was happening reflected their lack of understanding of what their people actually thought of them. Sam Tanenhaus makes the interesting suggestion that the masquerading of those feelings was the result of the influence of *ketman* (the Islamic tradition of hiding true feelings from religious authorities to avoid persecution).[10] Whether such an exotic explanation holds or not, the velocity of change, shedding communism like an old rag, was stunning.

Undoubtedly, some of the incredulity derived from self-delusion on the part of party officials who genuinely did not know the depth of popular animosity toward them. Moreover, the system had become so corrupt that public revelations that were certain to emerge would have caused them to crumble anyway. At the same time, the Brezhnev Doctrine had allowed the regimes the luxury of not concerning themselves with their own preservation; the Soviets were always there to bail them out. But suddenly they were gone, and "the Brezhnev Doctrine, oddly enough, undermined socialism though it was meant to protect it."[11] The crutch provided by the Red Army left the leaders defenseless once it was removed.

In this environment of uncertainty, "largely peaceful social movements"[12] acted with remarkable speed and with a minimum of violence except in Romania, where Ceausescu initially tried to use the secret police and the army to quell the revolution. According to Andrew Nagorski, we should have been able to predict the orderliness of events because there was a "seasoned generation of dissidents" in movements such as Charter 77 in Czechoslovakia, from which Vaclav Havel arose, ready to move into action when the opportunity came.[13]

The Gorbachev Influence

While the role of Mikhail Gorbachev in all this was crucial, there is great disagreement among observers about Gorbachev's motives, and Gorbachev himself is not saying. Essentially, three different interpretations have emerged. The first argues that Gorbachev had none of what happened in mind, that the "Gorbachev effect" of unintended effects indeed occurred. The second interpretation suggests that he indeed wanted to induce change, but change of a more moderate variety than what transpired. The third argument is that the whole operation was a carefully conceived and brilliantly executed plan to rid the Soviets of the last bogeyman of the Cold War. Each argument deserves at least a cursory examination.

The first group of observers believes that Gorbachev did not want any of what happened in Eastern Europe to occur, least of all the destruction of the Warsaw Pact. Ted Warner represents this line of reasoning, maintaining that the Soviet leader could not possibly have wanted massive change because he had "every intention" of maintaining the integrity of the Warsaw Pact and "keeping troop presence there until the year 2000."[14] Henry Kissinger agrees, arguing that what

Gorbachev wanted was to gain access to Western technology by instituting limited reforms that would be put in place in Eastern Europe with reformist Communists in power capable of "liberating, not overthrowing, existing institutions."[15] In this view, Gorbachev's actions essentially were a feint to convince a guileless West that more fundamental change was occurring than was indeed the case.

The second explanation has Gorbachev recognizing a deeper sense of malaise. In this view, part of Gorbachev's acquiescence in the revolutions of 1989 is explained by the Soviet Union's need for Western economic assistance, which required some image polishing. But that is not all. According to Brian Crozier,

> When the rot spread to the Eastern European colonies, Gorbachev and his closest advisors (especially his mentor, Yakovlev) made the bold decision to give the mounting revolt a shove in an effort to control events instead of being overwhelmed by them. There can be no doubt that the KGB helped to organize the mass demonstrations that brought down Honnecker in East Germany and Ceausescu in Rumania.[16]

Having reached this determination, the question for Gorbachev became how to pull the rug out from under the old guard while maintaining some control. The answer, reflecting at least some narcissism, was to turn to reformist Communists in Eastern Europe who shared his views. According to recently rehabilitated Soviet activist and Gorbachev biographer Zhores Medvedev, Gorbachev had attended Moscow State University with a number of Eastern Europeans who met the general criteria.[17] If Gorbachev was right for the Soviet Union, it must be the best thing to place Gorbachev clones in charge of the countries of the Warsaw Pact. Reformist Eastern European Communists, in turn, would come up with strategies for economic progress that would satisfy popular aspirations and, with any luck, improve conditions in the region in ways that the Soviet Union might emulate.

The problem for Gorbachev, of course, was that he got more than he bargained for when change began to occur. Probably limited by the same blinders that maintained his own faith in continuing Communist rule, he could not bring himself to see the bankruptcy of the system or the venality of the group he was pushing aside. As a result, the ultimate Gorbachev effect of unintended effects took over: he pushed for change, never intending to liberate Eastern Europe; rather, he simply set out to replace "hidebound, often corrupt viceroys with communist reformers like himself so he could give Moscow's satellites greater autonomy and reduce their drain on Soviet treasure."[18]

The third explanation says this was a well-conceived plan. Getting rid of puppet states in Eastern Europe not only removed the economic millstone of propping up those economies, it also served to transfer "to the West the economic burden of the Soviet Union's satellite states."[19] The Soviet Sergei Karaganov adds that this action was also a brilliant piece of geopolitics on Gorbachev's part:

> The events . . . of 1989 were in many respects the crowning success of Soviet European policy. . . . The Cold War system of bloc confrontation has started not only to show cracks, but actually to fall apart. That system was highly unfavorable to the Soviet Union, in that the USSR found itself in a position of opposition to states with a predominant economic wealth.[20]

According to another analyst, allowing the Eastern European states to cast their own lots represented Gorbachev's insight into what was needed to end a Cold War his country could no longer afford. Moreover, Gorbachev recognized that NATO was held together by the dread inspired by Moscow's handling of its own East European satellites. Thus, he reasoned "the bloc facing Russia could only be dissolved by reassurance."[21]

Although the three explanations overlap to some degree, they also diverge to the point that they cannot all simultaneously be correct. As any good politician would do, Gorbachev took credit only for what went right (and what he could not affect anyway), and he has not clarified what his own intentions were at the beginning. Doubtless he will not reveal what he had in mind unless he writes his memoirs and does reveal his motivations.

There is one explanation that borrows from and synthesizes the others. It is entirely possible, even probable, that at the beginning Gorbachev could identify three problems that Eastern Europe posed for his vision of the future. First, the regimes were increasingly at odds with his vision of the Communist order and thus needed replacing. The KGB must also have told him of the corruption that permeated the structures. Second, the economies of Eastern Europe were a burden that was cutting into the resources necessary for reform at home, a loss to be cut. Third, Gorbachev needed assistance from the West, notably in technology, and the continuation of Stalinist puppets in the Warsaw Pact was bad for his image.

If Gorbachev knew these things, then a logical answer from his perspective was Eastern European *perestroika* carried out by like-minded Communists in those states. As stated earlier, he was acquainted with some of them from collegiate days. It is extremely unlikely that he wanted to replace Stalinist regimes with noncommunist ones: in 1989, he was still resisting that prospect too vigorously in his own country to be suspected of anything else. As noncommunists came to power, he must have been in a quandary, faced with unacceptable alternatives. If he interfered in the process, in effect resuscitating the Brezhnev Doctrine, he would have been viewed as a monster, and his careful courtship of the West would have been a total loss.

In such a situation, he had no real choice. The lesser evil was accepting noncommunist governments that he did not want. Like any good politician, he went a step further and embraced the change as if it were his idea; since decommunization was powerfully supported everywhere else, why not claim to be the liberator of Eastern Europe? And, especially, why not get out ahead when there is really nothing you can do to stop the change that is occurring? This was a recurrent theme in Gorbachev's domestic strategy, so why not try it in the international realm and hope for the best?

Initially, the results were serendipitous. There was a visible improvement in East–West relations; Western Europeans began falling over themselves trying to come to the aid of Eastern European economies; and Gorbachev's "common European home," with its free-flowing Western aid and technology, was closer to becoming a reality. In that case, Gorbachev would have been a fool not to smile sweetly through what Andrei Gromyko once described as his "iron teeth."

But what has occurred still represents a gamble that may not pay off. For the gamble to provide lasting benefits to the Russians, and indeed to the stability of the new international system, the revolutions of 1989 must prove successful.

Neither success nor failure is preordained. The uniformity with which communism was shunted aside has not been matched by uniform movement toward market democracy throughout the former Communist world—Eastern Europe and the successor states. The process of change continues differentially.

Yeltsin, of course, has become the principal inheritor of this process and all its uncertainties. His performance and its acceptance by the Russian people have been mixed. Positively, he is the only person freely elected president of Russia, and approval of the constitution that places great power in his hands indicates a strong residue of continuing support. Clearly, no one in Russia currently has the personal political standing that Yeltsin possesses. Negatively, it is not at all clear that his personal standing extends to support for his policies, including the economic reforms. The strongest indication of this lack of support has been the electoral rejection of parties most clearly supporting reform in the 1993 elections. In the long run, Yeltsin's political fate—and that of those reformers who would succeed him—may well boil down to the perceived progress of reform by the Russian people.

The Process of Change in Eastern Europe

There are points of both similarity and dissimilarity between the processes of change set in motion in Eastern Europe and in the former Soviet Union. Both areas share the Stalinist past of command economies and authoritarian political systems. They are both on a course of economic and political reform where success in one area ultimately must extend to the other. Both realize that the alternative to reform is second-class status in the new Europe—relegation to the Second Tier.

Among the differences is the fact that the "nationalities problem" has its parallel in some, but not all, East European countries, where national minorities are found within existing states and the danger of irredentism clearly exists. As in the former Soviet Union, political repression dampened this problem while it existed; it is now up to political freedom to come to grips with it. Basically, however, the problem is much more severe in parts of the former Soviet Union than it is in Eastern Europe other than in the Balkans.

Communist rule obviously failed to take popular root in most of Eastern Europe. For one thing, communism was imposed on most of these countries (former Yugoslavia is a notable exception) by the Red Army of occupation and quislings trained in the Soviet Union. It was also of shorter standing, a matter of slightly over forty years. Operational communism was a Russian invention, a part of their heritage and artifact of part of their culture. In Eastern Europe, it was an alien intrusion.

The second point of dissimilarity has to do with the thoroughness with which the Communist past has been expunged and the trauma associated with the exorcism. The problem has clearly been more difficult within Russia and some of the other successor states. The Soviet Union gave birth to Marxism-Leninism as a functioning governmental system, the system existed there for nearly three-quarters of a century, and many saw their personal and the national lots improved under Communist rule. Thus, there existed—and continues to exist—a certain level of support for the old system that allows "former" Communists to remain in power and has energized nostalgia for the old order among those suffering from the new. There is hardly such a sentiment anywhere in Eastern Europe.

One of the difficulties of talking about the prospects for success in Eastern Europe arises from the fact that there really is no single entity called Eastern Europe. Rather, there are a whole series of distinct nationalities with differing, often conflicting, histories and cultures. Some form national societies (Poland), but others are fitted imperfectly into more or less multinational states. Some are more Westernized and prosperous now than others and thus have better opportunities for succeeding in the transformation to Western societies. This is generally true of the northern tier of the Warsaw Pact (Poland, Hungary, and the Czech Republic) and former East Germany, whose success is nearly assured by virtue of reunification. The southern tier states, Romania and Bulgaria, have more uncertain prospects; they suffered the greatest repression and the least prosperity, and their cultures are distinct, more affected by Byzantine influences. The northern tier states culturally resemble the rest of Europe much more closely, which helps explain why they are westernizing more quickly (a peaceful Croatia could probably be added to this list). By contrast, the southern tier states have known more of the Byzantine influence. The result is a split between the northern and southern tiers that falls generally within Samuel P. Huntington's "clash of civilizations" idea.[22]

Within this diversity, one can see some common threads that provide markers against which to measure progress. The purpose of the revolutions in the first place was shared: the peaceful achievement of democratic status. While in the abstract this is true, it is probably not enough to assure a peaceful transition to Western ways (just as democracy is a necessary, but not sufficient, long-term condition for Russian reform). The democratic tradition is not deeply embedded in most East European countries. For democracy to take hold, the precondition (or possibly corequisite) is economic success; the success of the new market economies will likely determine the "fate of democracy in all the states."[23]

The difficulty is the familiar lack of a road map to market capitalism. The problem is the same as that bedeviling Russian reform; no one prior to the last couple of years gave very serious thought to *how* one makes over a Socialist command economic system into a market system. Some favor a shock treatment of quick transformation (Poland), while others prefer a more gradual, Gorbachev-like pace (the Czech Republic). For that reason, the practical difficulties of transforming command economies into market economies "may dwarf the problems of shifting from dictatorship to democracy."[24] This brings out a contrast with the Russian experiment. By controlling the levers of state and party, Gorbachev was able, at least in the early days, to impose some democracy and economic reforms with the considerable weight of institutions—so-called top–down management. The East European revolutions, on the other hand, started from the masses as bottom–up movements. For the movements to maintain their momentum, the masses must continue their support, which is much easier if conditions of life improve. The alternative is stark. As Michael Brenner argues, if Eastern European countries "are to become prosaic, post-ideological, and conflict-averse societies for which the Western liberal democracies are the model, they must first become prosperous. If they fail economically, liberalism may be discredited throughout the region."[25]

The outcomes of these processes will affect the future politico-economic status of the various Eastern European states, and thus their association with the rest of Europe and the generalized international system. Those states where political democracy and market economy take hold most firmly have the best chances of joining the First Tier, probably through some variant of the model by which Spain and Portugal were allowed to join the European Community (a gradual, assisted period of change). The most obvious candidates are Poland, Hungary, and the Czech Republic. Once peace returns to the Balkans/former Yugoslavia, Croatia and possibly Slovenia could contend.

The prospects are not so bright elsewhere. Political democracy has had noticeably little impact in places like Bulgaria, Romania, and Albania, all of whose economies remain within the partially developed subtier of the Second Tier. It will take years to rebuild the Serbian economy and polity, as it will in what survives of Bosnia. The fates of the other splinter states (Montenegro, Macedonia, and Slovakia) are in limbo.

It is very important that economic reform occur in a way clearly beneficial to the people of Eastern Europe, both to implant support for political democracy and to dampen divisive forces lying under the surface. One author describes the worst:

> In the throes of economic and political crisis, derivative and other social movements could become vehicles of ethnic, nationalist, and class strife and rivalries—with unforeseeable consequences which could include dictatorial populist backlashes against newly won democracy.[26]

Fortunately, there appears to be an awareness in Western Europe of the momentous opportunity that the revolutions of 1989 afford. There is clearly a state of flux in the central region today that is slightly unsettling, because the postwar division of Europe did lend predictability to relations among European states. The new Europe already has produced the bonus of breaking down the Cold War military competition, thus opening the door of associational opportunities for those Eastern European states ready to go through it. There is an opportunity to grab the brass ring of peace and stability in Europe without military confrontation by coming to the material, economic aid of Eastern Europe in its transformation. It is difficult to imagine the states of Western Europe not responding to this historic chance.

There is, of course, unfinished business galore. One list of the requirements in the transition argues "liberal values and economic growth must be fostered in the regimes of Eastern Europe, the two military blocs must be reconstituted into a pan-European system, and a collective accommodation must be made to the power of a reunified Germany."[27] This is not a bad list, although I think it is slightly out of order. The emergence of a stable, westernized East Europe and the shape of German reunification are the qualifying or enabling conditions for the building of a new structure to encompass the changes in Europe. What kind of Germany emerges is key to all aspects: political, economic, and military.

German Reunification

Even as late as 1989, the idea that Germany would be completely reunified by October 3, 1990, would have seemed ludicrous to almost any observer. Yet, as the most dramatic effect of the revolutions of 1989, German de facto reunification occurred within a period of a few short months.

There could be no greater symbol of the breakdown of the Cold War system than a single Germany. Since its inception, the joint occupation and division of Germany was the focal point of the Cold War. The inability of the Western Allies and the Soviets to decide what kind of Germany they wanted after World War II was one of the precipitating events of the Cold War, and the periodic crises over Berlin, beginning with the blockade and airlift in 1948 and culminating with the construction of the wall in 1961, symbolized the Cold War at its most intense.

And suddenly it was over. In one sense, it was the completion of "part of a larger process which was bringing an end to the postwar era shaped by American hegemony, a Soviet threat, and a divided and dependent Europe."[28] The problem was that no one saw it coming, so no one quite knew how to adjust to the new reality.

Two points about the reunification process are worth making, because they represent examples of how the new international system operates differently from the Cold War system. First, the Cold War superpowers were unable to influence the process greatly. Reunification occurred essentially without prior consultation with the two nations who erected the old division; instead, Chancellor Helmut Kohl tried to issue adequate reassurances to both the Soviets and the Americans (especially the Soviets) that the process and outcome were not threatening. In particular, Kohl traveled to Moscow to assure Gorbachev that a reunified Germany, still a member of NATO, posed no threat to the Soviet Union in July 1990. Part of his peace offering was the promise of German economic assistance to aid the transformation of the Soviet economy.

The irrelevance of the superpowers in this matter reflects a basic change in how the system operates. If one accepts the premise that a docile and weak Germany was a cornerstone of Soviet policy since World War II, then reunification was the last thing the Soviets wanted, although it is exactly what they have gotten. Despite face-saving concessions to the Soviets in the form of German economic assistance, the Soviets were powerless to do anything but acquiesce. And, while a strong, pro-Western Germany does not threaten the United States, the U.S. role in its creation was also largely passive.

The change is in the relative balance and salience of power. In the old Cold War days, a movement toward reunification in East Germany would have been dealt with by Soviet occupation forces, which remained in the country as it reunified. Yet the potential price of crushing reunification by force was superpower confrontation and possibly a nuclear world war. Reunification was the final symbolic act following the fall of the Berlin Wall that also broke down part of the confrontation between East and West, thus providing the opening for Soviet economic and technological relations with the West. Hence, Soviet military force could not have been used to exercise power over the outcome, even if Gorbachev had desired to do so. From the U.S. viewpoint, the historic means of influencing events in Europe was American economic domination. But Germany, whose economy was as vital as that of the United States, could not have been coerced by economic threats should the United States have chosen to try to hamper reunification.

The second point about reunification is the way in which it occurred. In a very real sense, reunification was indeed a private act by the German people—and especially West German industry—acting almost without governmental direction. The population of East Germany simply walked across the border and joined the West, while West German corporations invested their money in the East and began the de facto process of economic unification ratified by the respective governments in the form of currency reform. To the extent that government played a leading role, it was in the form of West German politicians campaigning in East Germany for candidates of their own or related parties.

The dynamics leading to German reunification provide an example of *the privatization of international relations*. In this instance, governments did not take the lead in vital parts of the process making reunification possible; the Kohl government favored reunification and "greased the skids" by compensating the Soviets and drawing up the agreements. The lead, however, fell to private individuals and groups. To some extent, this was an extension of the popular uprisings in the rest of Eastern Europe in 1989, where governments thought to be impregnable and indomitable could not resist the popular tide. At the same time, this phenomenon may be a harbinger of the future actions of the large multinational, stateless private enterprises that can act first and ask governments for permission later.

The Consequences of Reunification

Now that a single Federal Republic of Germany is a fact, the question is, what difference does that fact make for the international system? A united Germany is the largest, most prosperous wholly European state, and it has the potential to dwarf its neighbors economically, at least after the integration of the east into the national economy has occurred (which is proving no small trick). The question becomes how to fit this large, dynamic country into a political, military, and economic framework that is comfortable for other Europeans and for the Germans themselves.

The problem would not be so severe were it not for the German past, and more specifically, the Nazi period. Were Germany Switzerland, reunification would pose no problem to anyone. But the stronger Germany has the prospect of once again becoming the most powerful continental state, and "nervousness about a dominant Germany is surfacing throughout the rest of Europe. No one is sure how to deal with it without provoking a West Germany that has been a steadfast ally for 40 years."[29]

The problems associated with reunification do not seem as vivid as they were portrayed at the time, for at least four reasons. First, the internal process of reconciling the east and the west have proven more difficult than was generally believed in 1990. Germany has visibly struggled with integrating the 16 million citizens of the old GDR with the 64 million westerners to the point that no one predicts a colossus of 80 million rising above and dominating the rest of Europe in the short run. Rather, Germany seems a more ordinary European state than some projected when unification began.

Second, the German economic miracle has sputtered as part of the general global recession that began in the latter 1980s and only started to lift in 1994. The image of a German economy so booming that it had to import large numbers of foreign workers to keep the factories rolling has given way to a more sober picture of high unemployment, an uncompetitive wage structure making German products too expensive (for instance, the decision by Mercedes-Benz to build a major automobile production facility in Alabama announced in 1993—the company's first production plant outside Germany—was partially justified by a desire to employ cheaper American workers), and layoffs and cutbacks among German workers.

Third, the government of Helmut Kohl has gone out of its way to reassure everyone, and especially the Russians, of its honorable intentions. With the possible exception of its premature recognition of Croatian independence in late 1991 (which helped trigger the Bosnian War), the Germans have been mostly passive and cooperative in foreign policy matters. They have taken a leadership role in promoting economic assistance and investment in Russia and the Eastern European states, and have pledged a constructive role in areas such as implementing the Maastricht Treaty.

Fourth, the system, including Europe, has had more important matters to concern itself with than a resurgent Germany. The continued turmoil in the successor states and what to do about the continuing carnage and horror in the Balkans are the two most pressing matters. Less dramatic, but in the long run of possibly greater import, is the shape of both the security and the economic architecture of Europe.

The New European Order

German reunification came at an especially pregnant time for Europe organizationally. Both the politicomilitary and economic institutions of the continent were undergoing overhaul. At the politicomilitary level, NATO was going through a debate about levels of future commitment activated both by an apparently reduced threat from the Russians and by U.S. domestic economic dictates to reduce defense spending. In addition, the Conference of Security and Cooperation in Europe (CSCE) has grown to encompass the emerging states of Europe (its membership in January 1994 was fifty-three states), and it has become an important part of the security scene. Competing for a place in the European security picture is the West European Union (WEU). In the economic realm, the twelve members of the European Community have moved steadily ahead to remove the remaining barriers to economic union implemented for 1992 (EC 92).

All of these negotiations originally proceeded on the assumption of two Germanys, and a single German state alters the calculations in each. The reunification of Germany certainly changes the problem NATO faces: for over forty years, NATO had been planning for a war beginning at a border dividing the two Germanys—a border that no longer exists. With the united Germany a full member of NATO, the dividing line—to the extent that it is meaningful—is the Polish-German frontier, and this affects force structure, as does the long-term presence or absence of U.S. and other foreign troops on German soil. Moreover, the implosion of the Warsaw Pact leaves NATO as a defensive alliance facing no offense. As a result, NATO has begun to lose its military *raison d'être* and struggles to find a way to justify its continuing existence. In the absence of its continuing rationale and with its members cutting back their troop commitments—both unilaterally and as the result of the Conventional Forces in Europe (CFE) accords, NATO looks for new roles. Full inclusion of former Warsaw Pact members such as Hungary and Poland has temporarily been put on hold, and the new Partnership for Peace remains an embryonic, vague construct the ultimate impact of which is conjectural.

The CFE process was similarly based upon the balance between NATO and the Warsaw Pact, with West German force levels counting as part of the NATO allotments and East German forces on the other side. The first hurdle, presented by what size forces Germany will contribute to NATO, has been surmounted, but that is not all. The demise of the Warsaw Pact has reduced the size of Eastern European military forces, and has provided an excuse for European NATO members to reduce the size of their forces as well. Finally, much of the CFE enterprise was directed at lowering the possibility that either side's forces could launch a rapid attack (because this prospect requires large standing forces). As the Russians have left former pact countries and the United States and other NATO countries have quit Germany, this task takes on less meaning. Moreover, economic restraints have impelled Russia to reduce greatly the size and offensive capability—especially outside its borders—of Russian forces.

The first step toward institutionalizing the new balance occurred in November 1990. At the Paris meeting of the CSCE, the twenty-two CFE states included in the CSCE signed the CFE I agreement, limiting the number of tanks, armored vehicles, artillery pieces, helicopters, and combat aircraft that NATO and the Warsaw Pact could retain. Under the terms of the agreement, both sides agreed to numerical limits well below the levels necessary for rapid offensive action; because of prior armament levels, the Soviets were forced to destroy, over a three-year period, many more weapons systems than the West.

Troop levels were not affected by the agreement, although negotiations began on November 26, 1990, to reach accord at considerably smaller numbers of men under arms. What CFE I did accomplish was to codify the disintegration of the Warsaw Pact; by placing numerical limits reflecting the changes that had already occurred (including counting former East German equipment within NATO forces), these changes were formalized. Moreover, the agreement stipulated that no more than two-thirds of the forces counted against each "alliance" could be American or Soviet.

These early actions contributed to the subsequent cascade of events that have dismantled the Cold War military confrontation. As noted, the Warsaw Pact voted itself out of existence in 1991, and the demise of the Soviet Union has atomized its former forces among the successor states. The CSCE process now incorporates all the successor states and all European states (Albania, the last holdout, joined in 1993) and has established a formal secretariat in Prague. At the same time, some proponents of an exclusively European defense system (now that American protection against evaporated enemies is unneeded) have suggested a new structure around the WEU, all nine of whose members are also members of the European Community.

A united Germany affects the European Community in at least two ways. First, Germany was already the predominant power in the European Community, and the addition of the former GDR can only enhance that position once full integration has occurred. Granting that it will take a number of years and much investment to bring the East up to the standards of living and productivity of the West, once that is accomplished, Germany will be even more formidable. Some wonder whether the new Germany might simply overwhelm the rest of the European Community. Second, the inclusion of East Germany via its amalgamation into the Federal Republic opens the EC membership question again. The emerging countries in Eastern Europe, as they adopt the market economies and the political systems of the West, are going to request membership in the institution of Western prosperity (Hungary and Poland have already petitioned for associate status). Having just absorbed, with some difficulty, two other relatively less developed members (Spain and Portugal), many EC member states are reluctant to consider more new, relatively poor members, especially with Greece now a member and Turkey clamoring for inclusion. At the same time, they all have a stake in a successful westernization of the East, which EC affiliation would promote.

Within the European Community, this has produced a debate over the future about whether to "widen" or to "deepen" the association. Basing their argument largely on seeking a more stable, homogeneous, and peaceful Europe, the wideners advocate extending membership to former Communist states—once they have achieved the dual criteria of democracy and market economy—as a way to coopt them into the First Tier. The deepeners, by contrast, seek to use the implementation of the Maastricht Treaty's provisions to further tie the members together through deeper forms of association, notably in the area of political integration, which has always been a stumbling block for the organization.

There is a larger question raised by German reunification: What is the shape of the organization of Europe in the new international system? As the Cold War has faded, organization on the old basis is clearly inadequate. The question is what should replace the old order. Before German reunification, there was some question about the inclusion of Eastern Europe and Russia in something like an economic union based upon Gorbachev's "common European home" concept, and this theme has been accentuated by the decommunization of the Eastern bloc. At the same time, there has been concern among Europeans about how to avoid U.S. "decoupling" from Europe, matched by fears of American exclusion from Europe expressed by Americans.

A united Germany obviously added yet another aspect to the organizational puzzle. On the one hand, some new associative institution raises the prospect of tying Germany firmly to the common destiny of Europe, thereby lessening the possibility that Germany will go its own way. On the other hand, Germany is the most vibrant state in the new Europe, and the further question is how to associate Germany without allowing Germany simply to take over the new structure.

There have been several suggestions about organizational pegs around which to build the new association. Three stand out: organization around NATO, the expansion of the European Community as the prime anchor, and the expansion of the CSCE. Each has advantages and disadvantages.

The NATO option represents the short-term but possibly not the long-term solution. Its primary advantage is that the United States is a full and active member, thereby assuring that the United States will not retreat from the new Europe. At the same time, the North Atlantic Council is an operating political body, and NATO has an organizational infrastructure in the form of its secretariat. Moreover, continuing

U.S. leadership also provides some leverage over Germany. The P4P has at least temporarily given new vitality to NATO.

NATO does, however, have some marked problems. First, although NATO does have a political dimension, it is primarily a *military* alliance whose political activities have been limited to coordinating security policies relevant to the defense of Western Europe. It is not, in other words, an all-purpose political body, nor does its administrative apparatus have any broad-ranging experience beyond the security area. Second, the continuing mission, the *raison d'être* for NATO, will become progressively cloudy as the military threat retreats—unless it can find a new role. No one expects NATO to disappear any time soon, but there could be conflict over what to do in the long term. Third, the question of association of the former Communist countries remains at issue. Northern tier Eastern Europeans want in, but this prospect is sufficiently troubling to Russia that their full participation has been deferred. These states are now associated with NATO through the P4P. Paradoxically, however, such an association would kick the last pin out from under NATO's reason for existing. Fourth, the performance of NATO outside its Cold War mission is less than promising. The situation for which NATO would have seemed a reasonable mechanism was Bosnia, but political divisions among the members paralyzed any response, thereby giving rise to doubts that there are *any* situations for which NATO is suited.

The second option centers on the European Community. Nine of the twelve members of the European Community are also members of the WEU, an organization that already performs security functions and has a security apparatus. As such, organizing the security system around an EC/WEU axis would create an exclusively European system that would also exclude those Europeans not members of the European Community.

This proposal effectively champions a United States of Europe, an idea that has been kicking around Europe since the end of World War II, but which normally founders on the rough shoals of nationalism. Granted that there is a greater sentiment for integration on the continent today than in the past, there are still some very real problems with the solution.

First, making the organization anything like universal would entail adding new members to the organization, especially the former Warsaw Pact countries, if it actually is to be viewed as a pan-European solution. The European Community has always insisted that its members share the homogeneity of political democracy and capitalist economies. While the states of Eastern Europe are moving in that direction, the precedents of Spain and Portugal—whose memberships were delayed until the others were satisfied that democracy was indeed established—means there will be a waiting period. Moreover, the European Community would then have to develop the economies of these countries to a level commensurate with the standards of the current members—no small task.

Second, the EC solution excludes the United States. U.S. membership would upset entirely the structure of the European Community because of the sheer size of the American economy. Moreover, the United States would likely view an even more invigorated European Community as more of a rival than a partner, and it has even been suggested that a stronger European Community might drive Japan and the United States together to form an "Amerippon"[30] to compete with an enlarged European Community.

Third, such an organization also excludes Russia and the other successor states, which could probably never become EC members and would most likely view an expanded European Community with considerable suspicion, mixed with envy, should Russian economic reform not prosper. Fourth, it is hard to see how Germany would not become the dominant force in an enlarged European Community, raising once again the question of how to maintain control over the new German state.

The third proposal is to use the institutional framework of the CSCE, set up as part of the Helsinki Final Act of 1975, as the mechanism for organizing the new European system. This proposal has been gaining adherents as events in Europe have swirled and old structures have seemed more and more out of touch with reality; the Paris summit focused public attention on this option for the first time.

The major advantage of using CSCE as the framework is that its membership is inclusive. All members of both NATO and the Warsaw Pact are included, as are prominent neutrals such as Switzerland, Sweden, and Finland, and all the successor states. With the inclusion of Albania, all European states are members. Thus, the CSCE is a forum that brings together the old antagonists and might align the European security structure with the growing demands for political and economic integration. In the absence of confrontation and division, the future holds the allure of "cooperative security," and according to John Steinbrunner, the CSCE framework is likely to become the increasingly obvious solution.[31] Such a package would, of course, go a long way in assuaging lingering Russian fears about German resurgence, since Germany and Russia would be members of the arrangement.

The proposal is not without its difficulties, most of which are structural and leave the CSCE "unwieldy and cumbersome. It has too many members. It has no structure, no staff, and not much of a headquarters. Its capability to function effectively as an administrator of a combined North American and pan-European political, economic and security policy is, at best, many years off."[32] The lack of structure was partly overcome in Paris, where the thirty-four participants agreed to institute a small secretariat and to regularize CSCE meetings.

All of these objections have merit but possibly go beyond what a pan-European/North American structure needs to do at this point. In the extreme state of flux in which Europe currently finds itself, imposing a large, inflexible structure would be premature and counterproductive, for the simple reason that no one quite knows where Europe will be in the next five or ten years. If what all parties need now is the simple stability of a forum to discuss evolving change, the inclusive nature of CSCE has proven to be an adequate umbrella for that to occur.

Conclusions

The lightning events of 1989–90 provide us with several points that are important in even a preliminary construction of the shape of the future.

The first and overarching effect of events is the structural end of the Cold War by the implosion of half the opposing alliance systems. As former members of the extinct Warsaw Pact imitate Western political and economic forms, there will be little if any reason for division.

Mikhail Gorbachev, for whatever reasons, was the central figure in all this, because he apparently made the crucial decisions leading to the dismantling of the pact. Raymond Garthoff dates the beginning of this process back to 1985 or 1986 as the Soviet Union engaged in introspection about its future role, and argues that movement away from the old Cold War structure accelerated with time. Garthoff maintains that Gorbachev personally set the objective of turning the Warsaw Pact into a primarily political alliance well before the revolution of

November–December 1989. The official decision to do this was made "in July, 1989, at a meeting in Bucharest of the Pact's Consultative Committee."[33]

Whatever Gorbachev's intentions may have been, the process of change is by now irreversible. Communism as an ideological system is dead, and a new confrontation based on the ideological divisions that marked the Cold War is no longer realistically conceivable. This is not to say that all will be easy and peaceful as particular nationalistic forces play themselves out, only that the old Cold War system is irretrievable—and hence the danger of system-threatening war has essentially disappeared.

Second, the evolution has revealed some new forces and debunked some old ideas. Primarily, the experience has reinforced two themes developed here: the role of necessary peace in altering the utility of military force, and the increasing salience of economic factors. A European war has always been the most plausible—or least implausible—situation in which the superpowers might reach a "rational" conclusion to employ nuclear weapons. The breakdown of the confrontation thus reinforces deterrence by reducing the likelihood of system failure that could lead to nuclear war.

The internationalization of economic activity is also cause and effect in the European mix. The need for economic reform and access to Western technology undoubtedly was a major factor in Gorbachev's decision to let the dice roll in Eastern Europe, as well as in the Soviet Union itself. As long as his nation remained the "enslaver" of Eastern Europe, the old inhibitions about dealing with the Russians would remain. He may not have anticipated the consequences of his actions, but any list of the benefits Russia receives currently from the West compared with a similar list compiled as late as 1989 will quickly reveal that it has not been a total loss.

The other side of economic internationalization is competition and the question of regulation. An invigorated Europe provides a deep challenge to the other economic powers of the First Tier, notably North America and Japan. How that competition evolves—as cooperative or conflictual activity—is far from assured. One of the trends, identified briefly in this chapter and developed at some length later, is the privatization of the system, as demonstrated in the early stages of German reunification. While the movement toward increased individual and private activity represents a democratization of economic activity, the experience of capitalist economies is not so uniformly perfect that it precludes the need for regulation. It will be a major task of the new international order to create mechanisms to regulate for the common good the dynamism of the evolving economic system.

One cannot avoid ending a chapter about the revolutions of 1989 on a note of optimism. The myth of the immutability and strength of authoritarian rule was successfully debunked. The exhilarating force of self-determination is the common theme of those events that threw out rulers who ignored the common will. The utter disbelief of the hard gray men of the Communist hierarchies as their populations toppled them from power is the single great legacy of the revolutions of 1989.

Notes

1. Mortimer T. Zuckerman, "The Gorbachev Effect," *U.S. News and World Report, 109*, 2 (July 9, 1990): 29–30.

2. Andre Gunder Frank, "Revolution in Eastern Europe: Implications for Democratic Social Movements (and Socialists?)," *Third World Quarterly, 12*, 2 (April 1990): 40.

3. Andrew Nagorski, "The Intellectual Roots of Eastern Europe's Upheaval," *SAIS Review, 10*, 2 (Summer–Fall 1990): 90.

4. Klaus von Beyme, "Transition to Democracy—or *Anschluss?* The Two Germanies and Europe," *Government and Opposition, 25*, 2 (Spring 1990): 173.

5. Christoph Bertram, "The German Question," *Foreign Affairs, 69*, 2 (Spring 1990): 45.

6. Frank, "Revolution in Eastern Europe," 41.

7. Nagorski, "The Intellectual Roots of Eastern Europe's Upheaval," 92.

8. Mikhail S. Gorbachev, "The International Community and Change: A Common European Home," *Vital Speeches of the Day, 55*, 23 (September 5, 1989): 707.

9. Valentin Falin, "The Collapse of Europe: Moscow's View," *New Perspectives Quarterly, 7*, 2 (Spring 1990): 22.

10. Sam Tanenhaus, "What the Anti-Communists Knew," *Commentary, 90*, 1 (July 1990): 36.

11. von Beyme, "Transition to Democracy—or *Anschluss?*" 177.

12. Frank, "Revolution in Eastern Europe," 39.

13. Nagorski, "The Intellectual Roots of Eastern Europe's Upheaval," 92.

14. Ted Warner, "A Crippled Warsaw Pact," *Deadline: A Bulletin from the Center for War, Peace, and the News Media, 5*, 2 (March–April 1990): 3.

15. Henry Kissinger, "Gorbachev: The Price of Survival," *Newsweek* (June 18, 1990): 37.

16. Brian Crozier, "Slouching toward Democracy," *National Review, 42*, 6 (April 11, 1990): 27.

17. Zhores A. Medvedev, *Gorbachev* (New York: W.W. Norton, 1986).

18. Zuckerman, "The Gorbachev Effect."

19. Anthony Hartley, "And the Wall Fell Down: Mr. Gorbachev and the New Europe," *Encounter, 74,* 1 (January–February 1990): 5.

20. Sergei A. Karaganov, "The Year of Europe: A Soviet View," *Survival, 32,* 2 (March–April 1990): 121.

21. Hartley, "And the Wall Fell Down," 3.

22. Samuel P. Huntington, "The Clash of Civilizations?" *Foreign Affairs, 72,* 3 (Summer 1993): 22–49.

23. von Beyme, "Transition to Democracy—or *Anschluss*?" 181.

24. Nagorski, "The Intellectual Roots of Eastern Europe's Upheaval," 99.

25. Michael J. Brenner, "Finding America's Place," *Foreign Policy, 79* (Summer 1990): 28.

26. Frank, "Revolution in Eastern Europe," 43.

27. Brenner, "Finding America's Place," 26–27.

28. Stephen Szabo, "The German Answer," *SAIS Review, 10,* 2 (Summer–Fall 1990): 55.

29. Rochelle L. Stanfield, "Under Europe's Umbrella," *National Journal, 22,* 14 (April 7, 1990): 828.

30. Zbigniew Brzezinski, "Europe and Amerippon: Pillars of the New World Order," *New Perspectives Quarterly 7,* 2 (Spring 1990): 18–20.

31. John D. Steinbrunner, "The Redesign of European Security," *Brookings Review, 8,* 3 (Summer 1990): 24.

32. Stanfield, "Under Europe's Umbrella," 826–27.

33. Raymond L. Garthoff, "The Warsaw Pact Today—And Tomorrow?" *Brookings Review, 8,* 2 (Summer 1990): 38.

6

The Changing Nature of Power

To those accustomed to the Cold War system, concerns about national security defined in military terms dominated thinking about international relations. The post–Cold War terrain provides some uncharted and uncertain grounds. One way in which the rules have changed is how we look at power. The new international system will be no less interested in power and its application than previous systems; where it will differ is in the sources of power and in how power can be used to promote national and other ends.

In some ways, the Cold War system worked so well that it put itself out of business. International relations were obsessed with the Cold War confrontation between coalitions headed by the military superpowers; hence, the system overprepared for an event, World War III, that could not be staged. The realization that war between the two cornerstones of the system could lead to nuclear holocaust sunk in, and the result was necessary peace. In turn, the need to perfect that peace led to actions that crumbled the symbols of confrontation and thus the basis for the old system. Many, if not most, of those actions were initiated by Mikhail S. Gorbachev.

It all happened with stunning suddenness. Although it is hard to remember or imagine, in the early fall of 1989, NATO was seriously debating the replacement of ground-to-ground tactical nuclear missiles in Europe with a follow-on system, the Lance. This system, as Joseph Kruzel recently reminded us,[1] was designed to support military operations in central Europe. By the spring of 1990, the suggestion seemed ludicrous, an example of "old thinking" that was going the way of the dodo bird. Senator Sam Nunn, in enunciating his proposals for a new military strategy for the United States, said of Lance that it was quite inconceivable that the United States would field a new system capable only of detonating on the soil of an ally or one of the newly democratic states of Eastern Europe.[2] A year earlier, of course, it had been more than conceivable to think of such detonations—they were key elements in the NATO strategy of Follow-On Forces Attacks (FOFA), designed to destroy second and subsequent echelons of Warsaw Pact attackers in their Eastern European staging areas. What a difference a year made.

Adapting to a changing world will not be without its hazards. In the immediate afterglow of the events that have unraveled the Cold War, there has been a tendency toward euphoria: the West is on a roll; its system has emerged triumphant; there are no viable ideological alternatives to Western-style political democracy and market economy. All of this is true to a large extent, but the new international system is not going to be any easier to deal with and understand. It is simply going to be different.

Essentially, there are three points to be made. First, there is almost certainly going to be a changed emphasis and ordering in the relative weights of the military and economic elements of national power. This observation applies most obviously to the relations among the major actors in the system, the First Tier. The leading economic powers are all political democracies and allies or partners in most important ways. It overstrains credulity to think of members of the Group of Seven (G-7) economic powers (the United States, the United Kingdom, Canada, Germany, Japan, France, and Italy) or other First Tier countries threatening one another militarily to gain compliance with some national objective, as suggested in chapter 1. Although Russia does not fall within the category of an economic power, it too is bound to nonmilitary means to accomplish its goals with the major powers. In order to gain entry into the world economy and overcome its former status as a rogue state, it must find nonmilitary ways to exercise power. A major question that continues to divide First Tier countries (notably those within the major First Tier security structure, NATO) is the extent to which they can or should try to assist Russian transformation without appearing overly meddlesome and stirring exclusionary Russian nationalism in the process.

Second, the distribution of power is changing and will continue to change. Just as World War II exhausted its major initiators and required others to step forward and assume leadership roles, so have forty years of "waging" the Cold War taken their toll on the leaders of the postwar period. Soviet "new political thinking" was an open admission of the price of the Cold War; while the American malaise is nowhere nearly as serious as that of the Soviet Union, it has entailed the loss of hegemony. As the Soviets and Americans figuratively slugged it out through pouring dollars and rubles into defense budgets, the losers of World War II, notably Germany and Japan, quietly built economic power that is the underpinning of a new system. G-7 may be the forum for power application in the future.

Third, it will be more difficult for national governments to wield power in the new international order. This is true for at least two reasons. On the one hand, economic power is more difficult to apply than is military power. It is subtler and more complex. Dropping 22,500 troops into Panama in a discrete operation was conceptually and operationally neat and tidy and, in terms of capturing Manuel Noriega, successful. Years of trying to apply economic power to the same problem failed. Part of the difficulty is also that using the economic levers of power almost always hurts groups within one's own country and is thus politically difficult to implement. A good example of this was the backlash against President Jimmy Carter's imposition of economic sanctions against the Soviet Union after its invasion of Afghanistan. The toughest sanction was the grain embargo, which caused the Soviets prematurely to slaughter those cattle that were to be fed by American grain. The result was several years of meat shortages in Soviet stores. The policy's problem was that the embargo cost U.S. farmers grain dollars. Finally, the embargo fell victim to the 1980 presidential election: Ronald Reagan campaigned vigorously in favor of lifting the ban and did so upon assuming office. Moreover, the track record of applying economic sanctions is unimpressive and sometimes counterproductive. The embargo against Iraq did not cause Saddam Hussein to leave Kuwait; armed force did. Similarly, embargoes made life miserable for the citizenries of Serbia and Haiti; they did not cause their governments to relent on obnoxious policies.

There is another limit that may, in systemic terms, be more important: *Increasingly, national governments do not control economic activity in their own countries and thus cannot manipulate the economy to serve national ends.* The beginning of this phenomenon was the emergence of the early multinational corporations (MNCs). These, however, were largely based and owned in one country. While they conducted business in lots of places, and often outside the view of the parent government, by and large they could be made subject to legal and political regulation.

The internationalization of economic activity has created new attitudes and new problems. A whole new way of thinking is entering the lexicon of international discourse, and it is at substantial odds with traditional ways of thinking and acting. For example, an executive of Northern Telecom of Canada exemplified the "new thinking" of international economics in a 1990 speech:

> Outmoded, nationalistic chauvinism and geocentric thinking have no place in the one-world economy ... where competition will be even more intense and universal ... and where a global perspective will increasingly be needed to compete and win. The global economy of the 90s approaches the world as if it were one, single market.[3]

While containing elements of boosterism, this way of looking at the world is in rather stark contrast to the world view of the national security state; the collision of traditional and contemporary perspectives will clearly be one of the major themes of the new system.

One can, of course, make too much of change and predict an apocalypse in no real danger of happening. Certainly, many of the predictions about nuclear war during the Cold War period were of this nature. In retrospect, it should be clear that the avoidance of nuclear war was not so much a matter of luck, thwarting the law of large numbers (which can "prove" such a war is inevitable), or genius; it was more precisely a matter of not doing something of supreme historical stupidity. In the new international system, the predictions of economic doom for the United States and the elevation, at least in some circles, of Japan as the United State's chief "enemy" are equally exaggerated.

The new international system will contain elements of the old and the new. Military force and war, for instance, are in no danger of extinction; the use of military force will simply be different in terms of the missions for which it is prepared and the places where it is used. Poverty in much of the Second Tier remains a part of the landscape; it will simply be more blatant as the rich get richer while ignoring the poor. Similarly, firms and nations will compete in economic markets; the rules will be different, but the objective, economic good fortune, will be the same.

The Future Role of Military Power

By now it should be obvious that a major theme of the new international order will be a diminished role for, and utility of, military force between the most important members of the international system, the states of the First Tier. Military force is simply irrelevant to most large power interactions; the limiting case is that both the United States and Russia retain large thermonuclear arsenals that they have agreed not to aim at one another.

The nuclear balance will probably remain, if at levels dictated in START II, at about 3,000 apiece. There are at least three reasons why this is likely to be true. First, nuclear weapons remain the distinguishing characteristic of those who have them; they remain a major criterion of claims to military power status. This is especially true for Russia, which is a major power by virtue of large conventional forces but a dominant power only in a nuclear sense. For the Russians, maintaining nuclear superiority is a matter of pride and status; until or unless the Russian economy can be propelled to world-class status (a distant prospect at best), the world would be remiss to want to rob the Russians of their major source of international status. As demonstrated by the flap over Russian sensibility at the prospect of admitting Poland into NATO during the 1994 NATO summit, there is little to be gained—and potentially much to be lost—by figuratively rubbing Russia's nose in the dirt and reactivating Russian nationalist paranoia over security.

Second, the nuclear weapons balance has helped move us beyond the Cold War, and the retention of that balance can only help keep us there. The prospect of nuclear war "focuses the mind" on the necessity of building peace. It makes us realize, as the late Soviet Marshall Sergei F. Akhromeyev eloquently put it, "States truly desirous of peace in the present situation have no alternative but the reaching of agreement on a radical lowering of the military confrontation level."[4] In other words, nuclear weapons continue to deter and to remind us why it is important to be deterred. They have contributed to the remarkable stability of the international system. During the current period of rapid change, they remain an intellectual anchor to help us direct change into nondestructive channels, and they provide us with some stability in looking at the world. Given the apocalyptical way in which people have viewed nuclear weapons in the past, thinking about them as familiar bulwarks in a stormy and unfamiliar sea may be difficult, but is nonetheless useful. As noted, this dynamic is particularly useful and stabilizing in a period of some uncertainty about Russia's future political directions.

Third, the nuclear genie is out of the bottle, and the problem of nuclear weapons spreading to other countries remains a concern between the United States and Russia. This problem of so-called horizontal nuclear proliferation has been with us for a long time, and the most dire predictions have been unfulfilled. This does not mean that proliferation will not occur in the future; if it does, then the maintenance of large nuclear forces remains useful to deter small attacks by third parties. Nuclear arsenals may also be useful instruments to deter the use by Third World countries of ballistically delivered chemical and biological munitions, which is now becoming a disturbing part of regional conflicts. Exacerbating this problem has been intra–Second Tier transfer of deadly weapons technologies and weapons themselves; an example is China selling missiles and missile technology to Pakistan.

Major powers, notably the United States and Russia, will likely be constrained by two other factors, one well documented, one not. The most obvious constraint is expense; a large measure of the economic problems that both countries faced was the result of the burden of national defense. For the Russians, the problem is clearly most severe, and its recognition was one of the major reasons for settling the Cold War. Thus, when Akhromeyev maintained that the Soviet Union "wants to see all controversial international relations settled by peaceful means, by political means alone,"[5] he was at least partially suggesting that talk (politics) is a lot less expensive than war. Moreover, the burden of large military forces and expenditures and the allocation of prime human and economic resources to defense continues to cripple Russian economic development.

The burden of past military spending continues to haunt Russia. In order to enhance economic change, Yeltsin has cut back sharply on the size of Russian forces and has begun retooling the old military production system to consumer production. The military and many other Russians resent this change in emphasis. Reduced military capability contributes to a sense of encirclement and vulnerability to ancient enemies that is a recurrent theme of Russian history. Converting a weapons production system that was the crown jewel of the overall productive system—building blenders and food processors on lines that once produced the most sophisticated weapons—offends Russian pride and feeds Russian paranoia.

Because the American economy is so much larger than the Russian, its economic strain is not as severe, but it is present. The enormous buildup in armaments by the Reagan administration—which its advocates claim caused the Soviets to back down and cancel a competition they could not win—has also been a major contributor to U.S. budget deficits that many agree form part of the problem of U.S. competitiveness in the emerging international economic order. Responding to this perceived problem has been a major priority of the Clinton administration's attempt to accelerate the military build-down and to convert resources to economic competition.

The second constraint on the major powers has not, to this writer's knowledge, attracted public attention. The internationalization of economic activity is symbolized by the increasingly international composition of products. What this means is that corporations acting in one country seldom make products of any complexity from components and subcomponents made entirely in the country where final assembly occurs. What is becoming far more common is for goods to be made from components produced in several different countries, and the goods themselves may be assembled in a country that produced few if any of the components. The reasons for this are almost entirely economic: it is most efficient to buy from the cheapest producer.

What makes this phenomenon important is that it is truest in the most advanced forms of production, such as computers and microelectronics generally, and in large, durable goods, such as automobiles and trucks. It is almost impossible to buy a new automobile or large electronic product that is produced exclusively within the boundaries of one nation.

This raises national security concerns that are rarely addressed publicly. The very kinds of things that large nations need to provide the wherewithal for military activity are precisely the kinds of goods that are being internationalized: microelectronics are the basic elements of so-called smart weapons, such as the munitions used to such great effect by the United States against Iraq. To put it bluntly, there are countries with whom it is becoming increasingly difficult for major powers to go to war because they depend upon those countries for the products needed to make war. To cite a farfetched example, can the United States go to war with Japan, a country upon whom we rely for almost all of the computer microchips on which our weapons depend? Moreover, this effective interdependence is likely to become more acute, because "the acceleration of change will tend to undermine governmental policy measures taken to limit or impede imports"[6]—with the consequence that internationalization will increase as time goes by. This phenomenon is particularly striking among the states of the First Tier.

There is a further aspect of internationalization. As states become progressively dependent on foreign sources for the components that are fashioned into weaponry, national interests will increasingly focus both on assured access to producing markets and on the secure ability to get those products back home, as in the safety of sea lanes of communication (SLOCs). Access to markets means that governments at least not inimical to trade must be in power, and the secure ability to trade means that nations will require access to the air and sea lanes through which vital products travel. This is particularly important because much of the internationalization process involves the movement of production facilities to the Second Tier, where lower labor costs allow things such as computer chips to be produced more cheaply than in the developed world. This kind of transfer has already occurred in some nations in the Pacific Rim—both the Four Tigers (Korea, Taiwan, Hong Kong, Singapore) and most ASEAN nations (Thailand, Malaysia, Singapore, Indonesia, Brunei, the Philippines)—meaning that the security of, say, the Straits of Malacca (the major choke point between the Indian and Pacific Oceans) becomes a more paramount concern than it was in the past.

If major powers cannot use military force in the old, large-scale ways, they may well be tempted to use it in smaller, more measured ways. Since the majority of opportunities for engagement in smaller wars are in the Second Tier, and since such wars rarely involve opposing vital interests on the part of the superpowers, engagement rarely poses the risk of escalation.

Raising the issue in this way, of course, sounds a bit like Cold War "old thinking," in which Second Tier involvement resulted from the desire to counteract or thwart gains by the opposing superpower. In the case of U.S. involvement in Grenada, for instance, this was rather clearly the case, but it will not necessarily be so in the future. The more clear analogy for the future may be the American "Just Cause" intervention in Panama. In that case, the motives for involvement had nothing to do with communism–anticommunism but with the removal of a corrupt regime in a country important to the United States (due to the impending cession of the Panama Canal back to Panama at the end of the century) that was also an important link in the drug flow into the country.

With major power confrontations waning, Second Tier involvement —small in the case of Panama, large in Saudi Arabia—is more likely. Partly, it is a matter of the necessity of having an ongoing role to play to justify budgets, force levels, and the like. For the Soviets, the primary uses of military force in the near future may be even more parochial—trying to maintain internal order and avoid the further fracturing of the union.

Second Tier Dangers

The security concerns of the Second Tier are both continuations of the Cold War and relatively new occurrences. The continuations are found especially in so-called regional conflicts between historical enemies such as India and Pakistan or Iran and Iraq. These were very much a part of the Cold War mosaic; the United States would place itself in close cooperation with one side, the Soviet Union with the other. In one sense, this juxtaposition was restraining; neither side wanted any of those situations to get out of hand to the point that the superpowers might be drawn into direct confrontation with escalatory potential. In another sense, however, superpower rivalry also meant that large and continuing stocks of arms were available to the contestants at low prices.

The restraints and the supplies are gone, as is the superpower competition. Getting out of the Second Tier as quickly and thoroughly as possible has been a prime way for Russia to rid itself of old drains on Russian treasure so desperately needed at home. Second Tier countries like Mozambique and Angola have been set adrift by the Russians, as have Communist states like Cuba. With the need to counter Soviet/ Russian influence gone, the United States has largely followed suit. In the absence of such problems, the United States finds itself in an interest–threat mismatch in the Second Tier: American vital interests are hardly threatened by violence and instability there. The interests, in other words, are hardly threatened, and the threats are hardly interesting.

A new, and potentially more ominous, set of problems has arisen in the Second Tier that directly affects regional conflicts: the spread of nuclear, biological, and chemical (NBC) weapons of mass destruction and ballistic missile delivery capability to Second Tier nations. This phenomenon and its potential has been the subject of considerable First

Tier effort to prevent these forms of arms proliferation among First Tier countries—with Russian assistance. The G-7 states, for instance, created the Missile Technology Control Regime (MTCR) to try to prevent missile spread, and conventions on existing NBC weapons have been strengthened (for instance, International Atomic Energy Agency inspections of suspected nuclear weapons programs in places such as Iraq and North Korea). Most of the violations are occurring in rogue states such as Iraq, but the problem is exacerbated by the fact that a number of Second Tier states themselves have gotten actively into the business of producing and exporting these capabilities to other Second Tier states. This practice by China has been the source of much of the strain in its relationship with Washington and has been a prime source of debate over its continuing most-favored nation (MFN) trade status with the United States.

The end of the Cold War and its accompanying emphasis on freedom have also spawned and heated a series of internal wars within Second Tier states. Some are ongoing artifacts of the Cold War, such as those in Mozambique and Angola. Some are occurring in the so-called failed states (places that seem perpetually incapable of constructive self-rule), such as Haiti, Rwanda, and Somalia. Others represent the expression of national self-determination run amok, resulting in "ethnic cleansing" in places such as Bosnia, parts of the former Soviet Union like Armenia and Azerbaijan, and even states like Sri Lanka. The potential for more of this kind of violence in other places seems ripe.

The new international system has not quite decided how to deal with these problems. In traditional terms, internal wars are off limits for outside interference on the grounds of sovereignty. The very public savagery that often occurs, and which is chronicled in deadly detail by global television, creates an urge in First Tier publics to assist, to do something when it is not clear what—if anything—effectively can be done. The United Nations has been a prime sponsor, under the active direction of its Secretary-General Boutros Boutros-Ghali, to intervene on the basis of so-called humanitarian vital interests that demand the restoration of order wherever it is breached. The Somali experience has considerably cooled international ardor for such involvements, as has the shame of Bosnia. This problem will, however, be the subject of continuing concern. As a major future issue, responding to internal war will be discussed at length in chapter 8.

Economic Competitiveness in the New World Order

As economics comes increasingly to affect international political concerns, the question of shifting power and influence follows closely behind. This changing emphasis is a primary result of military paralysis. One of the major reasons the Soviets were forced to abandon the Cold War was because their economy, and the economies of those countries forced to emulate them, became increasingly unable to compete.

Increasingly, the operative language of what constitutes power mixes economic and technological terms. One author provides the flavor of change in defining the components of the "informatics" revolution: "semiconductors, computers, fiber optic communications, high-definition television, industrial control systems, robotics, office automation, globally integrated financial trading systems, military C3I . . . smart weapons, and electronic warfare."[7]

This list defines the cutting edge of technology, the ability both to provide the goods and services that people want at the most competitive cost and to generate further knowledge on which future technologies and applications are based. Successful competition in technology is important in determining the U.S. position as a world leader, its ability to provide a rising standard of living for the American people, national security, and the ability of government to fund domestic programs.[8] Moreover, technological distinctions are a core component of the economic differentiation between the First and Second Tiers, and one measure of the relations between the tiers will focus on the extent to which the First Tier encourages near–First Tier states to attain the most advanced technologies.

The United States in the New World Economy

The United States emerges in the new international system as the world's only superpower, based upon the new order's definition of that status. In the Cold War (and before), major-power status was largely defined in military terms; possession of nuclear weapons was the membership card.

The rules have changed. It is now possible to argue that the most important powers—the superpowers—are those states possessing the broadest range of so-called instruments of power. Those instruments are both economic and military in nature. Some states in the new order have one form or the other; the United States' uniqueness—and claim to being the sole remaining superpower—is that it possesses both. This creates special leadership responsibilities for the United States; it also highlights the vitality of economic competitiveness.

Generously infused with U.S. dollars and exempted from the burdens of heavy defense spending, the world's economies recovered from World War II and began to become competitive with that of the United States. Since revitalizing the world's economy was the American purpose all along,[9] the competitiveness problem is in important ways the result of the triumph of U.S. foreign policy. Because competitiveness sometimes manifests itself in the inability of American firms successfully to compete against foreign manufactures and services, however, it has also sparked something of a national debate about how the United States can either recapture the competitive edge or, more modestly, at least stay in the competition.

One of the leading students of this phenomenon is Harvard economist and Secretary of Labor Robert Reich, who captures the heart of the current competitiveness malaise facing the United States. He argues that it lies in the "inability of American companies (or, more accurately, the U.S.-based portions of what are fast becoming global technological firms) to transform discoveries quickly into high-quality products and into processes for designing, manufacturing, and distributing such products."[10] It is, in other words, a matter of coping with the rapid evolution of the knowledge-to-commercial application cycle described in chapter 3, an accelerating competition that will increasingly define global success.

There is a long list of potential villains in what were signs of the relative U.S. decline during the 1980s. Two, however, stand out: the need for greater attention to scientific and technical education and research support, and the role of government in the support of private industrial development and activity. These two areas are related. One observer argues that a nation's innovative capacity can be gauged by the answers to two questions: Does the environment spur the creation and use of new knowledge and improved ways of doing things? Are effective macroeconomic policies in place that provide a healthy climate for investment, growth, and commercial success?[11]

What many had come to see as an American decline has apparently begun to be reversed. One reason is a revitalization of U.S. firms, which have become leaner and more productive by trimming costs (for instance, the size of their work forces) and adopting more state-of-the-art production designs and methods. The resurgence of the American automobile industry is a well-publicized case in point. A second reason has been recession and stagnation in counterpart industries—like cars—in Japan and Germany.

Traditionally, the education process has been the great source of American competitive strength, but that lead has slipped, particularly in the areas of science and technology. Joseph S. Nye, Jr., hardly a partisan of "declinism," contends that the United States needs more investment in mathematics and the sciences (one-fifth of U.S. engineers are foreign or foreign-born).[12] The problem of education at the higher levels of knowledge and skill is worsening, as former Colorado Governor Richard Lamm pointed out starkly in 1988: fully 50 percent of the Ph.D.s in mathematics granted by U.S. universities over the past decade have been to foreign students.[13] Many of these students remain in the United States after graduation; if they all decided to go home in one mass exodus, the American base would be in trouble.

On the positive side of all this, the United States continues to enjoy "the advantage of the best scientific and technological infrastructure"[14] in the world, principally through the superiority of American graduate education in the nation's universities. The problem, however, is that increasingly those graduate programs are becoming the training centers for non-American students. Even a casual stroll across the science and engineering parts of any major American graduate institution reveals that this situation continues. Moreover, nondefense spending to support those programs, principally by underwriting graduate research, needs attention, because American public support for civilian research and development lags behind equivalent support by the United States' principal rivals, Germany and Japan, although the Clinton administration is committed to greater funding for nondefense research.

Because government, especially the federal government, has historically been the chief source of funds supporting research, this raises the question of appropriate governmental intrusion into the competitiveness realm. More specifically, the question addresses the propriety or desirability of using federal dollars to stimulate the competitiveness of specific industries—what is loosely known as industrial policy.

Industrial policy is an intensely controversial and highly partisan issue in the United States. Imposing some kind of government guidance and support on the direction of U.S. industry, which is the heart of industrial policy, has been vigorously opposed by the Republican administrations of Ronald Reagan and George Bush on the philosophical grounds that it would interrupt the natural forces of the market, and on the practical belief that businessmen will make better judgments on economic matters than will government officials.

Advocates, including many of Bill Clinton's closest economic advisors, argue that the United States has no real option but to concentrate its efforts, and this entails cooperation in which government must take the lead. The Young Commission appointed by Reagan, for instance, took the position that U.S. technological leadership and industrial competitiveness depend on the ability of government, industry, and academia to cooperate in creating, applying, and protecting U.S. technological innovation.[15] Such an emphasis would entail a new, long-term investment strategy for technology, capital, and people, and federal leadership in education, research and development, export finance, and direct help for key industries.

There are two other good reasons for the U.S. government to take the leadership in directing or, at the least, assisting the American economic effort. First, there is a long history of separation and even antagonism among the key institutions in the process—government, business, and academia. Government supports academic researchers who are inherently (some would argue pathologically) averse to direction, businessmen want proprietary control over research that they underwrite, many academics view research directed at producing goods for profit as little more than prostitution, and so on. Although government is not always the most trusted of institutions, it does have the grease to take some of the squeaks out of the relationships in the form of funding. The Clinton administration has sought to nurture these relations in selected areas such as environmental waste technology and clean-up.

The second reason for adopting an industrial policy is that the United States' competitors have already done so. Former Defense Secretary Harold Brown argues that the existence of Japanese industrial policy provides the Japanese with an advantage in developing new technologies and products that "makes much precompetitive cooperation difficult."[16] The chief mechanism for Japanese industrial policy is the Ministry of Industry and Trade (MITI), which has aggressively coordinated the activities of Japanese industrial sectors to their comparative advantage by helping companies and industries define very far in advance the consumer goods for which they think there is a market, and derive the necessary technologies to service these markets.[17] The HDTV fiasco noted earlier has taken some of the bloom off the rose with regard to MITI, since that organization helped convince the giant Japanese electronics firms to reject digitization for signal transmission.

In the case of Japan, it has been argued that the Japanese government does more than simply promote its own industries; this remains a constant irritant to U.S.–Japanese trade relations. The charge is frequently made that the Japanese regularly and consistently engage in adversarial trade, the practice of creating "conditions in which one country uses trade barriers combined with policies favoring certain industries to obtain advantages over a trading partner." The result of adversarial trade is "that a country tends not to import any of the products it exports."[18] In the Japanese–American relationship, this allegation is most often made about Japanese policies that virtually exclude American automobiles from the Japanese market. The removal of some of the more egregious aspects of adversarial trade—such as barriers on the importation of American rice—was a major accomplishment of the December 1993 GATT accords.

In addition to Japan, the third partner in the emerging economic tripolar system is the European Community. Traditionally, the European Community has lagged slightly behind in the competitive race. This has partially been the result of national policies and rivalries that have made collaboration between corporations and individual scientists and researchers in different countries difficult, and because, according to Italian entrepreneur and conglomerate specialist Carlo De Benedetti, "Too much emphasis was placed on basic research, too little on the channels for bringing scientific research from the laboratories to the marketplace."[19]

The implementation of economic union under the Maastricht Treaty promises to remove most of the historic barriers. According to one European observer, the revolutions of 1989 have added to the growing sense of optimism in three ways. First, the extension of the market economy to Eastern Europe will provide a new impulse investment by Western European businesses in the Eastern European economies. Second, 140 million new customers from the East are expected to generate massive demands for goods and services. Third, the end of the Cold War is expected to free at least 0.8 percent of Western Europe's GNP, formerly spent on defense, for new investment.[20] Leading Europe's challenge to American and Japanese preeminence, of course, will be Germany; West Germany's trade surplus was already larger than that of Japan (at $70 billion annually), and now that Germany is unified, it will produce about one-third of the total output of the European Community. This rosy picture must be balanced against the stubborn problem of integrating the old GDR into the German mainstream and the stubborn recession in Europe, of which Germany is a prominent part.

A great deal, and probably too much, has been made of economic competitiveness as a race among three major players, where one country "wins" and another "loses." This implies a degree of adversarial relationship that is not present between Japan, Germany and the rest of the European Community, and the United States; it suggests that economic success is a zero-sum game in which one advances at the other's detriment, and that international economics is still largely controlled at the national level. None of these premises is true; as argued in chapter 1, the members of the First Tier have far more in common than that which divides them.

While there are indeed disagreements among the economic superpowers of the First Tier over issues such as terms of trade, the three are fundamentally similar in important areas such as political and economic philosophy. Moreover, the new international order is one of collaboration across borders where scientists and engineers regularly cooperate and where the results benefit everyone; the system has considerable positive-sum aspects. Finally, economic activity is no longer solely national. The phenomenon of the stateless corporation is the clear wave of the future. The world economy, especially among the First Tier countries and those who aspire to that status, is becoming so intermingled that it is increasingly difficult to determine the national origin of success and hence to produce "standings" of who is winning and who is losing. To cite just one simple example, when an automobile built by Honda America is sold somewhere in Latin America, is that a "victory" for the American workers who built the car or for the Japanese who own the corporation and hence get the profits?

The Role and Dynamism of Technology

The lifeblood of the new international economic order is high technology, which both made internationalization possible and provides the

frontiers for advance. At the forefront of high technology is the production and application of knowledge. This is important to the point
that "in the late 20th century, knowledge is the primary determinant of
comparative advantage."[21]

The technological revolution has, in essence, snuck up on the lay
public and political leadership. It is axiomatic that public policy will
almost always lag behind scientific invention for the simple reason that
it is impossible to predict discovery. In more tranquil days, this lag was
tolerable because the pace of change was more leisurely. In the contemporary world, however, invention and expansion of physical capabilities are happening so rapidly that the most basic rules of the
international game are being altered almost without reaction by national governments. In essence, we have created a process of innovation that is self-sustaining and is changing the ways we do things,
whether we like it or not.

This process is largely a creation of the 1980s, and, in retrospect, its
roots and dynamics are understandable. As one student of the process
constructs it, there were three basic elements—one economic, one
technological, and one political—that underlay the high-technology
revolution and that largely describe the economic motor of the First
Tier. Economically, the cost of computing power and memory de-
clined rapidly throughout the decade. Technologically, the digitization
of information through the binary code and digital switching of data
transmission brought about the convergence of the telecommunications, electronics, and computing industries. Politically, the worldwide
wave of deregulation and the privatization of public monopolies
sparked an explosion of entrepreneurial and corporate activity.[22]

We have witnessed no more than the tip of the iceberg of change.
Harald Malmgren, for instance, provides a list of six likely developments in the next decade or so that will fundamentally alter the
human condition and, in the current context, change the conditions
in which international relations are conducted. The list, along with
some of its implications, is momentous enough to warrant reproduc-
tion and exploration.[23]

First, the development of new, man-made materials will increasingly compete with, and substitute for, traditional materials generated
from natural resources. If accurate, this is a change with enormous
geopolitical implications. If, in essence, almost anything can be made
from almost anything else, then dependence on natural resources

shrinks, and factors such as the strategic locations of mineral and other natural resources decline in importance. Much of this change relates to advances in plastics and ceramics, however, meaning that access to the basic building blocks of those materials, notably petroleum, actually becomes more vital.

The second technological thrust is in accelerating advances in computers, telecommunications, and information processing, which provide enormous economies of scale in supply services and transferring technology. There is widespread agreement on this point among those in the relevant industries, and the changes predicted seem to come from science fiction. Fiber optics and optoelectronic technology, for instance, promise an increase in several orders of magnitude over today's predominantly copper networks, expanding telecommunications networks as the building blocks of the information superhighway. In this context, the four "building blocks" in this technological explosion will be personal computers, public television networks, data communication networks, and television.[24] In this latter regard, the distinction between a computer monitor and a television set will largely disappear. Moreover, the kind of television capable of serving as a "terminal" in such a system falls into the category of HDTV, which will clearly be a great deal more than a passive device on which to watch situation comedies. The most visible sign of this trend has been the virtual merger of telecommunications firms (e.g., the Baby Bell regional companies), cable television, and computer hardware and software, all under the regulating eye of the Clinton administration in the United States. This spate of activity, which burst onto the public stage in 1993, has washed like a *tsunami* over former Japanese advantages in these areas.

The implications are breathtaking. Progress to date has already contributed to the possibility of the stateless corporation by creating instantaneous, real-time global communication that facilitates a coordination of economic activity heretofore impossible. With the kinds of developments being discussed, one can easily envision a truly global corporate board meeting with members located around the world in front of computer consoles that project their visual images instantly to one another. The globalization of economic activity will clearly be accelerated by these trends.

Quantum increases in communications and information sharing will also surely contribute to the privatization of international relations. It is increasingly evident that advances in telecommunications have already made it impractical or impossible to regulate a good deal of economic activity, because potential regulators can so easily be bypassed. As the capability expands, there will undoubtedly be expanded sharing of scientific findings, making national control of information and knowledge more difficult. At the same time, governments will find it increasingly difficult to regulate the information citizens receive, thereby decreasing the possibility of lying to those citizens.

Obviously, these advances will not be shared uniformly over all parts of the globe. What these advances will likely do is widen the gap between the most and least developed regions, although some of the advances can be applied widely to alleviate the worst of the human condition. At the same time, inclusion in the First Tier "club" of those most advanced states who are producing and benefiting will be critical to staying atop the wave. It is in this regard that the efforts of Boris Yeltsin take on special meaning. The game, however, may already be over for the Russians, because the pace is simply going to be too fast for anyone with a late start.

The third prediction suggests that industrial activity will increasingly occur within the framework of computer-integrated manufacturing (CIM) and flexible manufacturing systems (FMS). This particular area poses a special challenge to the United States. The prototype of the U.S. manufacturing system is and has been the Ford automobile assembly line, where a huge investment was made in a large, relatively static manufacturing process designed to produce a maximum number of like products, such as the Model-T Ford.

The new technological frontier reverses that trend. Because of the speed with which technology alters the realm of the possible, we are more likely in the future to see manufacturing centers constructed in easy-to-assemble-and-disassemble modules that can either perform several manufacturing tasks at the same time or be quickly reconfigured for changing product needs. Computer assistance and even regulation of the manufacturing enterprise are the key here. Moreover, as these kinds of enterprises mature into the production of repetitive goods, one would expect to see global corporations move such plants to appropriate Second Tier countries, such as the NICs, where lower wage costs will lower the price to consumers. The effect of such "trickle-down" development can be to enhance movement through the various subtiers of the Second Tier.

This is clearly a sophisticated business that will require the increasing globalization of economic practices. It will also require a greater degree of collaboration between the scientific and business communities to assist industries in their adaptations to rapidly changing realities in a world "where technological innovations are increasingly more valued than basic research."[25] If the United States' largest and most ossified industries do not adapt to the challenge of the new manufacturing environment, the result will be decreasing market shares across a widening variety of products. The virtual rebirth of the American automobile and electronics industries provides some indication this revival is occurring.

The fourth prediction is that there will be improvements in transportation, especially in aircraft technology, that will bring production centers closer in terms of time and relative cost. There are three obvious consequences of this phenomenon. First, it will tend to increase the internationalization of the manufacturing process by making it easier to aggregate components and subcomponents produced around the globe for final assembly and distribution. One would assume this would also spur the further development of the transnational, stateless corporations as well. Second, aerospace and avionics comprise a historic area of American advantage, but the new trend suggests that it will become a competitive field. The Japanese, as demonstrated in the flap over joint production of the so-called FSX jet as Japan's newest fighter aircraft, have indicated their intention to enter the aerospace game along with the Americans and the Europeans. The spectacular success of American airplanes and the sophisticated weaponry that they employed in the Gulf War may provide a welcome relief for an American aerospace industry that was falling progressively farther below peak capacity. Third, if the result of this trend is further acceleration of trade generally, then the protection of the air and sea lanes of communications will take on even more importance as a component of national security.

The fifth and sixth predictions can be considered together. The fifth suggests that rapid advances in the life sciences are likely to alter demographic profiles and to enhance human capabilities across all age brackets. This is clearly an area of importance to both the First and Second Tiers: it could reverse some of the adverse effects of aging populations in First Tier countries, but could actually exacerbate problems of young populations in Second Tier countries by creating even more competition for scarce jobs.

The sixth prediction encompasses biotechnological advancements, which may open the way for major advances in the production (and location of production) of food and improvements in such diverse areas as industrial processes, management of wastes, and even in animal and human characteristics. Although distribution, not the sheer quantity, of food has been the source of widespread malnutrition and even starvation in the Second Tier, breakthroughs in food production offer hope for those outside distribution centers to produce their own food, thereby bypassing current physical and political impediments to adequate diet in places such as Africa.

A number of these technological thrusts have the potential for great good in parts of the Second Tier at a time when some concerted effort there is sorely needed. The urgency is caused by growing disparities in the distribution of resources between rich countries and poor countries, and within poor countries. Whether this needs to be depends, to a great extent, on whether the fruits of the Third Industrial Revolution are applied "with a human face," suggesting some form of equity, or whether the unfettered pursuit of profit becomes the underlying value, by design or default.

Conclusions

The answer to the equity question is open. The international economic system, driven as it is by quantum increases in science and technology, is changing the world. There is absolutely no reason to believe that the forces unleashed by this dynamism will abate. The dynamics of this change are acting as both cause and effect of the transformation of the international system. Those countries astride this process will continue their successful affiliation with the First Tier; those that are not, will not. At the same time, technological advances have made possible phenomena such as the stateless corporation.

These trends are moving the "battlegrounds" of international politics from the trenches to the laboratories. As the Young Commission warned, "The security of the United States, both militarily and strategically, depends on advanced technologies. . . . U.S. technological leadership . . . is a critical element of deterrence."[26] Written in 1985, those remarks had a Cold War ring that is no longer applicable to the world today. Nonetheless, because economic competitiveness will be a key element in economic well-being and the capacity to wield some form of power, technological preeminence and the infrastructure underlying it (for instance, the educational system) will be important measures of power in the future.

The internationalization, including privatization, of the world economic system raises the question: Who is going to be in charge? Who, if anyone, will regulate what goes on, and to what values will the system be directed? The problem is that all this has happened very rapidly, to the point that few political leaders understand the process of innovation or grasp the direction of technologically driven change. Apparently, very few leaders or analysts have yet come to appreciate the impact of privatization on their own power and the ability of national governments to regulate their own and international affairs. Because of the kinds of economic advisors (including some cited or consulted in these pages) with which he has surrounded himself, President Clinton comes much closer than do most world leaders on this score. His impassioned insistence on NAFTA as part of the globalizing future in contrast to an isolationist past that would have accompanied rejection highlights that awareness.

The warnings are there, but they are coming primarily from the very community that is either reporting or carrying out these changes. Thus, one member of the international business community maintained matter-of-factly before a business audience that "national boundaries and regulations tend to be much smaller hurdles than in the past."[27]

That is a momentous assertion for the operation of the international *political* system, a realization that only a relative handful of academic observers have to this point grasped: "Governments . . . have lost the power to manage stable economies within their frontiers, because national economies have, for all practical purposes, ceased to exist."[28] This position is, of course, overstated, but it does correctly point to the profundity of change.

The privatization of international economics due to technology has happened at a time of unprecedented world (at least developed world) prosperity, which it helped create, and at a time when the market economy philosophy that underpins it has triumphed over socialism. The evolving system behind this combination of prosperity and triumph has represented such a "roll" for the states of the Western world that hardly anyone has thought to look at it critically. Yet the privatization of international relations does raise some important underlying questions that will have to be worked out in the new international order. Richard Barnet frames the issue nicely:

The fundamental challenges posed by the age of globalization are how to make economic actors accountable to political communities and how to modernize government so it can protect the public interest in the territory that it is expected to govern. . . . Global corporations, whatever flag they fly, have outgrown national laws and national cultures, and the world has not yet begun to address the problem.[29]

Raising the question in this manner does not suggest that the phenomenon of economic change—privatization—represents a conscious or unconscious conspiracy to undermine political authority. Rather, it rephrases my own question concluding the previous section. If social equity (socialism) and economic efficiency (capitalism) are the two poles at the ends of the economic value spectrum, who is going to make the decisions about where on the spectrum the system will land? The values of a market-based economic system will tend toward the efficiency end of the scale. Yet, if the stability of the international political system requires that the members be at least basically satisfied with the outcomes of system dynamics, then some form of equity must also intrude. This is particularly the case for those who lose in a system driven by efficiency, which means specifically the countries of the Second Tier. The basic problem is whether the *political* system can regain control of the *economic* system before the transfer of effective power is so complete that it is a *fait accompli*.

This concern can be placed within the general framework of a world of tiers. The dynamics of a globalizing economy based in the market and the general lowering of trade barriers regionally (EC, NAFTA) and globally (GATT) will contribute to the ongoing prosperity of the First Tier, partly because these dynamics promote efficiency. Those Second Tier states nearest the First Tier—the Pacific Rim states associated with APEC, for instance—could share in the prosperity. The benefit, judged solely in terms of economic efficiency, will likely not extend very deeply into the Second Tier. If those states are to enjoy the benefits of the First Tier's prosperity, it will have to be because politically based notions of equity are entered into the equation.

Notes

1. Joseph Kruzel, "From Whence the Threat of Peace," in Joseph Kruzel (ed.), *American Defense Annual*, 1990–91, 6th ed. (Lexington, MA: Lexington Books, 1990), 1.

2. Sam Nunn, "A New Military Strategy," *Congressional Record—Senate* (Washington, DC: April 19, 1990), S4451.

3. Donald K. Peterson, "Globalization and Telecommunications Leadership: The Future Ain't What It Used to Be," *Vital Speeches of the Day, 56,* 17 (June 15, 1990): 529.

4. Sergei Akhromeyev, "The Doctrine of Averting War and Defending Peace," *World Marxist Review, 30,* 12 (December 1987): 44.

5. Ibid., 40.

6. Harald B. Malmgren, "Technological Challenges to National Economic Policies of the West," *Washington Quarterly, 10,* 2 (Spring 1987): 29.

7. Charles H. Ferguson, "America's High-Tech Decline," *Foreign Policy, 74* (Spring 1989): 123.

8. John A. Young, *Global Competition: The New Reality,* vol. 1 (Washington, DC: The Report of the President's Commission on Industrial Competitiveness, 1985), 1.

9. Peter Tarnoff makes the same point in "America's New Special Relationships," *Foreign Affairs, 69,* 3 (Summer 1990): 67–69.

10. Robert B. Reich, "The Quiet Path to Economic Preeminence," *Scientific American, 261,* 4 (October 1989): 42.

11. Frank Press, "Technological Competition in the Western Alliance," in Andrew J. Pierre (ed.), *A High Technology Gap? Europe, America and Japan* (New York: New York University Press, 1987), 16.

12. Joseph S. Nye, Jr., "Understanding U.S. Strength," *Foreign Policy, 72* (Fall 1988): 121.

13. Richard Lamm, "Crisis: The Uncompetitive Society," in Martin K. Starr (ed.), *Global Competitiveness: Getting the U.S. Back on Track* (New York: W.W. Norton, 1988), 24–27.

14. Press, "Technological Competition in the Western Alliance," 34.

15. Young, *Global Competition,* vol. 2, 59.

16. Harold Brown, "Competitiveness, Technology, and U.S.–Japanese Relations," *Washington Quarterly, 13,* 3 (Summer 1990): 93.

17. Jacques Attali, "Lines on the Horizon: A New Order in the Making," *New Perspectives Quarterly, 7,* 2 (Spring 1990): 7.

18. David Brock, "The Theory and Practice of Japan-Bashing," *National Interest, 17* (Fall 1989): 33; and Chalmers Johnson, "Their Behavior, Our Policy," *National Interest, 17* (Fall 1989): 22.

19. Carlo De Benedetti, "Europe's New Role in a Global Market," in Pierre (ed.), *A High Technology Gap?* 67.

20. Gianni De Michelis, "From Eurosclerosis to Europhoria," *New Perspectives Quarterly, 7,* 2 (Spring 1990): 12.

21. Robert D. Hormats, "The International Economic Challenge," *Foreign Policy, 71* (Summer 1988): 108.

22. Tom Forester, *High-Tech Society: The Story of the Information Technology Revolution* (Oxford: Basil Blackwell, 1987), 1–2.

23. Malmgren, "Technological Challenges to National Economic Policies of the West," 24–27.

24. G.A. Keyworth II, "Goodby, Central," *Vital Speeches of the Day, 56,* 12 (April 1, 1990): 361.

25. Joseph Berger, "Universities and Their Scientific Research: A Question of Commercial Profits," *New York Times* (September 16, 1988): 16.

26. Young, *Global Competition*, vol. 2, 307.

27. Peterson, "Globalization and Telecommunications Leadership," 529.

28. Richard J. Barnet, "Reflections (on the Age of Globalization)," *New Yorker* (June 16, 1990): 57.

29. Ibid., 59.

7

The Changing Power Map

The year 1989 was the year of revolution. The years that have followed are witnessing the transformation of the international system into a new set of relationships. The dynamic impacts of the new international economic order and the altered role of military force, focused on both the First and Second Tiers and their intersection, will form the basis of that system.

One major result of this process is a changed power map of the world, a set of relationships that supersedes the militarily based bipolarity of the Cold War years. Whether the result will be greater stability or instability depends on how that alteration of power occurs. While the dynamics of international economic change provide some possibility of being a positive-sum game where the gain of one does not have to come at the expense of others, some will clearly benefit more than others.

How the power map configures will largely determine the stability of the new order. It is axiomatic that those who are most satisfied with a given set of relationships, including those that constitute an international order, are likely to be most supportive of those relationships, and that those who feel they suffer are most likely to oppose them.

The language and distinctions of a world of tiers are useful in organizing how changes in power will occur. From an internal vantage point, the First Tier is likely to be relatively tranquil. Its basic, underlying agreement about the world, its common democratic and economic philosophy, and its increasingly intertwined economy all militate against fundamental disagreements. Because the most central international players are First Tier members, this produces a basis for system stability not evident in the Cold War system.

This does not mean that there will not be problems or needs for adjustments among First Tier members and areas. Within the First Tier, answers to three important questions will have to emerge: (1) the organization of a post–Cold War security structure for the European continent; (2) how or whether to incorporate the formerly Communist states of Eastern Europe into Europe; and (3) how or whether to assist Russia and the other successor states through their political, economic, and nationalities crises.

The major challenges to the new order will occur in selected areas of the Second Tier where instability and violence will remain. With the exception of renewed violence in the Persian Gulf or possibly the Korean peninsula, this pattern will not necessarily convulse or ensnare the First Tier. It will, however, provide an often vivid and bloody irritant to which the system will have to make adjustments, which are currently identifiable only as possibilities.

Parts of the First Tier power equation are reasonably easy to predict and hence do not require elaboration. The United States will remain the single major actor in the system by the simple virtue of being the only state that is simultaneously a military and an economic superpower. The status of the United States will not be hegemonic in either realm, as it was during the period immediately after World War II.

In the system of tiers, the term "superpower" itself is somewhat misleading, connoting a level of coercion and force arising from overwhelming military power that is not relevant within the First Tier. Rather, the U.S. role is to provide leadership and coherence to First Tier action, primarily toward the Second Tier in security matters. The pattern is already clear: the rest of the First Tier already looks toward the United States for leadership, even if it does not always like the advice it receives. In some ways, however, the responsibility is even greater than it was in the conceptually simple Cold War, as the Clinton administration has come to learn in places like Bosnia.

In quantitative terms, American military might will decline as the threat recedes, and the United States' preeminence will have to be premised on a technologically and professionally superior force. The United States will still be a nuclear "superpower," although at lower levels of thermonuclear and nonnuclear armament as prescribed by arms control agreements that will come into being quickly now that the old Soviet arsenal is entirely in Russian hands. Because of both the declining Russian threat that necessitated large standing armed forces and the budgetary drain those forces create, conventional might is likely to shrink in the aftermath of the Persian Gulf crisis with Iraq and adversaries such as Somalia.

Japan's place in the new system is similarly well established. Notwithstanding that the Japanese face some difficulties in the future arising from demographics—an aging work force—and the lack of natural resources, Japan will remain an economic superpower and the world's principal financier for the foreseeable future. The questions that arise about Japan's future will largely be determined internally: whether Japan should look primarily westward or eastward and whether Japan should carve out a larger international political role to match its prominent economic position. The 1994 economic and political crises in Japan notwithstanding, Japan will be called upon to assist in the economic modernization of the developing world. The fact that Japan is financially in such an advantageous position to respond will provide the basis for considerable leverage should it decide to exercise its power.

The power equations in other parts of the world are not quite so settled, and each area has different problems and prospects. In Europe, the prospect is for a Pax Europa unknown in modern European history. Key elements in the evolution of the new Europe include the institutional structure that supersedes the edifices created for the Cold War, the place and behavior of the unified Germany, the progress (or lack thereof) of Eastern European westernization and hence participation in the greater Europe, and the impact of the continuing crisis in Russia and the successor states on the rest of Europe.

The years since 1989 have been humbling and traumatic for Russia. The crisis that had been brewing and was fully exposed by *glasnost* has produced both internal and international repercussions. Internally, the Russians continue to be plagued by the overlapping and mutually exacerbating problems of political legitimacy, economic nonperformance, and ethnic unrest. Progress in one area continues to aggravate the others. The current backlash of Russian nationalism plagues the domestic scene. Freedom of speech is expressed in increasingly chaotic rancor; the failure of the economy is exacerbated by political timidity in attacking old but popular vestiges of the old system such as inefficient state-run enterprises that protect lots of jobs but produce few quality goods or services. In the international arena, domestic travail has forced Russia to pull back from an aggressive foreign policy that had often made it a pariah state—especially in the advanced economic realm to which it aspires—and to accept international outcomes that it clearly would not have acceded to in time of strength, such as a unified Germany within NATO. How the Russian crisis resolves itself will largely determine the prominence of Russia in the new international order.

Then there is the matter of the Second Tier. As already pointed out, current trends, especially in the economic arena, are widening even further the already enormous gap in wealth between rich and poor nations. In a privatized international system where corporate profit is the operating value, that condition can only worsen, because the marketplace has no use for the losers. If the new economic order dominates the new international political system and its values are those of capitalist market economics, the result may be that the poorest countries of the Second Tier become the international equivalent of the homeless in America.

Ignoring the Second Tier's problems is, of course, something with which the international system has had a lot of experience. Three things are, however, different from before. First, the situation is much more public and obvious to both rich and poor thanks to the telecommunications revolution, which has made the poor well aware of the benefits they are not receiving. The plight of the poorest countries is as obvious as the huddled figure of a homeless person in midtown Manhattan.

Second, these are the countries that, by virtue of being losers in the post–Cold War, are most likely to reject the rules of the new system, including its rejoinders against the recourse to violence. The nations of the Second Tier, in other words, have less stake in the ongoing prosperity of the First Tier as long as they are excluded from it.

Third, this time the Second Tier comes to the party well armed. Ironically, modern technology has produced the great equalizer to nuclear weapons and sophisticated conventional weaponry in the form of widely available arsenal components such as intermediate-range surface-to-surface ballistic missiles carrying chemical and ABO (agents of biological origin) munitions, which were used effectively in the Iran–Iraq War. This suggests that if some way is not found to include the Second Tier in the coming economic plenty of the First Tier, the system will have an element of instability that would otherwise not be there.

Power in the First Tier

If the prior analysis is correct, the First Tier will have a virtual monopoly on economic and military power at the same time that conflicts with military potential will be absent in the relations among First Tier nations. This seeming anomoly reflects both the economic and the technological superiority of the First Tier (which produces economic *and* military superiority) and their general agreement (which results in the absence of conflicts with violent potential).

This does not mean that there will be total tranquillity within the First Tier. As already noted, economic skirmishes will persist at the margins over matters such as terms of trade. The collapse of the Cold War raises questions about the adequacy of the security system that was the Cold War's centerpiece. At the same time, the map of Europe is changing politically, and the process of adjustment to new political realities—including their security implications—remains to be determined.

The Prospects of Peace in Europe

The postwar organization of Europe was the direct result of the Cold War confrontation between East and West that divided the continent. The revolutions of 1989, as they have evolved, have invalidated the distinctions: communism–anticommunism is no longer an issue. All that truly divides the two halves of the continent is economics; the East is uniformly poorer than the West, and it is only in the early throes of conversion from a Socialist to a market base.[1]

The previous organization by bloc had political, economic, and security dimensions. For the East, the Warsaw Pact and the Council for Mutual Economic Assistance (Comecon) were the primary vehicles; in the West, organizations such as the Council of Europe, the European Community, and the North Atlantic Treaty Organization have performed the three roles. The only overarching organization has been the Conference on Security and Cooperation in Europe (CSCE), which is just coming into being as an organization and is expanding as fast as the map changes.

What will replace this pattern is the first question facing the new Europe. As discussed in chapter 5, CSCE provides an opportunity for continentwide political discussions, since it includes not only the former antagonists but also the neutral states of Europe. Similarly, the prospects for economic organization exist within the structure of the European Community. The question is how fast and in what direction association will occur. Whether change and inclusion (if any) are dragged by the economic mechanisms or by the security architecture is similarly up in the air. Inclusion beginning in the European Community would be slower, because it will take longer for outsiders to meet the membership requirements. Change beginning from the security system must come to grips with terms of association and the acquiescence of Russia. Where will the Partnership for Peace (P4P) lead, if anywhere?

To reiterate, several questions remain about this evolution. First, it depends on the pace and success of economic and political change in Eastern Europe and hence the region's status with the European Community. Second, there is the question of the U.S. role in such a Europe. Third, there is the question of balance of power and influence within the organization, which is really a question of the balance between Germany and the rest. Finally, the new integrated Europe will be much more diverse than Western Europe was, including not only significant economic disparities but also the clash between the principles of market economy and Socialist expectations that are certain to survive socialism, as they are in Russia.

Does NATO Have a Future?

What will be even more difficult is defining the new security order. With the implosion of the Second World's Warsaw Pact, NATO looks strangely like an alliance without a mission, brave talk about its continuing vitality notwithstanding.

President Clinton's maiden European foray in January 1994, which began at NATO headquarters in Brussels, highlighted the problem and the need for a new focus. On the major European violent upheaval of our time—Bosnia—the alliance again failed, asking Clinton to take the lead in posing a bombing threat against the Serbs that he had earlier proposed and they had rejected. Fearful of a negative Russian domestic reaction, the alliance demonstrated its myopic vision of the future by passing the interim, innocuous P4P initiative, which offered association but no airtight security guarantees for Eastern Europe.

The two issues mirror the underlying malaise. Bosnia demonstrated the absence of anything like common will and vision outside the traditional East–West confrontation (an extension of the alliance's inability to act "out of area" during the Cold War). The P4P "solution" suggests that NATO members have no common agreement about pan-European security. This malaise makes many wonder about the attractions of an alternative framework like the CSCE.

Unless NATO can find some plausible new *raison d'être*, it is going to be in trouble, because a military alliance requires both a workable strategic concept that defines the probable dangers and the means to deal with them.[2] Absent a revived Russian expansionist threat that is difficult to imagine conceptually (what would prompt a Russia desperate for Western aid?) and physically (how could they afford it?), there is no clear focus for the alliance.

There are reasons to try to keep NATO alive, at least during the period of system transition. On the one hand, a U.S. presence on the continent provides continuity and credibility to the American deterrent at a time of transformation and instability in Eastern Europe and Russia.[3] On the other hand, the U.S. presence makes other European processes easier by allaying somewhat the visceral fears of Germany. Henry Kissinger argues that NATO is the only organization that relates the United States to Europe and Germany to a superpower. Thus, "The American presence reassured West Europeans that they have a safety net should Germany—against all expectations—return to the road of nationalism."[4] These reasons, while valid, are transitory in nature and could easily be superseded by a security organization based around the CSCE membership.

The linchpin in any European arrangement is the status of the new Germany and Russia. Germany is the most powerful European nation, its economy is by far the most robust among European nations, and its combined population of slightly over 80 million gives it the potential to be a military power that could, as in the past, challenge to dominate the Eurasian landmass. Given all these attributes, the shape of Europe is bound to be heavily influenced by Germany.

The process by which Germany reunified and ended the postwar occupation demonstrates the position of strength from which Germany operates. The Germans did not, in essence, ask anyone's permission to unify; they simply accomplished the task and informed the world of the outcome. As a measure of Germany's standing, Gorbachev and the Soviets could merely accede meekly to the *fait accompli*. The current appeal of Zhirinovsky suggests that the Russian people retain some sense of unease at the transition.

Because of its history, a strong Germany makes many people nervous. Given over forty years of political democracy and a population of which hardly any participated in the Nazi period, the fear is largely instinctive rather than substantive; but it is present nonetheless. This nagging fear, which Germans understand but which still annoys them, creates a strong desire to tie Germany to organizations in which others can have some influence over the direction of German policy. Periodic outbreaks of neo-nazism feed these fears, despite the German government's attempts to snuff them out.

This desire is particularly true with respect to Germany's military potential, creating a continued interest in NATO that can hardly be justified otherwise. Thus, it can be argued that economically and politically integrating Germany into a European security system with substantially lower levels of armaments offers the most credible strategy for containing any future German threat to world peace.

If the formerly Communist countries continue to modernize and to aspire to inclusion in the prosperity of the First Tier, the rationale and momentum of NATO are almost certain to decline. This progress is by no means universally certain; the southern tier formerly Communist states are hardly making progress toward market democracy, and the large-scale bloodletting in former Yugoslavia precludes progress in the successor states to that former union. The world's understandable fascination with progress—or its absence—in Russia obscures the snail's pace of change in the other successor states of the Soviet Union.

Does NATO have a positive role to play in these dynamics? Northern tier Eastern European states clamor for inclusion to protect them from a potentially expansionist Russia; Russia objects to having NATO near its boundaries; and NATO members (who are not quite certain they are ready to shed their blood for Polish or Czech independence anyway) demur to the Russians. NATO's impotence in the Balkans is well established.

In spite of all this, NATO is unlikely to go away anytime soon. It *is* there, and its sheer presence comforts its members. Moreover, P4P has breathed new life into the organization. In all likelihood, a Europewide organization that encompasses both the European successor states of the former Soviet Union and the United States, probably based on the CSCE membership and extending the rudimentary structure authorized at the Paris summit of 1990, will emerge in the long run. Such an organization would complete the obsolescence of NATO and allow it to slide into oblivion along with the other edifices of the Cold War.

The Fate of the Second World

How the European part of the First Tier organizes its future will both affect and be affected by whether the old Second World succeeds in modernizing and joining the First Tier or whether the Second World slides into the Second Tier. What happens is important to all of Europe because of physical proximity and historical relationships. A formerly Communist world gladly embraced by and embracing the glow of market democracy can add visibly to systemic prosperity and stability. Those same countries sullenly falling into the Second Tier will add to the system's problems, not their solutions.

The prospects, of course, are highly differential and generally dim. The Socialist economic systems produced residual structures that were partially developed at best, uncompetitive with both First and near–First Tier states. The situation is particularly dire in the southern tier states of Eastern Europe (including most of the Balkan states that were not part of the Warsaw Pact) and a number of Soviet successor states (especially in the Central and East Asian regions). The situation is slightly less bleak for Russia and the other large successor states (Ukraine, Byelarus, and Kazakhstan). The prospects are brighter (or less dim) for the northern tier states of Eastern Europe and the Baltic states.

Eastern Europe

The economic and military shape of Europe will depend in great measure on the progress of the countries of Eastern Europe toward democratization and integration into the rest of Europe. Despite the hopeful start provided by the revolutions of 1989, the success of these varied states, with hardly any democratic experience and even less with modern market economies, is not assured.

Jacques Attali, the chief adviser to French President François Mitterrand, lists three criteria for these countries to be integrated into the West: "a civil society, with the rule of law and the constitution of democratic institutions; the development of market economies; and a 'political culture' of tolerance."[5] These criteria, of course, are very similar to those describing membership in the First Tier.

As in Russia, these problems interact with and aggravate one another. All relate to the task of trying to build democratic political systems at a time of economic transition "complicated by the kind of massive economic problems faced today by the new democracies."6 Moreover, because there is no clear set of guidelines on how to make the transition from socialism to capitalism, mistakes continue to be made that exacerbate difficulties inherent in the switchover.

The relative pace of economic change varies in tempo and in mixture (political versus economic change), but one thing is clear: the new leaderships do not maintain the ideological attachment to communism that Gorbachev had. The process may thus be easier than in the former Soviet Union. Adam Ulam argues, "Communism has the notions of autocracy and imperialism embedded in its dogmatic scheme, and wherever Communism triumphs it tends to produce a tyrannical system. . . . The key to the tyranny of Communism is Communism, not the country in which it is enacted."7 Rejecting the fallen ideology thus serves as the necessary precondition for successful democracy. As noted, authoritarianism shorn of the Communist mantra remains in a number of the least promising states (Bulgaria and Serbia, to name two).

Eastern Europe will have a great deal of assistance in making the transition. Western Europeans clearly want the democratic regimes to succeed and make the transition to westernization for economic, political, and security reasons. At the economic level, the institution of political democracy and market economy is prerequisite to inclusion in the European Community, and the success of democratic forces carries with it the possibility of an ideological homogeneity on the continent that could produce lasting peace coupled with economic prosperity. Understanding that the chief barriers will be economic and that the transition can be softened with the generous application of money, West Europeans, led by the Germans, will certainly respond with a generosity born of self-interest.

The problems of transition are manifest. They are least severe in those states like Poland, Hungary, the Czech Republic, and the Baltic states, which are culturally and historically most like the First Tier states of Western Europe, and thus have the least traumatic changes to make, as is evident from their desire for greater association with the West. It does not stretch credulity to its limits to imagine their medium-term elevation to the First Tier, broadly fertilized and nurtured by Western investment. The southern part of the region remains highly underdeveloped (Bulgaria, Romania, and Macedonia, for instance) and/or war torn to the extent that, with the possible exception of Croatia, most of it will slide into the lower rungs of the Second Tier.

Russia and the Successor States

The lurching attempts to fill the vacuum created by the peaceful implosion of the former Soviet Union represents the other major European challenge to the First Tier. Fifteen states of varying size, importance, and stability stand where there once was one. Of those that remain, only Russia, armed with nuclear weapons, poses a potential threat to the international system. Russia was, after all, the core and instigator of the Soviet empire, and it remains by far the largest block of residue. Change is more visible, more fractious and contentious, and ultimately of greater consequence for the First Tier in Russia than elsewhere in the old union.

How the process of change works out in Russia is crucial to the new order. At the most optimistic and positive end of the process is a democratic, popularly supported state integrated into the global economy and fully sharing the values of a democratic world order that can form a model for the other successor states. Such a system would have the potential for maximum stability and would allow the system's attention to be turned to integrating the Second Tier into meaningful participation. At the other extreme is a Russia in flames, further secessions fueling the return of authoritarianism, the economy worsening to economic anarchy, and the state facing the world as a suspicious and resentful outsider.

The crisis has two basic dimensions. On the one hand is the problem of internal change within Russia. On the other hand is the nationalities problem, an element with importance within a number of the successor states, in the international relations among the successor republics of the old USSR, and possibly for the broader international system.

The Domestic Crisis

The outcome of the domestic crisis has been the subject of much impassioned debate, particularly in light of the well-publicized resurgence of Russian ultranationalism that has caused a number of observers to hypothesize a dark future for Russia.[8] Suggestions of the possibility of reversion to the authoritarian past are widespread. I think this outcome is unlikely (although hardly impossible, especially in the short run for a brief period) for the following reasons.

First, people rarely voluntarily forfeit their freedom. There are occasional points in history when peoples choose a Faustian bargain, but those are rare exceptions, particularly in this world of instant telecommunications. The second reason is that the leadership that will follow Yeltsin is almost certain to be more radical and prodemocratic than the current leadership. Yeltsin is politically and generationally a transition figure. Those who would reassert authority are remnants of the Brezhnev years, by and large; they are old, and they are by now well out of power. The leadership that will follow is younger than Yeltsin, and there is evidence that younger Russians have a more tolerant outlook and are strongly attracted to Western values, especially consumer values, rather than to traditional nationalist ones. Although admittedly a carefully selected group, the young people who participated in the Clinton town meeting in Moscow—a consciously bright, westernized assemblage—are the future. This is not to suggest that there will not continue to be eccentricities and challenges to democratic growth, as the Zhirinovsky phenomenon has demonstrated. Those challenges, however, must be taken in light of current circumstances: economic hard times that would raise questions about support for any regime; and the companion fact that the Russians are amateurs at democracy.

The third reason reversion is unlikely is that it is difficult to imagine who would support such a movement. Normally, the military would seem an apt candidate, but the upper leadership of the military has been remarkably supportive of (or at least quiescent about) change, and the rank and file that would be the sword of reimposed authority would have to come from the masses of the population that support change. The military made its decision when it supported Yeltsin against the renegade parliament in October 1993.

Fourth, it is hard to imagine that a movement could be organized with sufficient strength to threaten the new political institutions without being exposed and discredited. One of the more remarkable aspects of Soviet reform has been the emergence of an increasingly impressive and independent media corps who would quickly identify the culprits in any attempt to reimpose the old system.

The economic dimension of the internal crisis is even more problematic. The transformation of an economy the size of Russia's from a command to a market basis is a chore unprecedented in economic history. The Russians are being forced, to borrow the British phrase, to "muddle through," and they face several barriers to their success.

A first barrier is embedded in Russian culture and tradition.[9] The economic dependency and lethargy that marked Socialist practice were fundamentally in tune with the virtual serfdom from which the average Russian emerged from the Russian/Bolshevik Revolution; both were paternal, command structures in which individual initiative was neither encouraged nor rewarded. What little entrepreneurial class existed (the *kulaks*) was systematically eliminated by the Communists. One can scarcely imagine a population less suited for grasping the dynamics of capitalism and market economy than the Russians.

Second, a substantial segment of the Russian population clings to its old economic system, and especially to the old "social net" of entitlements. This is particularly true of the elderly, who served their time under the old regime and expected to be taken care of by it. The rough-and-tumble uncertainties of the contemporary scene can only be highly unsettling to these people. It is hardly surprising that they form much of the voting opposition to reform.

Third, change is proceeding within the context of a fractured economic as well as political system. The Soviet Union was an economic unit wherein component parts supported and relied upon one another. Ukrainian grain fed urban Russians, and the Ukrainian winter was warmed by cheap Russian energy through an elaborate system of economically artificial subsidies. With the political breakup, all these relations are now subject to negotiations among the successor states wherein market forces make talks more difficult (what is Russian natural gas "really" worth, for instance).

Fourth, the situation is exacerbated by the absence of a legal and political framework within which to channel and regulate the transition to a free enterprise system. Since the state in essence owned everything under communism, there were essentially no provisions for selling or otherwise transferring public assets to private individuals, for instance. The result is a kind of frontier capitalism where the participants have to make up most of the rules as they go. In that circumstance, the emergence of mafia and mafia-like criminal organizations is hardly surprising.

Fifth, the system is so large that its conversion will require a massive influx of capital well in excess of that readily available. The ability of the system to absorb the amounts needed is itself suspect; at the middle and upper levels of government, for instance, the same old *nomenklatura* of the Communist age remain in place, providing barriers to be leapt with considerable frustration (a major problem discouraging foreign private investment). All this simply adds to the general chaos of the system.

The immensity of how far the Russians have to go to join the world economic competition is described by Bialer, who says Soviet "priorities lie not with the futuristic technology of the Third Industrial Revolution, but with the unfulfilled tasks of the First and Second Industrial Revolutions—infrastructure, abundant food, cheap but durable consumer goods, labour discipline, financial management, and an efficient services industry."[10] The failure to move sequentially through the various "revolutions" and to extend the resulting benefits to the population will almost certainly destroy support for the regime. Moreover, the gap is likely to widen for two reasons. First, the Russians are already far behind in an era of accelerating change. Second, a barrier to competition remains in the weakness of support industries in the vital areas of electronics and computer technologies.[11]

This technological gap extends to the military realm as well and helps explains why the Soviet military has been generally supportive of Gorbachev's economic program. According to Dale Herspring, the Soviet high command understands "the increasing danger of the military's technological obsolescence"[12] in relation to the West. Another writer argues that this is particularly difficult for the Soviets. Because of the technological component of modern military power and the importance of military strength to Soviet claims to superpower status,[13] the technological gap is particularly threatening to them. This fear is accentuated by what former U.S. National Security Council official Condoleeza Rice calls their "almost pathological respect for U.S. technology,"[14] which was reinforced in the Kuwaiti desert.

The Nationalities Crisis

The most dangerous and explosive problem facing the Russians is the so-called nationalities problem. *Glasnost* had the unintended effect of allowing citizens of the non-Russian areas of the Soviet Union to express their suppressed nationalist beliefs. The result of providing a modicum of freedom was not to produce democracy, but rather to reignite primordial, exclusionary nationalisms expressed in terms of national self-determination run amok and exclaimed in bloody ethnic conflict.

This problem, of course, demonstrated the most glaring aspect of the weak society of the former Soviet Union. It revealed there really was no such thing as a Soviet "society" in the sense of a broadly based set of common beliefs and loyalties shared by all citizens of the old union. Instead, there are a whole series of more parochial societies based in ethnicity and nationalisms of the various Soviet peoples. The attempt to impose a common vision based on the Great Russian model was a dismal failure.

In Stalinist days, smoldering nationalism did not matter greatly, because the coercive power of the strong state compensated for the weak social base. When control was removed and the old system crumbled, people were left without bearings to which they could attach and identify; order was gone. In the process, many reverted to ancient identifications such as ethnicity and religion. Unfortunately, those designations divided neighbor from neighbor in ways that have become murderous.

As a Great Russian, Gorbachev probably had little idea of the hatred that much of the citizenry feels toward ethnic Russians, and the instruments of coercion covered any evidence of Russophobia. Moreover, "Gorbachev's career prior to becoming party leader . . . gave him no experience in managing ethnic relations. He was, therefore, slow to recognize the explosive potential of ethnic tensions within the country."[15] Of particular note, his career was devoid of any experience with agencies such as the KGB, which were the suppressors of ethnic expression.

As the Soviet Union dissolved, the nationalities problem quickly turned nasty and violent, as discussed in chapter 4. Overt violence has so far been isolated to the southern tier of successor states, where ethnic and religious differences intermingle to light a particularly volatile mix whose resolution is nowhere apparent.

The extent and depth of this crisis has received less attention than it probably deserves. This is at least partially true because we have been so totally focused on Russia and its travails. Ethnic cleansing has not been one of the immediate problems that Yeltsin and his opponents have been forced to confront within Russia itself, although it is probably only a matter of time until ethnically distinct regions of Asian Russia decide they would prefer to go their own way. Moreover, the regions where the violence is occurring are physically and psychologically remote from the international consciousness. Occasionally, Nagorno-Karabakh gains fleeting public attention, but it quickly and quietly fades from view.

This inattention is curious. The fighting, killing, and dislocations are certainly real and on a scale to match more public suffering, such as that in Somalia, but even the United Nations and its activist Secretary-General Boutros-Ghali have been remarkably quiet. It is as if the system has enough other matters to worry about; let the Russians worry about this one.

The nationalities problem will not go away, and it has real consequences for the evolution of the former Soviet Union and the broader international system. For the Russians, the problem has two major ramifications. First, it points to their embarrassment at the demise of the old Soviet structure: things like this simply did not happen under the old regime. Second, the 25 million ethnic Russians living in the other successor states could, in principle, become victims of the same kind of violence directed against Azeris and Armenians. What is Russia to do in such circumstance?

To many in the successor republics, the answer to the latter is clear: the Russians would rapidly come to the relief of beleaguered Russians, a fact reinforced by the November 1993 adoption of a new Russian military doctrine in which controlling attacks against Russians is a prominent part. The fear in many successor states is that such action could be the guise for reimposing Russian rule and, in effect, recreating the empire. Some of the ultranationalists in Russia have already suggested as much, and there is no doubt that guarantees against Russian imperialism were a prominent part of the Clinton administration's efforts resulting in Ukraine's agreement to surrender nuclear weapons, which they had been keeping partly as a hedge against this very thing.

The international system has taken very little notice of these problems, nor have there been clear appeals for international efforts through the United Nations or elsewhere to become involved. This may be partially out of deference to Russia, for whom the problem is most real; and it is probably partly due to the absence of any interest in shedding blood for places like Nakichevan (if one cannot marshall force for Bosnia, why would one do so for Tblisi?). In this circumstance, any action devolves to Russia, a recognition that gives pause to many in the successor states.

How this works out has both regional and broader implications. Regionally, there is the danger that the old Soviet Union's neighbors could be drawn in. This is most likely in the case of the Islamic states; the Azerbaijanis of former Soviet Azerbaijan and its Iranian provincial counterpart are, after all, of the same ethnicity and religion. Could Iran stand idly by in the event of a decisive victory by Armenia over Nagorno-Karabakh? The answer is unclear.

The outcome is also interesting for those other areas where nationalities problems continue. As noted, there are a number of African states where centrifugal forces are important, and systemic actions could be instructive. Of more fundamental importance, however, is the precedent for the world's two largest, and most diverse, countries, China and India. The Chinese, as previously noted, hold up Soviet disintegration as the rationale for continued political repression; would a loosening of control result in the Balkanization of China and its own nationalities problem? Similarly, India is a patchwork of different nationalities and religions with great disintegrative potential, wherein ethnic violence is already evident (Kashmir, the Tamil regions, for instance).

The outcome of change in the former Soviet Union is vital to the shape of the international system that succeeds the Cold War system. A Russia that emerges successfully from reform politically democratic, economically strong with a market economy, and more or less intact physically could become a major link in the new system, helping to enforce the values of the new order rather than acting as an agent of change. A Russia diminished—democratically fractious, with an economy in perpetual disarray and with its boundaries shrinking—is less likely to have the kind of stake in the new system that will make it a major supporter of stability.

The Russian crisis is deep and complex. Because the Russians' problems do interact in mutually destructive ways, it is exceedingly difficult for them to deal simultaneously with their dilemmas. Also, because of this interaction and complexity, it is hard to prescribe actions that other nations can take to help the Russians solve their difficulties.

The Second Tier

The most troublesome part of the world in the new international order is the collection of nations that constitute the Second Tier. Most of these are in Latin America, Africa south of the Sahara, and Asia; most are politically and economically underdeveloped.

The most prosperous states, notably the states of the Pacific Rim, will succeed in gaining First Tier status. In addition to the Pacific Rim states that fall into this category, a number of other nation-states are potential members. A list would include a number of South American states (Brazil, Argentina, Chile, Venezuela), Mexico (by virtue of its membership in NAFTA), and a few African states (Nigeria, South Africa). The great barrier in most cases is foreign debt, which both saps investment capital and keeps these countries from the kind of infrastructure development that will make them attractive to private investment.

At the other extreme are the poorest and least developed countries, which have little prospect of development due to a dearth of both human and natural resources. These are often referred to as "Fourth World"; we have characterized them as undevelopable. Countries such as Mali and Bangladesh head the list. Countries in this situation have little stake in the ongoing system, but are generally too weak to challenge the inequities they perceive in a manner that could upset the system. These countries constitute the international system's equivalent of the homeless; in an international system that has adopted—if implicitly—the values of the market as its primary norms, their condition is unlikely to improve; if anything, it would worsen.

Between these extremes are the states that create the problems for the evolving order. Poised between the most developed and the least developed Second Tier nations, this layer of countries has undergone some economic but usually little political development. Concentrated in the Middle East, Southeast Asia, and parts of Latin America and Africa, these states feel aggrieved by the structure of the international system and consequently have little reason to uphold the rules of the game when they can avoid doing so.

In the past, there was relatively little reason to worry about states in this category. During the days of Cold War competition, usually the United States or the Soviet Union exercised some restraint over these countries by virtue of military or economic aid programs, and these countries were only armed at levels adequate to suppress their own populations or to harass their immediate neighbors.

That has changed, at least partly as a result of the breakdown of the Cold War and the privatization of international economic activity. The most notable way in which the situation has changed is that these countries are now heavily armed to the point that they pose grave risks to their regions and beyond. The great symbols of change are the proliferation of ballistic missiles to an estimated eighteen to twenty nation-states[16] and the possession of chemical and biological weapons by many of those states.

Iraq, of course, is the exemplar of this troublesome category, and the Iraqi conquest of Kuwait in August 1990 was the most vivid example of the kind of international mischief that these nations can create. Coming on the heels of the long and exhausting Iran–Iraq War (1980–88), the Iraqi action against the tiny state of Kuwait demonstrated that naked military force can still be employed to great effect.

Prior to the breakdown of the Cold War, Iraq's action would probably have required the approval of the Soviet Union, which served as Iraq's principal armorer: without continued Soviet military assistance, Iraq could not have sustained military action. In August 1990, Iraq's Saddam Hussein could view the world from a different viewpoint. With nearly a million men under arms—many of them battle-hardened, but also battle-weary, veterans of the Iran–Iraq War—he had the largest army in the region. Iraq also possessed heavy armor (mostly tanks) in superior numbers to anyone else in the region and more than the major powers could bring to the region rapidly.

The possession of advanced weaponry only adds to the volatile mix. According to one source, the Iran–Iraq War was important in transforming the nature of Second Tier regional conflict for three reasons. First, the use of chemical weapons by the Iraqis demonstrated the tactical utility of those weapons. Second, large numbers of surface-to-surface tactical ballistic missiles were used effectively. Third, during the period the war was being fought, a number of states in the Third World developed the capacity to produce both ballistic missiles and chemical or biological weapons.[17] As an example of how troubling this prospect may be, the list of countries known to be capable of producing chemical weapons includes Iran, Iraq, Libya, Syria, China, the Koreas, Taiwan, and possibly Israel and Egypt,[18] in addition to the traditional Western powers.

Regional conflict thus represents one of the most dangerous military problems facing the post-1989 world. Now, what one author calls "small states with large grievances or large ambitions"[19] cannot be ignored by the system as a whole. Moreover, the locales where regional conflicts will be played out are physically remote from all of the traditional seats of power, save, in some Asian cases, the former Soviet Union. It will be difficult, in some instances impossible, for the West to mount effective ground actions in many regional conflict arenas, thereby rendering hollow the effectiveness of threats to intervene in such situations.

Moreover, the encompassing nature of preparation for World War III in Germany that highlighted the Cold War period has left all states, but especially the United States and Russia, with force structures arguably inappropriate to fight in most Second Tier regional conflicts at precisely the time when budgetary constraints make it unlikely that additional resources will become available to convert those structures. This is especially true regarding adequate airlift and sealift capability to transport large numbers of troops and supplies to distant theaters. The successful expulsion of Iraq from Kuwait may prove to have been the last battle of the old order rather than the first battle of the new order.

The Persian Gulf War also demonstrated the enormous imbalance in military capabilities between the tiers. Iraq's forces were large, but they were not very effective. They were battle tested, but against another Second Tier army that did not prepare them in anything resembling an adequate manner for the onslaught of the United States–led coalition.

The lesson for the future of intertier involvement in regional conflict is ambivalent. The outcome of the Gulf War clearly showed that the First Tier can impose its will on Second Tier conflicts when it chooses to do so; if a Second Tier action produces a First Tier response, the Second Tier nation will lose. At the same time, it is not at all clear *when* the First Tier will respond. In Kuwait, the one unambiguous vital interest of the First Tier in the Second—access to petroleum—was involved. In other circumstances, where interests are less clear, how will the system respond? A major factor here is to remember, as pointed out in chapter 1, that First Tier military capability is mainly limited by public opinion. The interest of that opinion in Second Tier conflicts is untested.

Regional conflict is not the only source of continuing instability in the Second Tier. As long as there remain grinding poverty and inequity in many Third World nations, political conditions will continue to be ripe for violence. The process of nation building (consolidating popular support around a nation and its government), which was extolled widely in the literature of the 1950s and 1960s, is still largely incomplete in much of the developing world. Until it is complete, there will be sources of challenge and instability from a number of sides.

First, it must be realized that democracy, where it exists at all in the Second Tier, is exceedingly tentative. Strong traditions of participatory democracy—which seems to thrive in conditions where there is at least some economic well-being to nurture participation in the affairs of state—are not deeply rooted in many Second Tier states, where the simple struggle to survive overwhelms more abstract notions of political democracy. At the same time, the desire of people of a single ethnic group to reunite under common rule—irredentism—remains a smoldering sentiment from the Horn of Africa to the outer boundaries of Russia (Moldova, Azerbaijan). Finally, internal discontent still finds vent in traditional insurgencies and counterinsurgencies in places as diverse as Cambodia and Peru.

This problem has changed somewhat. During the Cold War period, much of the active encouragement and sponsorship of guerrilla movements seeking to overthrow noncommunist governments—so-called wars of national liberation—came from the Soviet Union. As a result, U.S. opposition in the form of support for whoever opposed the side the Soviets backed was justified in Cold War terms. This, of course, was the basic model for the United States' involvement in Vietnam, as well as less active support of a number of other anticommunist movements. Under the Reagan Doctrine, this competition was extended to active American support for (even creation of) the anticommunist Nicaraguan Contras and to the Afghan *mujahadin*.

Cold War rationales are no longer relevant. While insurgencies and opposition to them continue, they continue on other grounds. For instance, the recently concluded (for the time being) struggle for control of Cambodia by the hated and genocidal Khmer Rouge and various opposition groups has become now more a struggle over human rights and the dread prospect of the Khmer Rouge coming back to power and reinstituting its murderous policies. Settling that war is currently being extolled as the major triumph of United Nations peacekeeping efforts. Until the Khmer Rouge are reconciled to the new arrangement or are destroyed as an effective force, the settlement will be subject to potential reversal.

There is a second new variant that arises from the drug problem identified in chapter 6. That is the rise of a new phenomenon known as the "drug-insurgency nexus," defined by one investigator as "the formation of politico-military enclaves controlled by [drug] traffickers allied with leftist guerrilla groups."[20] The major contemporary example is *Sendero Luminoso* (Shining Path) in Peru, where the United States has proposed to assist Peruvian government efforts to eradicate these pro-Maoist anarchists. What makes a movement like the Shining Path unique is that it is self-sustaining; it requires no outside assistance (it gets its money by taxing the *narcotraficantes* whose business it protects) and can appeal to the peasantry because it protects them from a government—and outsiders like the Americans—who would deprive them of their coca-derived livelihoods. Since a side effect of ending the Cold War will be the evaporation of ideologically based funding for Second Tier insurgents and terrorists, new sources of funds will be necessary. Crime and crime-related activities, as in alliance with the drug trade, are but one possibility.

Bosnia and Somalia have introduced the system to a whole new genre of internal violence—not unlike that going on in former Soviet areas like Nagorno-Karabakh—that both fascinates and sickens us. It is near-genocidal warfare among ethnic groups, born of deep and abiding national hatreds and seeking to "cleanse" the body politic of offensive others. It seems to thrive in the so-called failed states like Haiti, Rwanda, and Somalia. The violence is bloody, often gruesome, and inconclusive.

Former Yugoslavia, the southern successor states, and Somalia may offer little more than a harbinger of things to come in other parts of the Second Tier. Ethnic difference interlaced with religious division infects a good deal of central Asia and is virtually epidemic in much of the heart of Africa; the renewed carnage between the Hutu and Tutsi in Burundi during the summer of 1993 and in Rwanda in 1994 may offer a chilling forewarning of the future unless the passions of rampant self-determination can be brought under control. Doing so may represent the single most important security problem facing the new system.

Finally, the challenge of Third World misery manifests itself in migration—people swimming, sailing, or even walking away from the sources of their poverty to the richer parts of the globe. This migration, often illegal but difficult to deny on humanitarian grounds, has been felt in the United States largely in terms of an influx from Central America and the Caribbean, and increasingly from Asia. Haiti represents this problem in its most difficult fashion. Certainly an implied motive underlying NAFTA is to help create enough jobs in Mexico to convince potential illegal aliens to stay home. Former European colonialists such as Britain have experienced similar problems with people from the old empire. The problem can only get worse until people feel a genuine desire, based in hope and well-being, to stay home.

All of these problems—regional conflict, the various forms of internal violence (insurgency, narcoinsurgency, failed states, migration)— stand at the intersection of the tiers. Terrorism and the flow of drugs could be added to that list of concerns with the potential for intertier violence, and transnational issues like the environment clearly have importance in how the tiers relate to one another outside the mainstream of the global economy. It is not clear how (or whether or where) the First Tier will choose to address or to try to solve the problems of the Second Tier; nor is it easy to judge how most affected parts of the Second Tier will respond to First Tier action or inaction. The pattern, however, will be important in determining the tranquillity and stability of the new order.

If talking about the problems of the Second Tier sounds a bit like old-fashioned moralizing, there are "stronger" reasons based in the self-interest of the states of the new order. If there is one commodity that will be increasingly valued by the major actors in the new system, it is stability, both for the conduct of business and for international political tranquility. Stability, in turn, requires that the membership basically support the system and its maintenance. In the evolving order, those with the least stake are the countries of the Second Tier who are not swept up in the wave of the Third Industrial Revolution. If these states are left aside, "we will all lose the chance for peace the world has won."[21]

Conclusions

The outcomes of the three major "variables" identified in the preceding pages will have a good deal to do with the shape and stability of the post–Cold War international political system. All could work out happily for international peace and stability: Germany shows every sign of emerging as a peaceful and constructive economic superpower whose might is devoted to system maintenance and improvement; Russia may work through its crisis and emerge as a viable participant in the world democratic order of market economies; and the Second Tier may be gradually brought into the global order of prosperity and hope.

The chances of these things happening vary. The prospects for a tranquil Europe with Germany as a major anchor are best. Despite some suggestions that Europe will revert to its old fractious patterns of internecine struggle,[22] the simple fact is that the old divisions of Europe are overshadowed by a commonality of ideology and aspiration to the Western models so loudly trumpeted at the November 1990 CSCE summit. All aspire to political democracy and economic prosperity resulting from market economy. This glue is stronger than the old wounds that divide. Moreover, as democracy takes hold where it previously has not, the simple dynamic that free people do not make war upon one another becomes an even more powerful force. For Europe, the questions are not about *whether* association and greater integration will occur; rather, they center on the forms such association will take, the pace at which the process will proceed, and who will and who will not be included and hence gain or be denied First Tier status.

Although this smacks of false optimism, the long-term prospects for Russia may not be as dire as some would have it. Certainly, Russia's problems are crushing, particularly in their synergistic combination, and it is unlikely that Russia will emerge as a full-blown economic competitor with the First Tier; the structural problems and temporal disadvantages are simply too great.

Even if all this is true, one cannot avoid being genuinely impressed with the degree of political development in Russia. Certainly the process of democratization is far from complete, yet the amount of progress has been staggering, and it is difficult to imagine the Russian people and the institutions they have created being reversed. If the West can find ways to help Yeltsin engineer the transformation of the economy to a market basis, they will have at worst a fighting chance of success.

The pessimism that accompanies the vicissitudes of Russian politics should be taken with a grain of salt. The confrontation between Yeltsin and his parliamentary-based cabinet in the spring of 1994 will almost certainly slow movement toward transformation to the market; it does not necessarily signal the end of political and economic change. The Russians are a perpetually pessimistic people whose mood swings are frequent but transitory. And, to repeat a point made earlier, much of the rough-and-tumble we are witnessing is the result of amateur politicians learning the trade of parliamentary politics.

It is most difficult to be optimistic about the Second Tier. The problems there are so diverse and so deep that change across the board is almost impossible. Forgiving Second Tier debt, a difficult and complicated problem, would ease the inhibitions to economic development that are probably a necessary precondition to political development. For the Second Tier to gain a truly meaningful stake in preserving the system, much more will have to be done, and that will require massive investment of the kind that financially strapped governments are in no fiscal position to make.

The scene is not completely bleak. Processes like APEC and NAFTA may assist the top two subtiers of the Second Tier to make legitimate claims to First Tier status in the years ahead, and as they rise, they may pull some of the partially developed states (India, for example) upward. The democratization of South America is a positive sign, and the future, especially if NAFTA membership extends beyond current applicants Chile and Argentina to greater parts of the continent, is promising. Although the true globalizing of the economy will be gradual as the circle of market democracies grows, it is those parts of the Second Tier where violence remains a viable option that pose the greatest systemic difficulty.

Notes

1. Richard J. Barnet, "Reflections (The Age of Globalization)," *New Yorker* (June 16, 1990), 48.
2. Henry A. Kissinger, "Germany, Neutrality, and the 'Security Trap' System," *Washington Post* (April 15, 1990), D7.
3. Peter Tarnoff, "America's New Special Relationships," *Foreign Affairs, 69*, 3 (Summer 1990): 73.
4. Kissinger, "Germany, Neutrality, and the 'Security Trap' System," D7.
5. Jacques Attali, "Lines on the Horizon: A New Order in the Making," *New Perspectives Quarterly, 7*, 2 (Spring 1990): 8.
6. Theodore C. Sorensen, "Rethinking National Security," *Foreign Affairs, 69*, 3 (Summer 1990): 15.
7. Adam Ulam and George Urban, "What Is 'Soviet'—What Is 'Russian'?" *Encounter, 74*, 4 (May 1990): 48.
8. Two recent *Foreign Affairs* articles capture the debate. See Dimitri Simes, "The Return of Russian History," *Foreign Affairs, 73*, 1 (January–February 1993): 67–82; and Stephen Sestanovich, "Russia Turns the Corner," *Foreign Affairs, 73*, 1 (January–February 1993): 83–98.
9. Bruce Parrott, "Gorbachev's Gamble: Political, Economic and Ethnic Challenges to Soviet Reform," *SAIS Review, 10*, 2 (Summer–Fall 1990): 70.
10. Seweryn Bialer, "The Passing of the Soviet Order?" *Survival, 32*, 2 (March–April 1990): 118.

11. Richard F. Kaufman, "Economic Reform and the Soviet Military," *Washington Quarterly, 11,* 3 (Summer 1988): 206.

12. Dale R. Herspring, "The Soviet Military and Change," *Survival, 31,* 4 (July–August 1989): 321.

13. Sergei Zamascikov, "Gorbachev and the Soviet Military," Rand Library Collection Papers P–7410 (Santa Monica, CA: RAND Corporation, January 1988). 31. See also John P. Hardt and Jean Farreth Boone, "Gorbachev's Economic Prescriptions: Goals and Expectations," in Arthur B. Gunlicks and John D. Treadway (eds.), *The Soviet Union under Gorbachev: Assessing the First Year* (New York: Praeger, 1987), 82.

14. Condoleeza Rice, "Defence and Security," in Martin McCauley (ed.), *The Soviet Union under Gorbachev* (London: Macmillan, 1987), 198.

15. Parrott, "Gorbachev's Gamble," 67–68.

16. See Janne Nolan and Albert D. Wheelon, "Third World Ballistic Missiles," *Scientific American, 263,* 2 (August 1990), 34; and Harvey J. McGeorge, "Bugs, Gas and Missiles," *Defense and Foreign Affairs, 17,* 5–6 (May–June 1990): 18.

17. Ibid., 15.

18. Nolan and Wheelon, "Third World Ballistic Missiles," 39.

19. Barnet, "Reflections," 53.

20. Scott D. MacDonald, *Mountain High, White Avalanche: Cocaine and Power in the Andean States and Panama* (New York: Praeger, 1989), 12.

21. Barnet, "Reflections," 60.

22. John J. Mearsheimer, "Why We Will Soon Miss the Cold War," *Atlantic Monthly, 266,* 2 (August 1990): 35–50.

─── 8 ───

The Shape of the Future

Since the dramatic events began unfolding during the last quarter of 1989 in Eastern Europe, the international system has changed radically in ways that no one suspected at the time. The result has indeed been a "sea change" in the rules of international relations, as fundamental as the changes that normally attend the outcomes of major hot wars.

The shape of the future, so murky five years ago, has begun to become clear. In some ways the successor system—for which we have yet to devise a title—represents a radical departure from the system it supersedes; in other ways, it is not so different at all.

The clearly radical change is the essential disappearance of the old Second World and hence the ideological, political, and military confrontation it spawned. Remnants remain: the anti-Marxist Leninists continue to rule China, and isolated Socialist regimes hang on tenuously in a few other places. They all look progressively anachronistic. Another part of the radical change has been to leave international relationists with a vocabulary that does not describe the system: terms such as "tight" and "loose bipolarity" or "multipolarity" are curiously inappropriate depictions of the contemporary scene.

With the Second World removed from the equation, what remains is familiar: the First and Third Worlds (our First and Second Tiers) have endured, as have the relations within and between the tiers. Lifting the Cold War veil simply brings the remaining elements into sharper focus, devoid of the distorting and diverting influence of the Cold War competition.

In a very real sense, the revolutions of 1989 were more effects than causes of change. The paralysis in East–West military relations that was economically draining both superpowers had been in place for a decade or more, making continuation of an East–West "confrontation" increasingly hollow and meaningless. Marshall Shulman was entirely correct in typifying the relationship as a "dance of the dinosaurs"[1]; the problem was how to stop the music.

Breaking the Cold War required the incentive to do so; for the Soviets that incentive came in the form of their economic crisis. As Western nations embraced the Third Industrial Revolution and raced ahead into greater growth and economic prosperity, a stultified Soviet society lagged further and further behind. As parts of the Soviet intelligentsia and at least some politicians recognized their dilemma and its consequences for continued superpower status, the appeal for fundamental change—including all the risks that change entails—became increasingly compelling. The only way to break into the dynamics of the new technologically based system was to renounce Stalinism and the Cold War, just as Andrei Sakharov had warned in 1970.

The pace and extent of change have been intellectually and physically breathtaking. That a nation-state the size and importance of the Soviet Union would simply dissolve itself into fifteen successor states without bloodshed was beyond our conception. That an operational idea like communism—whose strength and vitality were being widely extolled as it was about to disintegrate—would simply disappear without a eulogy was overwhelming. Russian democracy, despite its tumultuous aspects, was an oxymoron when Gorbachev suggested it; yet here it is.

This unpredicted (future historians will have to decide if it was unpredictable) cascade of events has left observers dumbfounded and tentative. The most basic yet least realized reason for this tentativeness is the enormous dynamism of change created by the revolution in high technology. Its effects have been discussed in previous pages and need not be repeated. Three aspects of this impact, however, demonstrate why it is so difficult to predict where technology is leading the system. Cumulatively, these factors indicate that no one really understands the totality of the impact or the direction of change associated with technology.

First, the pace of technology-driven change is so rapid as virtually to defy comprehension. If one goes back no more than a decade, the explosion in knowledge production and dissemination that underlies high technology was virtually nonexistent. Phenomena such as the stateless corporation were impossible because the communications tools needed to manage truly global enterprises were unavailable. If such capabilities came into being in a decade, what will the future hold in the decade to come? More important, what will the unforeseen consequences be?

Second, high technology is occurring simultaneously across a broad range of activities that make keeping up with all of it extraordinarily difficult. Moreover, the highly technical nature of many of these advances makes them opaque to the policy community, which scarcely understands even small parts of the whole, much less the whole itself. Spearheaded by Vice President Gore, the Clinton administration has attempted to organize and understand these dynamics and to reverse this situation through constructs like the information superhighway.

Third, the rapidity and scope of change have far outstripped any policy guidance or framework for dealing with change. To repeat an example, it is becoming apparent that the next generation of supercomputers will have as their communications and operational centers (or work stations) HDTVs, making preeminence in that technology tantamount to leadership in the technology race itself. The rapidity of technological change generally, however, suggests that the preeminence that HDTV currently affords may well be overcome in short order by some new technological strain.

This is all to say that our collective cognitive capacity has been overwhelmed by the pace of change. Technology is changing the environment faster than we can comprehend, faster than we are able to judge its impact on reality.

The area of new materials technology, one of the derivative technologies of the high-technology revolution, illustrates this point. To the lay observer, this may seem a prosaic area; in fact, progress in new materials chemistry and physics may alter fundamentally the way people live and some long-held precepts of international relations and national security.

Advances in this scientific area are rapidly reaching the point of freeing humankind from a dependence on natural resources. Two scientists describe the situation in a way that is both so breathtaking yet matter-of-fact as to warrant quotation:

> For most of history we have been constrained by the materials produced by nature, modified by our intelligence and artifice. *We are now able to select the properties we desire in a material and have it engineered to order.* [Emphasis added.][2]

In other words, modern materials science will allow us—figuratively, of course—to produce just about anything from just about anything, without reference to the presence or absence of some naturally produced material. The dream of the alchemist has been realized.

The potential effects of this scientific advance on international relations has not even been considered, largely, I suspect, because most students of international relations are unfamiliar with and overwhelmed by technology. Yet what does this breakthrough portend for traditional notions of geopolitics, all of which have some element dealing with access to natural resources? What does it mean for a resource-poor country like Japan to be able to produce materials with all the properties of the best steel without having iron ore? If science can produce fuel without petroleum, what happens to the leverage of the Persian Gulf states on the international order? The possibilities are endless.

Stating that the problem is difficult is no excuse for not trying to divine the shape of the future; rather, it means the effort must be somewhat tentative and subject to amendment. Within those limitations, this discussion proceeds, looking first at some ways in which power balances are likely to be changed in the new system, then at some issues with which the new system will have to come to grips, and ending with some possibilities for the future.

The Changing Power Balance

The power map of the world will continue to change in at least three fundamental ways that will define the transformation from one kind of international system to another. The first aspect of that change is the distribution and nature of power: Which states have the most power? The second aspect deals with what kinds of power can and cannot be employed effectively to serve national interests. The third aspect has to do with the limits of power: will states be more or less effective in their application of the tools of power to national ends? Each of these questions has been addressed in describing a world of tiers. What follows is an attempt to systematize and project the implications into the future.

The Distribution of Power

There are two important parts of the question of the distribution of power. On the one hand, there is change in the military equation. The

Cold War international system was distinguished by the military confrontation between the two superpowers, which was made more antagonistic by the fact that the United States and the Soviet Union had opposing world views which they sought to promote globally. In this situation, military force occupied center stage, and military threats were central to power relationships.

The end of the Cold War defused this system. Exhausted by the competition, the Soviets and later the Russians and other successor states have pulled back militarily, both literally and figuratively. The size—and, one suspects, the quality—of Russian and other successor state forces have been slashed. Even if somehow they could be aggregated under the banner of the CIS, they would be a mere shadow of the forces of the old union. In the meantime, the Russians and the others prepare militarily to deter or repel one another (especially Russians), and the Russians prepare to rescue other Russians living outside Russia. In the absence of significant change, it is hard to imagine Russia projecting conventional military forces outside of the boundaries of the old Soviet Union, although many in Eastern Europe worry about the prospect, and this fuels their interest in NATO.

It is different for the United States. The end of the Cold War has relieved the United States of the need to maintain forces of a counterbalancing size and nature to former Soviet forces. The result is a process of active-duty force reduction from a Cold War level of about 2.1 million in uniform to a Clinton administration projection of 1.4 million by the end of 1995. Despite debates about how much is too much in cutbacks, the United States remains the only military and economic superpower: not the hegemon but the most central player.

Although Russian–American balance will hardly be the dominating characteristic of the post–Cold War system, the two powers will remain major global military powers. This is so partially because, even with START reductions, the two retain the world's largest and most potent nuclear forces. Since nuclear weapons cannot be disinvented, and since the knowledge of how to build them has spread to the Second Tier, nuclear disarmament is a hollow and reversible gesture. Since nuclear weapons have indeed created necessary peace, they clearly have had some utility, and their continuing presence can serve as a mind-clarifying reminder of potential consequences to those who might upset the peace. The image of Saddam Hussein and his chemical arsenal comes immediately to mind as someone for whom necessary peace needed enforcing.

At a slightly more subtle level, continued nuclear balance will likely be of tremendous symbolic importance to the Russians in the future—possibly more so than in the past. Nuclear weapons possession was the passkey to major-power status in the past; although economic measures will likely have more prominence as status symbols in the future, nuclear weapons remain a potent symbol of great-power status. This symbolism is likely to be more important to the Russians if their economic decline is not swiftly reversed, as no one thinks it will be in the near term. Especially in light of revived nationalism at least partly fueled by the embarrassment of perceived decline as a global power, it makes no sense to add to that embarrassment by trying to deprive or downplay Russia's claim to major-power status based on nuclear weapons possession.

The second part of the distribution equation has to do with the balance of power between the tiers. The absence of superpower military confrontation does not mean that military power will lose its salience in the new order. As long as the new order fails to coopt all member states, there will be those who will challenge the status quo and who, as a result, will have to be brought to heel. The example of regional conflict, as in the Iraqi invasion and annexation of Kuwait in August 1990, with the threat of Iraqi chemical-weapon–tipped ballistic missiles looming in the background, is an adequate reminder that the world remains a militarily dangerous place where force must sometimes be used.

Does the international response to Iraqi aggression provide a glimpse of the future, or the conclusion of a Cold War past? By invading Kuwait and threatening the Kingdom of Saudi Arabia, Saddam Hussein challenged the evolving order. In the past, he might have been constrained by his former Soviet "allies"; in the future he may well be constrained by a collective security system in which the United States and possibly Russia are the bulwarks. In the interim, he gambled. His action was found unacceptable and resulted in the assembly of a remarkable coalition of states led by the United States and several Arab states to frustrate his further ambitions.

The Iraqi invasion of Kuwait and the international reaction it spawned activated and energized the United Nations as well; the assemblage of forces in Saudi Arabia resembled a collective security action (as envisaged in the U.N. Charter) of a kind not seen since the 1960 Congo (Zaire) operation. The effort, at least in the immediate aftermath of the Gulf War, was to elevate the role of the United Nations as a central actor in the collective security system, with particular emphasis on policing the Second Tier. Boutros-Ghali spoke effusively of "empowering" the world organization to enforce the peace.[3] The United Nations' difficulties in Somalia in 1993 cooled that ardor considerably, but the United Nation remains a potential player in the evolving peace and security system.

Certainly, it is not difficult at all to envision future joint American–Russian military agreements on how to stem regional conflicts in the Second Tier. And while it is doubtless true that military force is not as easily "translated into influence"[4] as in the past, major-power military might is likely to be harnessed progressively for enforcement—much as those who drafted the United Nations Charter envisaged in a world of Soviet–American cooperation.

Military bipolarity will largely disappear in the future. The size of forces possessed by the superpowers will undoubtedly shrink, partly because they will no longer have the justification of joint opposition, and partly because shrinkage will allow diversion of resources to other problems. At the same time, the United States and Russia will continue to be distinguished by the size and sophistication of their forces, especially their retention of nuclear arsenals much larger than those possessed by anyone else. In nonnuclear terms, the United States will be the only power with global reach; Russia will, for a time, be more regionally focused.

The Effectiveness of Power

The military balance is likely to be progressively overshadowed by economic internationalization featuring the progressive evolution of the global economy where a United States-led NAFTA, the European Community, and Japan (possibly in greater cooperation with an APEC-based regional arrangement) are the major players within the dominant First Tier. Some aspects of this relationship will be competitive—if not openly adversarial—and the degree to which globalization spreads to successive subtiers of the Second Tier will be an important factor in global stability. Joseph S. Nye, Jr., concluded that "the real problems of a post-cold-war world will not be new challenges for hegemony, but the new challenges of trans-national interdependence."[5]

The economic element of power is attractive in several ways. At one level, the possessor of technological superiority will have processes, products, and knowledge that, if transferred to other states, could add measurably to the prosperity of those on the receiving end. A number of the ASEAN states, for instance, have benefited from the importation of Japanese and Western assembly plants based on CAD/CAM (see chapter 3) and other computer-based processes. The use of economic carrots can be a powerful tool for coopting Second Tier states into the evolving system's First Tier.

Economic preeminence also hits close to home. The states that are most competitive will also be the most prosperous, leading Edward Luttwak, in his assessment of the new world of "geo-economics," to suggest that the goal of geo-economic activity "could only be to provide the best possible employment for the largest proportion of the population."[6]

The most important question about economic globalization is whether it will engender cooperation or conflict among the First Tier states and between those powers and the rest of the world. Economic competition, after all, has led to some of history's great military conflicts, and it is not prima facie evident that an economically intertwined world is necessarily a more tranquil world. Many of the optimistic predictions about the effects of interdependence were also made before World War I, after all, although in admittedly different political circumstances.

There are, however, hopeful signs. First, the internationalization of the global economy has in fact intertwined the world's economies to an extent never seen before. The stateless corporation is the best example of this. At the same time, the large-scale adoption of market economics, political democracy, and activity in the Third Industrial Revolution is enormously homogenizing for the First Tier. Kenichi Ohmae, long a proponent of the beneficial effects of what he calls the "borderless economy," argues that the new order will have two major characteristics—global commonality in terms of economic values, and regional differences culturally.[7] Moreover, conflict is bad for business in the sense that interruptions work against overall prosperity, so another characteristic of what Francis Fukuyama calls the "common marketization" of the international system is "the diminution of the likelihood of large-scale conflicts between states."[8] The tranquillity of the First Tier, in other words, is likely to deepen.

All this suggests that economic globalization will likely be much less confrontational than was military bipolarity during the Cold War. The confrontational aspect of military bipolarity was enlivened by an ideological division that has largely disappeared. In the economically advanced world (the First Tier), there is no philosophical disagreement equivalent to communism–anticommunism to embitter the competition. Certainly there will continue to be disagreements on matters such as terms and balances of trade, but they are likely to be marginal rather than central to the overall system. The likely dynamic is "no longer a collaboration for the sake of military security, but collaboration for the sake of growth, prosperity, and stability."[9]

The larger question is about the relationship between the major economic players and the rest of the world. It is possible that some of the newly emerging Eastern European democracies and even some Soviet successor states will be able to overcome formidable obstacles to absorption into the general prosperity. The admission price for cooptation, as noted, is adherence to the principles of the new order—political democracy and market economics. In the case of formerly Communist Europe, the questions revolve around, not whether they want to be included or whether they are welcome, but whether these countries can overcome the barriers to association and how long the process will take.

It is not so clear what the relationship between the old First and Third Worlds will be. Very few Second Tier countries can meet the dual criteria being applied to Eastern Europe: only a few have been political democracies long enough to have great confidence in the permanence of democratic institutions (India, for instance), and only some Pacific Rim and South American countries have economic philosophies or economic systems that are congruent with the evolving order.

The case is most severe in the Islamic Middle East, where religious and cultural barriers are added. Many of the tenets of market economics, such as the concept of interest, are at odds with strict Islamic thought; traditional Islamic theocracy and Western political democracy are political belief systems out of tune with one another. It is difficult to envision how states of that region can be brought into the new order without the serious compromise of deeply held beliefs.

Whether or not cooptation occurs is also partly a matter of the second aspect of power—its effectiveness. In the old order, the Soviet Union and the United States deterred one another with nuclear threats, the Soviet Union exercised military power to keep its bloc in line, and elsewhere, before the rise of Japan and Germany, American economic hegemony meant the United States normally had its way. None of these conditions obviously hold in the future.

The effective employment of military power is likely to be more specialized in the future. With great-power confrontation nullified, conflicts such as they occur are likely either to be between regional powers (India–Pakistan, Iran–Iraq), between regional powers and major powers often acting in concert (the coalition formed against Iraq after its invasion of Kuwait), or wars *within* states (the ongoing struggle in what is left of Somalia, or the Shining Path in Peru). While some of these will be exceedingly dangerous because of the kinds of weapons now available in parts of the Second Tier, they do not threaten the system in the way the prospect of global nuclear war has. In some cases, such as Cambodia, they may produce a united international response.

This also means that military force possessed by major powers will be of a narrower utility. In the past, its major purposes were deterring strategic nuclear war or "conventional" war in Europe, or, should deterrence fail, fighting such wars. At a somewhat lesser level were so-called low-intensity conflicts in the Second Tier. Because there was never any evidence that superpower military force deterred anyone from starting an insurgency in a Second Tier country, the utility of force was in influencing the outcome.

The strategic nuclear and NATO missions have dissolved with the end of the Cold War. Some European-based security system (as discussed in chapter 6) will undoubtedly evolve in the place of NATO and the Warsaw Pact. It is likely to include an American presence, because "a credible Western security system must include a United States that is militarily a first among political equals."[10] In addition, the major powers need to find ways to isolate and solve such diverse phenomena as regional conflicts between Second Tier states, internal conflicts (insurgencies and counterinsurgencies), and specialized problems such as terrorism and the narcotics trade.

In this world of constrained military power, the economic element will be more important. Preeminence, as has been argued above, will fall to those who demonstrate the greatest competitiveness: those who demonstrate the capacity to innovate, to excel on the cutting edge of science and its application to technology and the commercialization of technology, and to seize opportunities to engage in economic opportunism, often to the greater benefit of mankind. The symbolic "battlefields" of this competition are clear as well. The competition is defined in areas such as microelectronics, telecommunications, biotechnology, advanced materials, avionics, robotics, computer software, and machine tools. Those who excel will prosper and have influence; those who fail will not. This is a visible way in which the First Tier can, if it chooses, positively influence the Second Tier.

Unfortunately, the exercise of economic power is not as simple as older conceptions based in military power. First, there is disagreement about what kind of economic competition exists. There are those, successors to the early advocates of economic interdependence, who argue that economic globalization is making the world more secure and less violence prone, because the intertwining of economies worldwide makes nations more alike and more dependent upon one another. Put another way, capitalist democracies rarely fight one another; this is partly because free peoples seldom freely choose war. Moreover—economic imperialistic arguments notwithstanding—war is good business only for a few, and interdependence compromises the independent ability to construct a comprehensive war machine.

The other side of the argument is not so optimistic. It holds that "foreign policy and national security now depend upon science and technology policy to a degree not seen since the advent of nuclear weapons."[11] In this view, scientific and technological competitiveness hold the keys to both economic and military preeminence, because so many of the new technologies are dual use. This problem, of course, is especially poignant for the Russians.

The second difficulty in thinking about the application of economic power is in measurement. This has two aspects. On the one hand, standard measures of preeminence are generally the aggregates of firm or sector preeminence, and international ownership and control make the translation to national advantage more difficult. To say, for instance, that the United States has an advantage (which it does) in mainframe computers is really to say that American-based firms such as IBM or Cray have an advantage. With clearly American firms, the U.S. government can transform this advantage into national leverage through influences such as contracts; faced with the stateless corporations, the basis of control for national ends is not at all clear.

The second aspect relates to the internationalization of economic activity. As privatization of economic activity increases, and multilateral ownership, management, and production increase, it will be more difficult to determine which countries have an economic advantage. To cite a prominent popular example, it is generally conceded that the Japanese have had great advantages in the automobile industry. But as U.S. corporations buy more shares in the Japanese automobile industry and more Japanese firms produce their cars in the United States, it becomes increasingly difficult to see how this translates into any exploitable power advantage for Japan.

As economic globalization occurs, what is more likely is that large economic trading blocks, with international intertwining among firms in the First Tier, will come to dominate the international economic scene.[12] In this sense, the combination of the major countries will gain increasing leverage over those in the Second Tier, but there will be relatively little power advantage among the members. Thus, economic power may evolve into a lever between the "haves" and the "have-nots," a familiar distinction. The major uncertainty in the new system is whether or not the old Second World (or parts thereof) will be able somehow to wriggle its way onto the list of beneficiaries.

The Limits of Power

Our discussion has anticipated the final aspect of the changing power balance, the limits of power. As the preceding discussion has at least suggested, the application of power in the new international system is going to be more subtle and more constrained than has been the case in the past. The brutish application of power has not disappeared, nor will it vanish quickly; Saddam Hussein clearly demonstrated that the thugs remain, as did North Korea's Kim il-Sung and others. However, it is also becoming more difficult to engage in loutish displays of force, and that trend will continue, for at least three reasons.

The first has to do with military force. Thanks in no small measure to necessary peace and the breakdown of the Cold War it helped activate, there are now sizable parts of the world—certainly the First Tier—where the use of force to solve problems among the member states has vanished as an option. As the Second World of former Socialist states blends into the new order, the residues of ethnic difficulties within the newly democratic states could lead to internal violence and instability. Yugoslavia is the prime example, but there are others in

Eastern Europe as well. A long-term result of the international reaction to Iraqi aggression in 1990 is that it will send a message that military force will not be tolerated in regional conflicts that affect the well-being of the First Tier.

That leaves the vestiges of Second Tier conflict as situations where military force remains a viable and usable option. In this part of the world, the major powers have not yet defined interests beyond the 1970s' and 1980s' competition for influence, although the Clinton administration's announcement in January 1994 of stringent guidelines for participation suggest a self-limiting role. These kinds of conflicts—regional wars, insurgencies, terrorism, narcoterrorism—will challenge the stability of the new international order, not by raising the specter of war between North and South, but by interrupting the more general tranquility. While serious, they pale beside the nuclear competition of the early Cold War days.

Second, the translation of the economic interests into meaningful power is made much more difficult by global intertwining that is "rendering it increasingly difficult to define just what constitutes the national interest."[13] Beyond the obvious constraints that internationalization places on national sovereign control of economic activity, however, there is an additional factor: the amazing homogenization of the globe that attends globalization. The economic values of the international economic order are universal wherever they are applied, and they create a homogeneity of economic and political outlook that moderates differences among peoples. (The Fay caning incident in Singapore reminds us that differences do not always disappear altogether.) In this sense, the interdependence theorists of the 1960s have been partially vindicated.

The third limit on power is the increasing transparency of international activity that is the direct result of the telecommunications revolution. In addition to facilitating the creation of the stateless corporation's ability to engage in global reach, the telecommunications revolution has also spawned the information revolution. In the contemporary world, international events have indeed become transparent, in the sense that there is now a global information society from which it is exceedingly difficult to hide the raw application of power. Stalin's purges and the atrocities of the Holocaust, to cite the most extreme examples, simply could not have been hidden from the contemporary world; there are simply too many camcorders and satellite dishes. If brutishness and bestiality cannot be hidden, they cannot be sustained for long. In this light, the Chinese action at Tiananmen Square was the beginning of the last hurrah for the thugs; only in the most isolated places is such behavior possible, and that will not last for long.

Issues for the Future Order

Several issues will have to be faced as a new order is assembled. From an American viewpoint, the first issue will be the reformulation of U.S. foreign policy. With the Cold War orientation of that policy overcome by events, this will require re-asking the basic question that any international construction must face: how to arrange the peace in such a way as to preserve stability.

The question of stability spawns three other issues that are direct consequences of current changes. On the one hand, the globalization of economic activity is a new phenomenon, whose political implications have not been thoroughly examined. Because globalization has prospered under the banner of privatization in a number of countries, the elevation of privatization as a principle of international relations will inevitably be advocated. This in turn raises two problems: (1) the impact on state sovereignty and the ability of the state to promote values that only the state can deal with, such as security, and (2) questions of who will regulate in the public interest.

The latter question raises the problem of international equity. Privatization, as the splurge of economic prosperity in the 1980s testifies, is a very effective system for the efficient creation of economic goods and economic expansion. That same system, however, has no inherent capabilities to deal with fairness and welfare; such ideas, part of the public agenda, are simply beyond the private agenda. The question of international equity, in turn, has to do with the inclusion of the Second Tier in the "action" of the new system.

In turn, the second issue has to do with preserving stability. There are two ways to maximize stability (minimize violent attacks aimed at altering the system): either through coercion or through cooptation of those who feel little stake in the ongoing system. In other words, will authority in the new system be based on legitimacy or coercion? In the evolving system, this boils down to the question of how to deal with the Second Tier.

The question of stability, in turn, raises the final concern, which is the nature of how or whether the new order will regulate violence and instability in the Second Tier. Within the First Tier, as already argued, the only major concern is how Europe will reorganize its security structure to accommodate or contain the crumbled communism of Eastern Europe and the former Soviet Union. The key variable in that mix is the near-term evolution of the major Soviet successor states, whose westernization process remains uncertain. Of greater concern is how to devise a security system that can attenuate or at least influence violence in the Second Tier.

The Future of U.S. Foreign Policy

The end of the Cold War has been traumatic for the intellectual base of U.S. foreign policy. In part, this is because absolutely no one saw it coming, and thus there was hardly any provision for an alternative to East–West confrontation. The geopolitical containment model of George Kennan was durable, and his prescriptions have largely been vindicated. Now that the Soviets, to borrow from Georgi Arbatov, have deprived us of an enemy, they have left us in an intellectual bind. We simply have no construct that encompasses the collapse of the opposition.

Several commentators have noted the effect of the Cold War's collapse. Sorenson, for instance, likens the current situation to the United States unexpectedly winning a lottery or being a surprise winner of an upset election,[14] and Charles William Maynes, editor of *Foreign Policy*, compares the situation to a ship that has lost its sextant.[15] The situation is particularly acute for the United States, according to Cold War critic Richard J. Barnet, because U.S. foreign policies have been defined by the Cold War "more than those of any other nation."[16]

The end of the Cold War reopens the old debate about foreign policy and the extent of American activism in the world. Within the context of the times, there are strong impulses to retreat: a domestic agenda neglected during the Cold War in areas such as infrastructure and education, a U.S. administration clearly more focused on domestic rather than on foreign policy which has added things like health and welfare reforms and crime to the domestic agenda, and reversals of foreign policy initiatives in places like Somalia.

Whether it prefers to or not, the United States cannot ignore a world that looks to and demands its leadership. The mantle of being the world's remaining superpower is also a tether that brings the United States back to center stage when it seeks to wander. The odyssey of the Clinton administration in its first year is instructive. The new president clearly prefers domestic policy, and his first six months were virtually consumed with trying to define the domestic agenda, from deficit reduction to health care reform. But foreign policy would not go away. Yitzak Rabin and Yasir Arafat came calling for an American guarantee for their peace; NAFTA, APEC, and GATT pressed the national attention, as did the crises in Somalia, Haiti, and Bosnia; January 1994 found the president winging his way to Europe, from NATO headquarters in Brussels to Prague and the Kremlin.

An evolving system from which retreat is impossible reactivates the traditional American foreign policy debate between idealists and realists. The idealists see the American role as that of exemplar, promoting the American system and its ideals globally as the best hope for a more stable order. The realists, by contrast, argue that American policy must be grounded solely in the protection and promotion of American vital interests. In the Cold War, these instincts led the idealists to a less aggressive posture. In a new system where American interests are rarely threatened but where misery abounds, the roles are largely reversed (the idealists favoring a more active stance). President Clinton has, after some early vacillation, cast his lot with the realists.

Until some determination is made about what image—realist or idealist—should dominate, U.S. foreign policy is almost certain to suffer from what former President George Bush called the "vision thing." It is difficult today to determine which principle will prevail. Critical to the question, however, is the matter of stability in the new order.

The Stability of the New Order

The stability of any international system is found in the relative balance between those who support the order and those who oppose it. Measured mainly in the relative power of the two groups, the larger the number and weight of the states supporting the system and the more powerful they are, the more likely it is that the system will be able to regulate itself peacefully. The smaller the number of supporters, the less likely is stability. In the Cold War system, the balance between those who supported the system (principally the West) and those who opposed it (the Communist world) was equal enough that no meaningful form of regulation was possible. The implosion of the Communist world, and indeed its movement toward cooptation within the dominant system, shifts the balance more strongly toward the supporters and thus provides hope for stability based in a consensus—at least among the major states and a growing number of Second Tier states who benefit from the new order.

The debate at the time the United Nations was formed is being revisited. The two images found in the charter, collective security and collective defense, were expressions of possible futures. Collective security presumed, indeed required, that overwhelming power would support stability and thus enforcement of the peace. The chief instruments were to be the triumphant allies, especially the Americans and Soviets, whose continued collaboration as the world's police would ensure the peace. When they could not agree on the shape of their future, they fell back to opposition in the form of collective defense, for which the charter also provided (Article 51; see the appendix).

In security terms, the most important aspect of the new order is that the ideological barrier to a common vision among the major powers has disappeared. As democratization continues, and *if* economic modernization occurs in the former Soviet Union and Eastern Europe, these nations will adopt the same values as the West and will develop a positive stake in the new order. The result could then be the requisite conditions for a true collective security system where the United States and Russia, with the financial backing of Germany and Japan, take the lead in organizing and enforcing the peace, *acting as partners*.

The ointment is not, of course, without flies. In the case of the evolving system, there is still opposition to the system in the form of those Second Tier states that are not included in the general prosperity and thus lack a stake in supporting the status quo. Although individually these states, primarily the regional actors, lack the physical capacity to bring down the system, they can cause trauma that would not otherwise be present. The dual facts that the plight of the outsiders is getting worse as inequalities increase and that many of the potential troublemakers are now very heavily armed with sophisticated and large supplies of arms only add to the problem.

It is not enough to talk about stability and instability within the Second Tier in the abstract. Rather, by combining Second Tier geographic regions with the six subtiers of the Second Tier and those areas where the potential for violence is greatest, one can define more pre-

Table 8.1

Second Tier Categories by Region

	Developed/ Stable	Developed/ Unstable	Resource-Rich	Partially Developed	Developable	Undevelopable
Asian and Pacific	1, 2	—	—	1, 2	—	1
Middle East	—	—	1, 2, 3	1, 2	—	—
Latin America	—	1	—	1, 2	1	—
Africa	—	—	—	1, 2	1, 2	1, 2
Formerly Communist Countries (former Soviet Union and Eastern Europe)	—	—	—	1, 2, 3	1, 2	—

1. Concentration of states
2. High violence potential
3. U.S. vital interests

cisely where the challenges to stability are greatest. Table 8.1 depicts these distinctions.

One may quibble with the precise designations, of course. Should, for instance, provision be made to place Asian countries such as Cambodia and Vietnam in the developable rather than the partially developed category? Does Haiti qualify as developable at all? What about the new South Africa (which I have omitted because its prospects are so unsettled)? Which of the formerly Communist countries (including the former Soviet Union and Eastern Europe) fall in which category?

For present purposes, the location of areas where there is potential for systemic violence is what concerns us. The table suggests three broad observations. First, among the top three subtiers, there are only two situations where major American and other First Tier interests may be involved. These, of course, are the Korean peninsula and the Persian Gulf. Second, the places with potential violence are concentrated in those countries (across the regions) that are at the partially developed level or below. Moreover, the vast majority of those situations are internal, where the efficacy of outside interference is most questionable.

Third, there are very few—if any—important First Tier interests in any of these internal conflicts. In a few cases, former colonists may retain enough residual interest (or guilt) to involve themselves in isolated situations. For the most part, however, traditional notions of vital interest are simply not engaged. This in turn limits the likelihood of significant First Tier involvement in collective security or other efforts.

Collective security, however, deals with the symptoms and not the disease. Moreover, it is only one possible organizational device for attempting to deal with the problem of peace and security. Discontent with the new order will be the result of exclusion from its benefits. If disparities continue to grow, the disease will only get worse. The ultimate solution to instability is to incorporate the dispossessed into the system. The question is whether the new order will have that capacity or that predilection.

Organizing the Peace: First and Second Tier Intersection

As has been noted already in several places, almost all the threats to tranquillity and stability in the new international order occur in select parts of the Second Tier in the form of either regional conflict or internal instability. Regional conflicts are the lesser problem numerically; internal conflicts form the core of the problem.

What will the attitude of the First Tier be toward Second Tier conflict? In one sense, the question is too broad to be answered categorically. There are, for instance, specific situations where one or a number of states might feel impelled to become involved for historical, including colonial, reasons or because some of its citizens might be placed in harm's way. Having said that, there would appear to be three broad options available.

The first is *benign neglect*—simply allowing Second Tier states to solve their own problems however they can. The principal advantage of such an approach is that it avoids entanglement in marginal places and affairs where there are problematic prospects for success and where critical public opinion will almost certainly turn on an operation of significant duration. The major disadvantage is the cold-heartedness of the approach, particularly where there is special outrage and atrocity, made very public by global television.

A second approach is *comprehensive involvement*—gearing the system and its capabilities to extinguishing violence and atrocity wherever they occur. The agency for such an approach would likely be an expanded United Nations capability, including something like a standing U.N. armed force ready to intrude when needed, whose existence would hopefully dissuade some who would break the peace. The principal disadvantages of this approach are that such a force would be terribly expensive (well beyond the resources currently available to the world body) and probably would not enjoy long-term popular support within First Tier populaces.

That leaves a third approach, *selective engagement*, as the sole standing alternative. On the face of it, willingness to engage some but not all of the time makes obvious sense: it relegates policy options to neither automatic inaction nor action, but preserves options when needed.

The question then shifts to what would trigger a selective action. The U.S. government, in the wake of Bosnia and Somalia, has grappled with this problem and come up with some stringent guidelines (described below). For the broader First Tier, however, there would seem to be two major concerns.

The first is the matter of interests involved. Traditional calculations of vital interest (situations and outcomes to which one would not willingly accede because of their negative effect on the national interest) will not, as argued, impel action often. The only way that interests will activate international action is by broadening the definition of what is worth fighting about. Within the past year or so, terms like "humanitarian interests" and even "humanitarian vital interests" have entered discussions, suggesting that the international community has an inherent vital stake in protecting and promoting the interests of humankind.[17] Boutros-Ghali has been a particular proponent of this view.

The other concern is how much of a stake the system has in overall stability. This is dual-faced. On the one hand, it asks how much particular outbreaks of violence threaten systemic stability. As argued, the answer is, normally not much, when that violence occurs in the Second Tier. On the other hand, it asks how much sacrifice First Tier countries are willing to endure in the name of stability. The answer again is, probably not much, as inaction to the 1994 carnage in Rwanda amply demonstrated.

The willingness or unwillingness of the First Tier to become involved in Second Tier violence also depends crucially on the kinds of politicomilitary situations for which action is contemplated. Setting aside regional conflicts, the internal situations that can be candidates for international involvements come in two varieties.

The first and easiest variety includes traditional *peacekeeping* missions of the kind frequently mounted by the United Nations in the past. These are relatively straightforward: a small, lightly armed United Nations force is interposed between two formerly warring parties that have agreed to a ceasefire and have also agreed to accept the force. The peacekeeper's function is to provide a shield between the parties to facilitate their reaching a permanent political settlement (although that may take a long time). As such, the peacekeeper must be a strictly neutral party who has the respect of all parties.

Most real Second Tier situations, however, are not of this sort—at least not when action may be deemed necessary. Rather, the situations are typically ongoing wars between factions within a country, often marked by atrocity and great human suffering, where the underlying political problem (which must be solved if peace is to occur) is control of the nation-state. Because one side or the other is winning and thus benefiting from the violence, that side is unlikely to appreciate interference that seeks to end the violence (unless the terms are overwhelmingly in its favor). Rwanda, again, is an extreme case in point.

These situations call for what the United Nations calls *peace enforcement*, the restoration of peace. It is a curiously inappropriate sobriquet, because it assumes there is a peace to enforce when there typically is not. The situation might be better described as *peace imposition*, the use of armed force to create peace between warring parties, a dynamic not unlike pulling apart two drunks fighting in a barroom.

Peace imposition is entirely unlike peacekeeping. First, peace imposition involves making war, not reinforcing peace. Second, peace imposers are not the invited guests of all involved, and the longer they stay, the more unpopular they become. Third, whether they intend to be or not, peace imposers are partisans, because their actions will inevitably strengthen one side or the other. Fourth, peace imposition must go beyond creating a peace to stimulating a viable political settlement on which an enduring peace can be built, which is inherently difficult and may be beyond the capacity of even the most dedicated outsiders.

Problems arise when situations are mistaken and the wrong kind of force is proposed or dispatched. Bosnia, for instance, has required peace imposition, but a classic peacekeeping force has been on the ground there proving perfectly impotent in a situation for which it was not designed. It is little wonder that the peacekeepers became disillusioned. The same dynamic, admittedly at a lower level of violence, has been the case in Somalia.

The difficulty is that there are no current mechanisms to make peace imposition decisions. This may well be because there is no international consensus that peace imposition is an activity to which the First Tier is committed. The United Nations Security Council can be, and has been over the past two or three years, the authorizing agency, but for a variety of organizational, financial, and philosophical (most U.N. personnel are opposed to armed violence) reasons, its propriety is suspect. The only other major First Tier security mechanism is NATO (or its long-term successor), but NATO has never been united outside the European theater; its inaction in its own backyard (Bosnia) raises concern about whether NATO could ever be useful in the Second Tier.

The role of the United States is critical. With the United States the remaining superpower, its acquiescence or support is critical for any major operation. Militarily, the United States has the only airlift and sealift capability that can project a sizable force in a short time. It is altogether possible that the United States will self-limit its involvement to transport and possibly intelligence and close air support, where needed. Economically, the United States pays approximately one-third of the bill for U.N. operations; unless the funding formula is amended (possibly as the result of giving permanent seats and vetoes on the Security Council to Germany and Japan), U.S. support will be needed.

The Clinton administration has announced stringent guidelines for its participation in peace imposition actions. The general conditions include a clear threat to international security, a major disaster requiring urgent relief, a gross violation of human rights, the guarantee that other important states would participate in any effort, and American operational control over all American forces. Moreover, traditional vital interests must be involved, and the planning process must be clear and explicit in terms of interests, prospects for success, cost, the ability to disengage, and public support.

The system's attitudes toward involvement in Second Tier situations is evolving. The year 1992 witnessed a spate of activity, whose ardor has cooled visibly in the face of the growth pains of the new system and the forces, including freedom and democracy, that it unleashed. How long the First Tier can let nature take its course or when it will feel impelled to change that course remains to be determined.

Resolving the Dilemma

We are left with a dilemma of sorts. The democratization of the international system that has been a major outcome of the revolutions of 1989 has created the possibility of a peaceful and stable order if the benefits of the First Tier can be extended to the Second. Only those who are conspicuously omitted from the general prosperity will have important incentives to overturn that order. If they can be coopted into having a stake in the game, then the prospects of general stability are enhanced.

The market system, however, which has been conceptually and functionally responsible for the prosperity, lacks the values of equity necessary to perform the cooptation. A globalized economy cannot deal by itself with the system's "losers," those who lack a stake in maintaining the stability and integrity of the system. Indeed, the gap from the top to the bottom will widen and become more intolerable to those on the lower rungs of the Second Tier that are unattractive to the market-based economic system. Even if Second Tier states desire to create the conditions necessary to enter the mainstream, it is unlikely that many can do so without considerable assistance from a source outside the value system of private enterprise.[18]

Fortunately, this dilemma is, in theory, resolvable. Prosperity and stability, after all, go hand in hand, with each nurturing the other. Providing developmental assistance to Second Tier countries and extending the benefits of market democracy may go beyond market values, but the creation of larger and more stable markets does not. By analogy, one of the great potential benefits of the end of the Cold War as perceived by Europeans is the prospect of the vast, largely untapped markets in Eastern Europe. The prospect of tapping those markets gives an actuarial—rather than a welfarist—basis for developmental assistance. Although the development of those markets will clearly take time, even longer in the case of those Second Tier states with the greatest instability, it is quite possible that even a privatized international order can evolve, through national and international political institutions, a set of equity values based firmly in self-interest.

A Hopeful Ending

Given the rush of events that began in 1989, it is impossible not to end on a note of some optimism. The events highlighted by change in the former Soviet Union and Eastern Europe have transformed the texture of international relations in ways that no one predicted even two or three years before the process began.

The revolutions were only obvious in retrospect. A few saw necessary peace as a stabilizing force in nuclear relations, but no one was bold enough to suggest that necessary peace had rendered the other symbols of the Cold War so hollow that the whole artifice could be easily swept aside, leaving hardly a trace. Some of the old structures linger because they are large and came with no disassembly instructions. Yet, even among those who defend the continuation of Cold War instruments such as NATO, the old justifications have simply vanished with stunning speed.

The impact of technology and economic internationalization has not been so easy to digest. Everyone is touched by the impact of the new technologies in day-to-day life, but the pace of change is so great as to defy capture. Since the impacts have apparently been beneficial, there has also been no great incentive to define the consequences in public terms, either national or international. Understanding technologically induced change and harnessing technology to solve the problems of the evolving order will clearly be major agenda items in the new international system.

The outcomes of the future are, of course, never clear until one gets there, but one cannot avoid some controlled optimism. The second half of the twentieth century has been, in large measure, a period of American might and hegemony. That condition has been modified, but the hope, even the promise, of the revolutions of 1989 may be the triumph of the American ideal of economic and political freedom.

It is indeed both the best and the worst of times. It is the best because the international system has been relieved of the enormous threat and burden of a nuclear-war potential Cold War, and because the glow of First Tier market democracy has begun to spread across the globe. It is in some ways the worst because the glow has not spread universally, because great uncertainties remain about the fates of people around the world, and because the ugly stain of violence remains the norm in many places. Nonetheless, the world looks far better today than it did a decade ago, when none of the changes described here had even begun. And that is something.

Notes

1. Marshall D. Shulman, "The Superpowers: Dance of the Dinosaurs," *Foreign Affairs, 66,* 3 (Winter 1987–88): 491–515.

2. Joseph Finkelstein and David Newman, "The Third Industrial Revolution," in Joseph Finkelstein (ed.), *Windows on a New World: The Third Industrial Revolution* (Westport, CT: Greenwood Press, 1989), 219.

3. Boutros Boutros-Ghali, "Empowering the United Nations," *Foreign Affairs, 72,* 5 (Winter 1992–93): 89–102.

4. Richard J. Barnet, "Reflections (The Age of Globalization)," *New Yorker* (June 16, 1990), 53.

5. Joseph S. Nye, Jr., "The Changing Nature of World Power," *Political Science Quarterly 105,* 2 (Summer 1990): 192.

6. Edward N. Luttwak, "From Geopolitics to Geo-Economics: Logic of Conflict, Grammar of Commerce," *National Interest, 20* (Summer 1990): 19.

7. Kenichi Ohmae, "Beyond Fiction to Fact: The Borderless Economy," *New Perspectives Quarterly, 7,* 2 (Spring 1990): 20.

8. Francis Fukuyama, "The End of History?" *National Interest, 16* (Summer 1989): 18.

9. Zbigniew Brzezinski, "Europe and Amerippon: Pillars of the New World Order," *New Perspectives Quarterly, 7,* 2 (Spring 1990): 19.

10. Peter Tarnoff, "America's New Special Relationships," *Foreign Affairs, 69,* 3 (Summer 1990): 73–74.

11. John P. Cregan, "Building an American Consensus: A National Interest Trade Policy," *Vital Speeches of the Day, 56,* 16 (June 1, 1990): 509.

12. This point is strongly made by Preston Townley, "Going Global in the 1990s," *Vital Speeches of the Day, 56,* 19 (July 15, 1990): 589–93.

13. Cregan, "Building an American Consensus," 511–12.

14. Theodore C. Sorensen, "Rethinking National Security," *Foreign Affairs, 69,* 3 (Summer 1990), 5.

15. Charles William Maynes, "America without the Cold War," *Foreign Policy, 78* (Spring 1990): 5.

16. Barnet, "Reflections," 47.

17. Much of the material in this section is taken from Donald M. Snow, *Peacekeeping, Peacemaking and Peace Enforcement: The U.S. Role in the New International Order* (Carlisle Barracks, PA: Strategic Studies Institute, 1993).

18. Charles Wolf, Jr., "The Third World in U.S.–Soviet Competition," Rand Paper P-7625 (Santa Monica, CA: RAND Corporation, February 1990), 3.

Key Security Provisions of the United Nations Charter

In the evolving new international order, the United Nations may gain new importance. Pertinent sections of the U.N. Charter are presented below. International operations against Iraq and in Somalia and Haiti, for example, were authorized by U.N. resolutions pursuant to Chapter 7 of the Charter.

CHAPTER I

PURPOSES AND PRINCIPLES

Article 1

The Purposes of the United Nations are:

1. To maintain international peace and security, and to that end: to take effective collective measures for the prevention and removal of threats to the peace, and for the suppression of acts of aggression or other breaches of the peace, and to bring about by peaceful means, and in conformity with the principles of justice and international law, adjustment or settlement of international disputes or situations which might lead to a breach of the peace;

2. To develop friendly relations among nations based on respect for the principle of equal rights and self-determination of peoples, and to take other appropriate measures to strengthen universal peace;

3. To achieve international co-operation in solving international problems of an economic, social, cultural or humanitarian character, and in promoting and encouraging respect for human rights and for fundamental freedoms for all without distinction as to race, sex, language or religion; and

4. To be a centre for harmonizing the actions of nations in the attainment of these common ends.

Article 2

The Organization and its Members, in pursuit of the Purposes stated in Article 1, shall act in accordance with the following Principles:

1. The Organization is based on the principle of the sovereign equality of all its Members.

2. All Members, in order to ensure to all of them the rights and benefits resulting from membership, shall fulfil in good faith the obligations assumed by them in accordance with the present Charter.

3. All Members shall settle their international disputes by peaceful means in such a manner that international peace and security, and justice, are not endangered.

4. All Members shall refrain in their international relations from the threat or use of force against the territorial integrity or political independence of any state, or in any other manner inconsistent with the Purposes of the United Nations.

5. All Members shall give the United Nations every assistance in any action it takes in accordance with the present Charter, and shall refrain from giving assistance to any state against which the United Nations is taking preventive or enforcement action.

6. The Organization shall ensure that states which are not Members of the United Nations act in accordance with these Principles so far as may be necessary for the maintenance of international peace and security.

7. Nothing contained in the present Charter shall authorize the United Nations to intervene in matters which are essentially within the domestic jurisdiction of any state or shall require the Members to submit such matters to settlement under the present Charter; but this principle shall not prejudice the application of enforcement measures under Chapter VII.

CHAPTER VI

PACIFIC SETTLEMENT OF DISPUTES

Article 33

1. The parties to any dispute, the continuance of which is likely to endanger the maintenance of international peace and security, shall, first of all, seek a solution by negotiation, enquiry, mediation, conciliation, arbitration, judicial settlement, resort to regional agencies or arrangements, or other peaceful means of their own choice.

2. The Security Council shall, when it deems necessary, call upon the parties to settle their dispute by such means.

Article 34

The Security Council may investigate any dispute, or any situation which might lead to international friction or give rise to a dispute, in order to determine whether the continuance of the dispute or situation is likely to endanger the maintenance of international peace and security.

Article 35

1. Any Member of the United Nations may bring any dispute, or any situation of the nature referred to in Article 34, to the attention of the Security Council or of the General Assembly.

2. A state which is not a Member of the United Nations may bring to the attention of the Security Council or of the General Assembly any dispute to which it is a party if it accepts in advance, for the purposes of the dispute, the obligations of pacific settlement provided in the present Charter.

3. The proceedings of the General Assembly in respect of matters brought to its attention under this Article will be subject to the provisions of Articles 11 and 12.

Article 36

1. The Security Council may, at any stage of a dispute of the nature referred to in Article 33 or of a situation of like nature, recommend appropriate procedures or methods of adjustment.

2. The Security Council should take into consideration any procedures for the

settlement of the dispute which have already been adopted by the parties.

3. In making recommendations under this Article the Security Council should also take into consideration that legal disputes should as a general rule be referred by the parties to the International Court of Justice in accordance with the provisions of the Statute of the Court.

Article 37

1. Should the parties to a dispute of the nature referred to in Article 33 fail to settle it by the means indicated in that Article, they shall refer it to the Security Council.

2. If the Security Council deems that the continuance of the dispute is in fact likely to endanger the maintenance of international peace and security, it shall decide whether to take action under Article 36 or to recommend such terms of settlement as it may consider appropriate.

Article 38

Without prejudice to the provisions of Articles 33 to 37, the Security Council may, if all the parties to any dispute so request, make recommendations to the parties with a view to a pacific settlement of the dispute.

CHAPTER VII

ACTION WITH RESPECT TO THREATS TO THE PEACE, BREACHES OF THE PEACE, AND ACTS OF AGGRESSION

Article 39

The Security Council shall determine the existence of any threat to the peace, breach of the peace, or act of aggression and shall make recommendations, or decide what measures shall be taken in accordance with Articles 41 and 42, to maintain or restore international peace and security.

Article 40

In order to prevent an aggravation of the situation, the Security Council may, before making the recommendations or deciding upon the measures provided for in Article 39, call upon the parties concerned to comply with such provisional measures as it deems necessary or desirable. Such provisional measures shall be without prejudice to the rights, claims or position of the parties concerned. The Security Council shall duly take account of failure to comply with such provisional measures.

Article 41

The Security Council may decide what measures not involving the use of armed force are to be employed to give effect to its decisions, and it may call upon the Members of the United Nations to apply such measures. These may include complete or partial interruption of economic relations and of rail, sea, air, postal, telegraphic, radio and other means of communication, and the severance of diplomatic relations.

Article 42

Should the Security Council consider that measures provided for in Article 41 would be inadequate or have proved to be inadequate, it may take such action by air, sea or land forces as may be necessary to maintain or restore international peace and security. Such action may include demonstrations, blockade, and other operations by air, sea, or land forces of Members of the United Nations.

Article 43

1. All Members of the United Nations, in order to contribute to the maintenance of international peace and security, undertake to make available to the Security Council, on its call and in ac-

cordance with a special agreement or agreements, armed forces, assistance and facilities, including rights of passage, necessary for the purpose of maintaining international peace and security.

2. Such agreement or agreements shall govern the numbers and types of forces, their degree of readiness and general location, and the nature of the facilities and assistance to be provided.

3. The agreement or agreements shall be negotiated as soon as possible on the initiative of the Security Council. They shall be concluded between the Security Council and Members or between the Security Council and groups of Members and shall be subject to ratification by the signatory states in accordance with their respective constitutional processes.

Article 44

When the Security Council has decided to use force it shall, before calling upon a Member not represented on it to provide armed forces in fulfilment of the obligations assumed under Article 43, invite that Member, if the Member so desires, to participate in the decisions of the Security Council concerning the employment of contingents of that Member's armed forces.

Article 45

In order to enable the United Nations to take urgent military measures, Members shall hold immediately available national air-force contingents for combined international enforcement action. The strength and degree of readiness of these contingents and plans for their combined action shall be determined, within the limits laid down in the special agreement or agreements referred to in Article 43, by the Security Council with the assistance of the Military Staff Committee.

Article 46

Plans for the application of armed force shall be made by the Security Council with the assistance of the Military Staff Committee.

Article 47

1. There shall be established a Military Staff Committee to advise and assist the Security Council on all questions relating to the Security Council's military requirements for the maintenance of international peace and security, the employment and command of forces placed at its disposal, the regulation of armaments, and possible disarmament.

2. The Military Staff Committee shall consist of the Chiefs of Staff of the permanent members of the Security Council or their representatives. Any Member of the United Nations not permanently represented on the Committee shall be invited by the Committee to be associated with it when the efficient discharge of the Committee's responsibilities requires the participation of that Member in its work.

3. The Military Staff Committee shall be responsible under the Security Council for the strategic direction of any armed forces placed at the disposal of the Security Council. Questions relating to the command of such forces shall be worked out subsequently.

4. The Military Staff Committee, with the authorization of the Security Council and after consultation with appropriate regional agencies, may establish regional sub-committees.

Article 48

1. The action required to carry out the decisions of the Security Council for the maintenance of international peace

and security shall be taken by all the Members of the United Nations or by some of them, as the Security Council may determine.

2. Such decisions shall be carried out by the Members of the United Nations directly and through their action in the appropriate international agencies of which they are members.

Article 49

The Members of the United Nations shall join in affording mutual assistance in carrying out the measures decided upon by the Security Council.

Article 50

If preventive or enforcement measures against any state are taken by the Security Council, any other state, whether a Member of the United Nations or not, which finds itself confronted with special economic problems arising from the carrying out of those measures shall have the right to consult the Security Council with regard to a solution of those problems.

Article 51

Nothing in the present Charter shall impair the inherent right of individual or collective self-defence if an armed attack occurs against a Member of the United Nations, until the Security Council has taken measures necessary to maintain international peace and security. Measures taken by Members in the exercise of this right of self-defence shall be immediately reported to the Security Council and shall not in any way affect the authority and responsibility of the Security Council under the present Charter to take at any time such action as it deems necessary in order to maintain or restore international peace and security.

CHAPTER VIII
REGIONAL ARRANGEMENTS

Article 52

1. Nothing in the present Charter precludes the existence of regional arrangements or agencies for dealing with such matters relating to the maintenance of international peace and security as are appropriate for regional action, provided that such arrangements or agencies and their activities are consistent with the Purposes and Principles of the United Nations.

2. The Members of the United Nations entering into such arrangements or constituting such agencies shall make every effort to achieve pacific settlement of local disputes through such regional arrangements or by such regional agencies before referring them to the Security Council.

3. The Security Council shall encourage the development of pacific settlement of local disputes through such regional arrangements or by such regional agencies either on the initiative of the states concerned or by reference from the Security Council.

4. This Article in no way impairs the application of Articles 34 and 35.

Article 53

1. The Security Council shall, where appropriate, utilize such regional arrangements or agencies for enforcement action under its authority. But no enforcement action shall be taken under regional arrangements without the authorization of the Security Council, with the exception of measures against any enemy state, as defined in paragraph 2 of this Article, provided for pursuant to Article 107 or in re-

gional arrangements directed against renewal of aggressive policy on the part of any such state, until such time as the Organization may, on request of the Governments concerned, be charged with the responsibility for preventing further aggression by such a state.

2. The term enemy state as used in paragraph 1 of this Article applies to any state which during the Second World War has been an enemy of any signatory of the present Charter.

Article 54

The Security Council shall at all times be kept fully informed of activities undertaken or in contemplation under regional arrangements or by regional agencies for the maintenance of international peace and security.

Bibliography

Abshire, David. "Strategic Challenge: Force Structures, Deterrence." *Washington Quarterly, 15,* 2 (Spring 1992): 33–42.

Aganbegyan, Abel. *The Economic Challenge of Perestroika.* Bloomington: Indiana University Press, 1988.

———. "The Economics of *Perestroika.*" *International Affairs* (London), *64,* 2 (Spring 1988): 177–85.

Akhromeyev, Sergei. "The Doctrine of Averting War and Defending Peace." *World Marxist Review, 30,* 12 (December 1987): 37–47.

Alan, Ray. "Can NATO Survive Gorbachev?" *New Leader, 73,* 6 (April 16, 1990): 5–6.

Allison, Graham T., Jr. "Testing Gorbachev." *Foreign Affairs, 67,* 1 (Fall 1988): 18–32.

Arbatov, Alexei G. *Lethal Frontiers: A Soviet View of Nuclear Strategy, Weapons, and Negotiations.* New York: Praeger, 1988.

Arno, Andrew, and Winral Dissayanake. *The News Media in National and International Conflict.* Boulder, CO: Westview Press, 1984.

Aron, Leon. "The Soviet Union on the Brink: An Introductory Essay." *World Affairs, 152,* 1 (Summer 1989): 3–7.

Asmus, Ronald D., Richard L. Kugler, and F. Stephen Larrabee. "Building a New NATO." *Foreign Affairs, 72,* 4 (September–October 1993): 28–40.

Aspin, Les. "Four Scenarios—Choose One." *Washington Post* (March 9, 1990): A23.

Attali, Jacques. "Lines on the Horizon: A New Order in the Making." *New Perspectives Quarterly, 7,* 2 (Spring 1990): 4–11.

Bandow, Doug. "Avoiding War." *Foreign Policy, 89* (Winter 1992–93): 156–74.

Bani-Sadr, Abolhassan. "Azerbaijan: The Muslims' Revolt against Moscow." *New Perspectives Quarterly, 7,* 2 (Spring 1990): 29–30.

Barnaby, Frank, and Marlies ter Borg, eds. *Emerging Technologies and Military Doctrine: A Political Assessment.* London: Macmillan, 1986.

Barnet, Richard J. "Reflections (the Age of Globalization)." *New Yorker* (June 16, 1990): 46–60.

Barone, Michael. "An Inquiry into the Health of Nations." *U.S. News and World Report, 108,* 24 (June 18, 1990): 35.

Battle, John. "In Search of Gorbachev's Revolution from Below." *International Perspectives, 18,* 3 (May–June 1989): 7–10.

Becker, Abraham S. "Gorbachev's Program for Economic Modernization and Reform: Some Important Political-Military Implications." Santa Monica, CA: RAND Library Collection P–7384, September 1987.

Bell, Daniel. "The World and the United States in 2013." *Daedalus, 116,* 3 (Summer 1987): 1–31.

Bell-Fialkoff, Andrew. "A Brief History of Ethnic Cleansing." *Foreign Affairs, 72,* 3 (Summer 1993): 110–21.

Beloff, Max. "A Premature Obituary?" *Encounter, 75,* 1 (July–August 1990): 5–6.

Benjamin, Gerald, ed. *The Communications Revolution in Politics.* New York: Proceedings of the Academy of Political Science 34, no. 4, 1982.

Berger, Joseph. "Universities and their Scientific Research: A Question of Commercial Profits." *New York Times* (September 16, 1988): 16.

Bergsten, Fred. "The World Economy after the Cold War." *Foreign Affairs, 69,* 3 (Summer 1990): 96–112.

Bertram, Christoph. "The German Question." *Foreign Affairs, 69,* 2 (Spring 1990): 45–62.

Bialer, Seweryn. "Gorbachev's Program of Change: Sources, Significance, Prospects." *Political Science Quarterly, 103,* 3 (Fall 1988): 403–60.

———. " 'New Thinking' and Soviet Foreign Policy." *Survival, 30,* 4 (July–August 1988): 291–309.

———. "The Passing of the Soviet Order?" *Survival, 32,* 2 (March–April 1990): 107–20.

Bialer, Seweryn, and Michael Mandelbaum, eds. *Gorbachev's Russia and American Foreign Policy.* Boulder, CO: Westview Press, 1988.

Birman, Igor. "The Imbalances of the Soviet Economy." *Soviet Studies, 40,* 2 (Spring 1988): 210–21.

Borden, William Liscum. *There Will Be No Time: The Revolution in Strategy.* New York: Macmillan, 1946.

Boutros-Ghali, Boutros. *An Agenda for Peace: Preventive Diplomacy, Peacemaking, and Peace-Keeping.* New York: United Nations, 1992.

———. "Empowering the United Nations." *Foreign Affairs, 72,* 5 (Winter 1992–93): 89–102.

Bowers, Stephen R. "East Europe: Why the Cheering Stopped." *Journal of Social, Political and Economic Studies, 15,* 1 (Spring 1990): 25–42.

Brandon, Harry. "In the Driver's Seat: EC or Germany?" *Brookings Review, 8,* 2 (Spring 1990): 28–31.

Brandt, Willy. "Will a United Europe Tilt Left?" *New Perspectives Quarterly, 7,* 2 (Spring 1990): 16–18.

Breckenridge, Scott D. *The CIA and the U.S. Intelligence System.* Boulder, CO: Westview Press, 1986.

Brement, Marshall. "Reflections on Soviet New Thinking on Security Questions." *Naval War College Review, 42,* 4 (Autumn 1989): 5–21.

Brenner, Michael J. "Finding America's Place." *Foreign Policy, 79* (Summer 1990): 25–43.

Brock, David. "The Theory and Practice of Japan-Bashing." *National Interest, 17* (Fall 1989): 29–40.

Brodie, Bernard. *Strategy in the Missile Age.* Princeton, NJ: Princeton University Press, 1959.

———, ed. *The Absolute Weapon: Atomic Power and World Order.* New York: Harcourt, Brace, 1946.

Brown, Harold. "Competitiveness, Technology, and U.S.–Japanese Relations." *Washington Quarterly, 13,* 3 (Summer 1990): 85–96.

———. "The United States and Japan: High Tech Is Foreign Policy." *SAIS Review, 9,* 2 (Summer–Fall 1989): 1–18.

Brown, Neville. "New Paradigms for Strategy." *The World Today, 46,* 6 (June 1990): 115–18.

Brzezinski, Zbigniew. "Beyond Chaos." *National Interest, 19* (Spring 1990): 3–12.

———. "The Cold War and Its Aftermath." *Foreign Affairs 71,* 4 (Fall 1992): 31–49.

———. "Europe and Amerippon: Pillars of the New World Order." *New Perspectives Quarterly, 7,* 2 (Spring 1990): 18–20.

Buck, Trevor, and John Cole. *Modern Soviet Economic Performance.* Oxford: Basil Blackwell, 1987.

Bundy, McGeorge, William J. Crowe, Jr., and Sidney Drell. "Reducing Nuclear Danger." *Foreign Affairs, 72,* 2 (Spring 1993): 140–55.

Burton, Daniel F., Jr. "High-Tech Competitiveness." *Foreign Policy, 92* (Fall 1993): 117–32.

Burton, Daniel F., Victor Gotbaum, and Felix G. Rohatyn, eds. *Vision for the 1990s: U.S. Strategy and the Global Economy.* Cambridge, MA: Ballinger, 1989.

Bush, George S. "Change in the Soviet Union." *Current Policy, 1175* (May 1989): 1–3.

Butson, Thomas G. *Gorbachev: A Biography.* New York: Stein and Day, 1986.

Central Intelligence Agency. *The Soviet Weapons Industry: An Overview.* Washington, DC: Central Intelligence Agency Document DI 86–10016, September 1986.

Chaffee, Steven H., ed. *Political Communication: Issues and Strategies for Research.* Beverly Hills, CA: Sage Publications, 1975.

Chalmers, Malcolm. "Beyond the Alliance System: The Case for a European Security Organization." *World Policy Journal, 7,* 2 (Spring 1990): 215–50.

Claude, Inis L., Jr. *Swords into Plowshares: The Problems and Progress of International Organization,* 4th ed. New York: Random House, 1971.

Clurman, Richard M. "Should TV Be Barred? Only Tyrannies Say Yes." *New York Times* (March 28, 1988): 21.

Corterier, Peter. "*Quo Vadis* NATO?" *Survival, 32,* 2 (March–April 1990): 141–56.

Cregan, John P. "Building an American Consensus: A National Interest Trade Policy." *Vital Speeches of the Day, 56,* 16 (June 1, 1990): 509–12.

Crozier, Brian. "Slouching toward Democracy." *National Review, 42,* 6 (April 1, 1990): 27.

———. "Was It Wrong to Be Right?" *Encounter, 75,* 1 (July–August 1990): 6–8.

Cullen, Robert. "Human Rights Quandary." *Foreign Affairs, 72,* 5 (Winter 1992–93): 79–88.

Dallin, Alexander. "Standing Lenin on His Head." *New Leader, 73,* 3 (February 5–19, 1990): 7–10.

Davison, W. Phillips. *Communications and Conflict Resolution: The Role of the Information Media in the Advancement of International Understanding.* New York: Praeger, 1974.

Defense Policy Panel. "General Secretary Mikhail Gorbachev and the Soviet Military: Assessing His Impact and the Potential for Future Changes." Washington, DC: Committee on Armed Services, U.S. House of Representatives (100th Congress, 2d Session), September 13, 1988.

Deibel, Terry. "Internal Affairs and International Relations in the Post–Cold War World." *Washington Quarterly, 16,* 3 (Summer 1993): 13–36.

De Michelis, Gianni. "From Eurosclerosis to Europhoria." *New Perspectives Quarterly, 7,* 2 (Spring 1990): 12–14.

Dentzer, Susan. "The Coming Global Boom." *U.S. News and World Report, 109,* 3 (July 16, 1990): 22–26, 28.

Dessouki, Ali E. Hilial. "Globalization and the Two Spheres of Security." *Washington Quarterly, 16,* 4 (Autumn 1993): 109–17.

D'Estaing, Valery Giscard, and Helmut Schmidt. "The Franco-German Axis: Core of the New Europe." *New Perspectives Quarterly, 7,* 2 (Spring 1990): 14–16.

Deutch, John N. "The New Nuclear Threat." *Foreign Affairs, 71,* 4 (Fall 1992): 120–134.

Doder, Duško. "Yugoslavia: New War. Old Hatreds." *Foreign Policy, 91* (Summer 1993): 3–23.

Douglass, Joseph D., Jr. "The War on Drugs: Prospects for Success." *Journal of Social, Political and Economic Studies, 15,* 1 (Spring 1990): 45–57.

Dyker, David A., ed. *The Soviet Union under Gorbachev: Prospects for Reform.* London: Croom Helm, 1987.

Egan, Jack. "Business without Borders." *U.S. News and World Report, 109,* 3 (July 16, 1990): 29–31.

Etzioni, Amitai. "The Evils of Self-Determination." *Foreign Policy, 89* (Winter 1992–93): 21–35.

Evangelista, Matthew. *Innovations and the Arms Race: How the United States and the Soviet Union Develop New Military Technologies.* Ithaca, NY: Cornell University Press, 1988.

Evans, Rowland, and Robert Novak. "Gorbachev's Pitch to Baker." *Washington Post* (August 9, 1989): A21.

Falin, Valentin. "The Collapse of Europe: Moscow's View." *New Perspectives Quarterly, 7,* 2 (Spring 1990): 22–26.

Ferguson, Charles H. "America's High-Tech Decline." *Foreign Policy, 74* (Spring 1989): 123–44.

Finkelstein, Joseph, ed. *Windows on a New World: The Third Industrial Revolution.* Westport, CT: Greenwood Press, 1989.

Forester, Tom. *High-Tech Society: The Story of the Information Technology Revolution.* Oxford: Basil Blackwell, 1987.

Frank, Andre Gunder. "Revolution in Eastern Europe: Implications for Democratic Social Movements (and Socialists?)" *Third World Quarterly, 12,* 2 (April 1990): 36–52.

Freiden, Gregory. "Reform or Else." *New Republic, 943,* 3 (August 13, 1990): 16–18.

Fromkin, David. *The Independence of Nations.* New York: Praeger Special Studies, 1981.

Fukuyama, Francis. "The End of History?" *National Interest, 16* (Summer 1989): 3–18.

————. "A Reply to My Critics." *National Interest, 18* (Winter 1989–90): 21–28.

Gaddis, John Lewis. "Coping with Victory." *Atlantic Monthly, 265,* 5 (May 1990): 49–60.

Galusza, Peter, William D. Marbach, and Rose Brady. "Soviet Technology." *Business Week, 3078* (November 7, 1988): 68–78.

————. "What Will They Do When They Get the Right Stuff?" *Business Week, 3078* (November 7, 1988): 82–86.

Garthoff, Raymond L. "The Warsaw Pact Today—and Tomorrow?" *Brookings Review, 8,* 2 (Summer 1990): 35–40.

Geremek, Bronislaw. "Which Way to Europe?" *National Review, 42,* 15 (August 6, 1990): 30–32.

Goble, Paul. "Soviet Citizens Blame System for Ethnic Problems." *Report on the USSR, 2,* 26 (June 29, 1990): 5–6.

Goldman, Marshall I. *Gorbachev's Challenge; Economic Reforms in the Age of High Technology.* New York: W.W. Norton, 1987.

————. "Gorbachev the Economist." *Foreign Affairs, 69,* 2 (Spring 1990): 28–44.

Gorbachev, Mikhail S. *The Coming Century of Peace.* New York: Richardson and Steirman, 1986.

————. "The International Community and Change: A Common European Home." *Vital Speeches of the Day, 55,* 23 (September 15, 1989): 706–11.

————. "Key Sections of Gorbachev Speech Given to Party Conference." *New York Times* (June 29, 1988): 8.

————. *Perestroika: New Thinking for Our Country and the World.* New York: Harper and Row, 1987.

————. "The Progress of *Perestroika.*" *World Today, 45,* 6 (June 1989): 94.

————. "Our Ideal Is a Humane Democratic Socialism." *Vital Speeches of the Day, 56,* 11 (March 15, 1990): 322–27.

Gunlicks, Arthur B., and John D. Treadway, eds. *The Soviet Union under Gorbachev: Assessing the First Year.* New York: Praeger, 1987.

Gurruti, Gustavo. "The War of the Philosopher-King." *New Republic, 935,* 3 (June 18, 1990): 15–22.

Halperin, Morton. "Guaranteeing Democracy." *Foreign Policy, 91* (Summer 1993): 105–23.

Hamman, Henry. "Soviet Defector on Origins of 'New Thinking.' " *Report on the USSR, 1,* 42 (October 20, 1989): 14–16.

Harris, Owen. "The Collapse of 'the West.' " *Foreign Affairs, 72,* 4 (September–October 1993): 41–53.

Hartley, Anthony. "And the Wall Fell Down: Mr. Gorbachev and the New Europe." *Encounter, 74,* 1 (January–February 1990): 3–7.

————. "Behind the Facade." *Encounter, 75,* 1 (July–August 1990): 17–18.

Hazleton, William A., and Sandra Woy-Hazleton. "Sendero Luminoso and the Future of Peruvian Democracy." *Third World Quarterly, 12,* 2 (April 1990): 21–36.

Heisburg, François. "The Future of the Atlantic Alliance." *Washington Quarterly, 15,* 2 (Spring 1992): 127–40.

Helman, Gerald B., and Steven R. Ratner. "Saving Failed States." *Foreign Policy, 89* (Winter 1992–93): 3–20.

Herspring, Dale R. "The Soviet Military and Change." *Survival, 31,* 4 (July–August 1989): 321–38.

Hewett, Ed A. "Is Soviet Socialism Reformable?" *SAIS Review, 10,* 2 (Summer–Fall 1990): 75–87.

———. *Reforming the Soviet Economy: Equality vs. Efficiency.* Washington, DC: Brookings Institution, 1988.

Heyns, Terry L. *American and Soviet Relations since Detente.* Washington, DC: National Defense University Press, 1987.

Hoffmann, Stanley. "What Should We Do in the World?" *Atlantic Monthly, 264,* 4 (October 1989): 84–96.

Holloway, David. "Gorbachev's New Thinking." *Foreign Affairs, 68,* 1 (1988–89): 66–81.

Holstein, William J. "The Stateless Corporation." *Business Week, 3159,* (May 14, 1990): 98–105.

Hormats, Robert D. "The Economic Consequences of the Peace—1989." *Survival, 31,* 6 (November–December 1989): 484–99.

———. "The International Economic Challenge." *Foreign Policy, 71* (Summer 1988): 99–116.

Howard, Michael. "The Gorbachev Challenge and the Defence of the West." *Survival, 30,* 6 (November–December 1988): 483–92.

Huntington, Samuel P. "Clash of Civilizations." *Foreign Affairs, 72,* 3 (Summer 1993): 22–49.

———. "Coping with the Lippman Gap." *Foreign Affairs, 66,* 3 (1987–88): 453–77.

———. "No Exit: The Errors of Endism." *The National Interest, 17* (Fall 1989): 3–11.

Husbands, J.L. "A Buyer's Market for Arms." *Bulletin of the Atomic Scientists, 46,* 4 (May 1990): 14–19.

Hyland, William C. "America's New Course." *Foreign Affairs, 69,* 2 (Spring 1990): 1–12.

———. "Setting Global Priorities." *Foreign Policy, 73* (Winter 1988–89): 22–40.

Inman, B.R., and Daniel F. Burton, Jr. "Technology and Competitiveness: The New Policy Frontier." *Foreign Affairs, 69,* 2 (Spring 1990): 116–34.

Jervis, Robert. *The Illogic of American Nuclear Strategy.* Ithaca, NY: Cornell University Press, 1984.

———. *The Meaning of the Nuclear Revolution: Statecraft and the Prospects of Armageddon.* Ithaca, NY: Cornell University Press, 1989.

Johnson, Chalmers. "Their Behavior, Our Policy." *National Interest, 17* (Fall 1989): 17–27.

Joint Economic Committee, Congress of the United States (100th Congress, 1st Session). *Gorbachev's Economic Plans,* vol. 2. Washington, DC: Government Printing Office, 1987.

Jones, David T. "NATO's Defense in the New Europe." *Foreign Service Journal, 67,* 4 (April 1990): 28–31.

Kagarlitsky, Boris. "Different Perestroikas for Different Folks." *New York Times* (September 7, 1988): 25.

Kaiser, Robert G. "The U.S.S.R. in Decline." *Foreign Affairs, 67,* 2 (Winter 1988–89): 96–113.

Kampelman, Max M. "Secession and the Right of Self-Determination: An Urgent

Need to Harmonize Principle with Pragmatism." *Washington Quarterly, 16,* 3 (Summer 1993): 5–12.

Karaganov, Sergei A. "The Year of Europe: A Soviet View." *Survival, 32,* 2 (March–April 1990): 121–28.

Kaufman, Richard F. "Economic Reform and the Soviet Military." *Washington Quarterly, 11,* 3 (Summer 1988): 201–10.

Kaufmann, William W. "Some Small Change for Defense." *Brookings Review, 8,* 3 (Summer 1990): 26–29, 32–33.

Keatley, Ann G., ed. *Technological Frontiers and Foreign Relations.* Washington, DC: National Academy Press, 1985.

Keller, Bill. "New Soviet Ideologist Rejects Idea of World Struggle against West." *New York Times* (October 6, 1988): 1–4.

Kennedy, Paul. *The Rise and Fall of the Great Powers: Economic Change and Military Conflict from 1500 to 2000.* New York: Random House, 1987.

Keyworth, G.A., II. "Goodby, Central." *Vital Speeches of the Day, 56,* 12 (April 1, 1990): 358–61.

Kirkpatrick, Jeane. "A Safer World?" *Washington Post* (May 28, 1990): A23.

Kissinger, Henry A. "Germany, Neutrality, and the 'Security Trap' System." *Washington Post* (April 15, 1990): D7.

———. "Gorbachev: The Price of Survival." *Newsweek* (June 18, 1990): 37.

———. "A Plan for Europe." *Newsweek* (June 18, 1990): 32–33, 37.

Klare, Michael T. "Wars in the 1990s: Growing Firepower in the Third World." *Bulletin of the Atomic Scientists, 46,* 4 (May 1990): 9–13.

Kober, Stanley. "Idealpolitik." *Foreign Policy, 79* (Summer 1990): 3–24.

———. "Revolutions Gone Bad." *Foreign Policy, 91* (Summer 1993): 63–84.

Kohl, Helmut. "A United Germany in a United Europe." *Vital Speeches of the Day, 56,* 18 (July 1, 1990): 546–48.

Kruzel, Joseph, ed. *American Defense Annual 1990–1991,* 6th ed. Lexington, MA: Lexington Books, 1990.

Lambeth, Benjamin, and Kevin Lewis. "The Kremlin and SDI." *Foreign Affairs, 66,* 4 (Spring 1988): 755–70.

Lankford, D. S. "High-Definition Television Technology." *Vital Speeches of the Day, 56,* 8 (February 1, 1990): 241–44.

Laqueur, Walter. *The Long Road to Freedom: Russia and Glasnost.* New York: Charles Scribner's Sons, 1989.

———. "Rediscovering the Truth." *Encounter, 75,* 1 (July–August 1990): 11–13.

———. "Why Stalin? A National Debate." *Society, 27,* 3 (March–April 1990): 26–42.

———. *A World of Spies: The Uses and Limits of Intelligence.* New York: Basic Books, 1985.

Larrabee, F. Stephen. "Gorbachev and the Soviet Military." *Foreign Affairs, 66,* 5 (Summer 1988): 1002–26.

Layne, Christopher, and Benjamin Schwartz. "American Hegemony—Without an Enemy." *Foreign Policy, 92* (Fall 1993): 5–23.

Lefever, Ernest. "Reining in the U.N." *Foreign Affairs, 72,* 3 (Summer 1993): 17–21.

Legvold, Robert. "The Revolution in Soviet Foreign Policy." *Foreign Affairs, 68,* 1 (1988–89): 82–98.

Lendvai, Paul. "In 'Mittel-Europa.' " *Encounter, 75,* 1 (July–August 1990): 8–9.

Levite, Ariel. *Intelligence and Strategic Surprise.* New York: Columbia University Press, 1987.

Lewin, Moshe. *The Gorbachev Phenomenon: A Historical Interpretation.* Berkeley: University of California Press, 1988.

Lewis, Flora. "The Return of History." *SAIS Review, 10,* 2 (Summer 1990): 1–11.

Liebowitz, Robert D., ed. *Gorbachev's "New Thinking": Prospects for Joint Ventures.* Cambridge, MA: Ballinger, 1988.

Ligachev, Yegor. "The Revolutionary Essence of Perestroika." *World Marxist Review, 30,* 2 (December 1987): 5–17.

Light, Margot. *The Soviet Theory of International Relations.* Brighton, Sussex, UK: Wheatsheaf Books, 1988.

Lucas, Michael R. *The Western Alliance after INF: Redefining U.S. Policy toward Europe and the Soviet Union.* Boulder, CO: Lynne Reinner, 1990.

Luck, Edward C. "Making Peace." *Foreign Policy, 89* (Winter 1992–93): 137–55.

Luck, Edward C., and Toby Trister-Gati. "Whose Collective Security?" *Washington Quarterly, 15,* 2 (Spring 1992): 43–56.

Luttwak, Edward. "From Geopolitics to Geo-Economics: Logic of Conflict, Grammar of Commerce." *National Interest, 20* (Summer 1990): 17–24.

———. "The Shape of Things to Come." *Commentary, 81,* 6 (June 1990): 17–25.

Lynch, Allen. "Does Gorbachev Matter Anymore?" *Foreign Affairs, 69,* 3 (Summer 1990): 19–29.

———. *Gorbachev's International Outlook: Intellectual Origins and Political Consequences.* New York: Institute for East–West Security Series (Occasional Paper Series No. 9), 1989.

Lyon, David. *The Information Society: Issues and Illusions.* Cambridge: Polity Press, 1988.

Mahnken, Thomas G. "America's Next War." *Washington Quarterly, 16,* 3 (Summer 1993): 171–88.

Mazarr, Michael J. "Nuclear Weapons after the Cold War." *Washington Quarterly, 15,* 3 (Summer 1992): 185–201.

McCauley, Martin, ed. *The Soviet Union under Gorbachev.* London: Macmillan, 1987.

McConnell, James M. "SDI, the Soviet Investment Debate and Soviet Military Policy." *Strategic Review, 16,* 1 (Winter 1988): 47–58.

MacFarquhar, Emily. "The Kashmir Question." *U.S. News and World Report, 108,* 23 (June 11, 1990): 42–44.

McGeorge, Harvey J. "Bugs, Gas and Missiles." *Defense and Foreign Affairs 17,* 5–6 (May–June 1990): 14–19.

McGowan, William G. "Telecommunications and Global Competitiveness." *Vital Speeches of the Day, 56,* 7 (January 15, 1990): 199–201.

Malmgren, Harald B. "Technological Challenges to National Economic Policies of the West." *Washington Quarterly, 10,* 2 (Spring 1987): 21–33.

Mandelbaum, Michael. *Restructuring the European Security Order.* New York: Council on Foreign Relations, 1990.

Markuson, Ann, Peter Hall, and Amy Glasmeier. *High Tech America: The What, How, Where and Why of the Sunrise Industries.* Boston: Allen and Unwin, 1986.

Maynes, Charles William. "America without the Cold War." *Foreign Policy, 78* (Spring 1990): 3–25.

Mead, Walter Russell. "The World Economic Order: Perils after Bretton Woods." *Dissent* (Summer 1990): 383–93.

Mearsheimer, John J. "Why We Will Soon Miss the Cold War." *Atlantic Monthly, 266,* 2 (August 1990): 35–50.

Medvedev, Zhores A. *Gorbachev.* New York: W.W. Norton, 1986.

Mercer, Derrik, Geoff Mungham, and Kevin Williams. *The Fog of War: The Media and the Battlefield.* London: Heinemann, 1987.

Merritt, Richard L., ed. *Communications in International Politics.* Urbana: University of Illinois Press, 1972.

Meyer, Stephen M. "The Sources and Prospects of Gorbachev's New Political Thinking on Security." *International Security, 13,* 2 (Fall 1988): 124–64.

Mikheyev, Dimitry. *The Soviet Perspective on the Strategic Defense Initiative.* Washington, DC: Pergamon-Brassey's, 1987.

Miller, Abraham H., ed. *Terrorism, the Media and the Law.* Dobbs Ferry, NY: Transnational Publishers, 1982.

Muravchik, Joshua. "Gorbachev's Intellectual Odyssey." *New Republic, 920,* 3 (March 5, 1990): 20–25.

Nacht, Michael. "Cold War: The Arms Race Isn't Over Yet." *Washington Post* (April 15, 1990): D1, D4.

Nagorski, Andrew. "The Intellectual Roots of Eastern Europe's Upheaval." *SAIS Review, 10,* 2 (Summer–Fall 1990): 89–100.

Nakasone, Yasuhiro. "Towards a New International Community." *Survival, 30,* 6 (November–December 1988): 493–98.

Naylor, Thomas H. *The Gorbachev Strategy: Opening the Closed Society.* Lexington, MA: Lexington Books, 1988.

Neumann, Robert G. "This Next Disorderly Half Century: Some Proposed Remedies." *Washington Quarterly,* 16, 1 (Winter 1993): 33–50.

Neuman, Stephanie G. "Controlling the Arms Trade: Idealistic Dream or Realpolitik?" *Washington Quarterly, 16,* 3 (Summer 1993): 53–73.

Nicandros, Constantine S. "The Innovation Imperative: Dynamic Societies." *Vital Speeches of the Day, 56,* 16 (June 1, 1990): 504–8.

Niiseki, Kinya, ed. *The Soviet Union in Transition.* Boulder, CO: Westview Press, 1987.

Nimroody, Rosy. *Star Wars: The Economic Impact.* Cambridge, MA: Ballinger, 1988.

Nolan, Janne, and Albert D. Wheelon. "Third World Ballistic Missiles." *Scientific American, 263,* 3 (August 1990): 34–40.

Nordenstreng, Kaarle, and Herbert I. Schiller. *National Sovereignty and International Communication.* Norwood, NJ: Ablex, 1979.

Nordlinger, Eric A. "Prospects and Policies for Soviet–American Reconciliation." *Political Sciences Quarterly, 103,* 2 (Summer 1988): 197–222.

Novak, Michael. "Democracy: The Collapse of the Alternatives." *Freedom at Issue, 114* (May–June 1990): 18–20.

Nozette, Stewart, and Robert Kuhn, eds. *Commercializing SDI Technologies.* New York: Praeger, 1987.

Nunn, Sam. "A New Military Strategy." *Congressional Record—Senate* (April 19, 1990): S4451.

Nye, Joseph S., Jr. *Bound to Lead: The Changing Nature of American Power.* New York: Basic Books, 1990.

———. "The Changing Nature of World Power." *Political Science Quarterly, 105,* 2 (Summer 1990): 177–92.

———. "The Misleading Metaphor of Decline." *Atlantic Monthly, 265,* 3 (March 1990): 86–94.

———. "Understanding U.S. Strength." *Foreign Policy, 72* (Fall 1988): 105–29.

———. "What New World Order?" *Foreign Affairs, 71,* 2 (Summer 1992): 83–96.

Odom, William E. "How Far Can Soviet Reform Go?" *Problems of Communism, 36,* 6 (November–December 1987): 18–33.

Ohmae, Kenichi. "Beyond Fiction to Fact: The Borderless Economy." *New Perspectives Quarterly, 7,* 2 (Spring 1990): 20–21.

———. "The Rise of the Region State." *Foreign Affairs, 72,* 2 (Spring 1993): 78–87.

Papp, Daniel S. *Contemporary International Relations: Frameworks for Understanding.* New York: Macmillan, 1984.

Parker, Richard. "Assessing Perestroika: Half Full or Half Empty." *World Policy Journal, 6,* 2 (Spring 1989): 265–95.

Parrott, Bruce. "Gorbachev's Gamble: Political, Economic, and Ethnic Challenges to Soviet Reform." *SAIS Review, 10,* 2 (Summer–Fall 1990): 57–73.

Peng, Ernest H. "Who's Benefitting Whom? A Trade Agenda for High-Technology Industries." *Washington Quarterly, 16,* 4 (Autumn 1993): 17–34.

Perle, Richard. "Too Many Guns, Too Little Butter." *U.S. News and World Report, 109,* 4 (July 23, 1990): 44.

Peterson, Donald K. "Globalization and Telecommunications Leadership: The Future Ain't What It Used to Be." *Vital Speeches of the Day, 56,* 17 (June 15, 1990): 527–30.

Pfaff, William. "Invitation to War." *Foreign Affairs, 72,* 3 (Summer 1993): 97–109.

Pfaltzgraff, Robert, Uri Ra'anan, and Walter Milberg, eds. *Intelligence Policy and National Security.* Hamden, CT: Archon Books, 1981.

Pickering, Thomas R. "The U.N. Contribution to Future International Security." *Naval War College Review, 46,* 1 (Winter 1993): 94–104.

Pierre, Andrew J., ed. *A High Technology Gap? Europe, America and Japan.* New York: New York University Press, 1987.

Pipes, Richard. "Why the Soviet Union Thinks It Can Fight and Win a Nuclear War." *Commentary, 64,* 1 (July 1977): 21–34.

Pires, Claudia. "Critical Condition." *Third World, 24* (February 1990): 7–12.

Prahalad, C.K. "The Changing Nature of Worldwide Communication." *Vital Speeches of the Day, 56,* 12 (April 1, 1990): 355–57.

Rand, Robert. "Perestroika Up Close." *Wilson Quarterly, 13,* 2 (Spring 1989): 51–58.

Reich, Robert B. "The Quiet Path to Economic Preeminence." *Scientific American, 261,* 4 (October 1989): 41–47.

Reichert, William, and Henry Sello. "Whole-Earth Technology." *High Technology Business, 9,* 7 (July–August 1989): 14–19.

Roberts, Brad. "Arms Control and the End of the Cold War." *Washington Quarterly, 14,* 4 (Autumn 1992): 39–56.

Roche, John P. "Ain't Going to Study War No More." *National Review, 42,* 5 (March 19, 1990): 27–28.

Rogov, Sergei. "International Security and the Collapse of the Soviet Union." *Washington Quarterly, 15,* 2 (Spring 1992): 16–28.

Rohatyn, Felix. "America's Economic Dependence." *Foreign Affairs, 68,* 1 (1988–89): 53–65.

Rosecrance, Richard. "A New Concert of Powers." *Foreign Affairs, 71,* 2 (Spring 1992): 64–82.

Rostow, W.W. "The Coming Age of Regionalism." *Encounter, 74,* 6 (June 1990): 3–7.

Rowen, Henry S., and Charles Wolf, eds. *The Future of the Soviet Empire.* New York: Institute for Contemporary Studies, 1987.

Russett, Bruce, and Harvey Starr. *World Politics: The Menu for Choice.* San Francisco, CA: W.H. Freeman, 1981.

Rutland, Peter. " 'Democratic Platform' Prepares for CPSU Congress." *Report on the USSR, 2,* 26 (June 29, 1990): 1–3.

Safire, William. "Restless Captives." *New York Times* (August 25, 1988): 23.

Sanger, David E. "U.S. Parts, Japanese Computers." *New York Times* (September 7, 1988): 27–28.

Schlesinger, James. "The Impact of Nuclear Weapons on History." *Washington Quarterly, 16,* 4 (Autumn 1993): 5–16.

————. "Quest for a Post–Cold War Foreign Policy." *Foreign Affairs, 71,* 1 (Winter 1992–93): 17–28.

Schmidt-Hauer, Christian. *Gorbachev: The Path to Power.* London: I.B. Tauris, 1986.

Schurmann, Franz. "After Desert Storm: Interest, Ideology, and History in American Foreign Policy." In Meredith Woo-Cumings and Michael Loriaux (eds.), *Past as Prelude: History in the Making of a New World Order.* Boulder, CO: Westview Press, 1993.

Shanker, Thom. "Gorbachev's New Ballgame." *Washington Journalism Review, 11,* 5 (June 1989): 18–21.

Shmelev, Nikolai, and Ed A. Hewett. "A Pragmatist's View on the Soviet Economy: A Conversation between Nikolai Shmelev and Ed A. Hewett." *Brookings Review, 8,* 1 (Winter 1989–90): 27–32.

Shub, Anatole. "Russia at the Crossroads." *New Leader, 73,* 3 (February 5–19, 1990): 3–6.

Shulman, Marshall D. "The Superpowers: Dance of the Dinosaurs." *Foreign Affairs, 66,* 3 (1987–88): 494–515.

Siegel, Lenny, and John Markoff. *The High Cost of High Tech: The Dark Side of the Chip.* New York: Harper and Row, 1985.

Singer, Max. "The Decline and Fall of the Soviet Empire." *National Review, 42,* 13 (July 9, 1990): 26–28.

Singer, Max. and Aaron Wildavsky. *The Real World Order: Zones of Peace, Zones of Turmoil.* Chatham, NJ: Chatham House, 1993.

Skolnikoff, Eugene B. "Technology and the World Tomorrow." *Current History, 88,* 534 (January 1989): 5–8, 42–46.

Smith, Tony. "Making the World Safe for Democracy." *Washington Quarterly, 16,* 4 (Autumn 1993): 197–218.

Smith, W. Y. "U.S. National Security after the Cold War." *Washington Quarterly,* *15,* 4 (Autumn 1992): 21–34.

Snow, Donald M. *The Necessary Peace: Nuclear Weapons and Superpower Relations.* Lexington, MA: Lexington Books, 1987.

———. *Peacekeeping, Peacemaking, and Peace Enforcement: The U.S. Role in the New International Order.* Carlisle Barracks, PA: Strategic Studies Institute, 1993.

———. "Soviet Reform and the High Technology Imperative." *Parameters, 20,* 1 (March 1990): 76–87.

Sorensen, Theodore C. "Rethinking National Security." *Foreign Affairs, 69,* 3 (Summer 1990): 1–18.

Stanfield, Rochelle L. "Under Europe's Umbrella." *National Journal, 22,* 14 (April 7, 1990): 826–31.

Staar, Richard. "The High Technology Transfer Offensive of the Soviet Union." *Strategic Review, 17,* 2 (Spring 1989): 32–39.

Starr, S. Frederick. "A Peculiar Pattern." *Wilson Quarterly, 13,* 2 (Spring 1989): 37–50.

———. "Soviet Union: A Civil Society." *Foreign Policy, 70* (Spring 1988): 26–41.

Stedman, Stephen John, "The New Interventionists." *Foreign Affairs, 72,* 1 (Winter 1992–93): 1–16.

Steel, Ronald. "The Rise of the European Superstate." *New Republic, 937,* 3 (July 2, 1990): 23–25.

Steinbrunner, John D. "The Redesign of European Security." *Brookings Review, 8,* 3 (Summer 1990): 23–25.

Stevenson, Jonathan. "Hope Restored in Somalia?" *Foreign Policy, 91* (Summer 1993): 138–54.

Stokes, Bruce. "High-Tech Tussle." *National Journal, 22,* 22 (June 2, 1990): 1338–42.

Sullivan, John D. "Democracy and Global Economic Growth." *Washington Quarterly, 15,* 2 (Spring 1992): 175–86.

Summers, Harry G. *On Strategy: A Critical Analysis of the Vietnam War.* Novato, CA: Presidio Press, 1982.

Szabo, Stephen. "The German Answer." *SAIS Review, 10,* 2 (Summer–Fall 1990): 41–56.

Tanenhaus, Sam. "What the Anti-Communists Knew." *Commentary, 90,* 1 (July 1990): 32–36.

Tarnoff, Peter. "America's New Special Relationships." *Foreign Affairs, 69,* 3 (Summer 1990): 67–80.

Taubman, Philip. "Soviet Chief Says Drive for Change." *New York Times* (September 26, 1988): 1, 7.

Teague, Elizabeth. "Is the Party Over?" *Report on the USSR, 2,* 18 (May 4, 1990): 1–4.

———. "The Twenty-eighth Party Congress: An Overview." *Report on the USSR, 2,* 29 (July 20, 1990): 1–3.

Todorov, Tzvetan. "Post-Totalitarian Depression." *New Republic, 936,* 3 (June 25, 1990): 23–25.

Townley, Preston. "Going Global in the 1990s." *Vital Speeches of the Day, 56,* 19 (July 15, 1990): 589–93.

Treverton, Gregory. *Covert Action: The Limits of Intervention in the Postwar World.* New York: Basic Books, 1987.

Trofimenko, Henry. "Ending the Cold War, Not History." *Washington Quarterly,* 13, 2 (Spring 1990): 21–35.

Ulam, Adam, and George Urban. "What Is 'Soviet'—What Is 'Russian'?" *Encounter, 74,* 4 (May 1990): 47–59.

Van Evera, Stephen. "The Case against Intervention." *Atlantic Monthly, 266,* 1 (July 1990): 72–80.

von Beyme, Klaus. "Transition to Democracy—or *Anschluss*? The Two Germanies and Europe." *Government and Opposition, 25,* 2 (Spring 1990): 170–90.

Waller, Douglas. "Risky Business." *Newsweek* (July 16, 1990): 16–19.

Warner, Ted. "A Crippled Warsaw Pact." *Deadline: A Bulletin from the Center for War, Peace, and the News Media, 5,* 2 (March–April 1990): 2–3.

Weinrod, W. Bruce. "Soviet 'New Thinking' and U.S. Foreign Policy." *World Affairs, 151,* 2 (Fall 1988): 59–64.

————. "Whatever He Does, Clap." *The Economist, 314,* 7646 (March 17, 1990): 11–12.

Weiss, Thomas G. "New Challenges for UN Military Operations: Implementing an Agenda for Peace." *Washington Quarterly, 16,* 1 (Winter 1993): 51–66.

————. *Whence the Threat to Peace,* 3d ed. Moscow: Military Publishing House, 1984.

Wettig, Gerhard. " 'New Thinking' on Security and East–West Relations." *Problems of Communism, 37,* 2 (March–April 1988): 1–14.

Wines, Michael. "Soviets Said to Pull Nuclear Arms from Restive Ethnic Areas." *New York Times* (June 23, 1990): 5.

Wright, Karen. "The Road to the Global Village." *Scientific American, 262,* 3 (March 1990): 84–94.

Wriston, Walter B. "Technology and Sovereignty." *Foreign Affairs, 67,* 2 (Winter 1988–89): 63–75.

Young, John A. *Global Competition: The New Reality.* Washington, DC: The Report of the President's Commission on Industrial Competitiveness, 1985.

"Z." "To the Stalin Mausoleum." *Daedalus, 119,* 1 (Winter 1990): 296–343.

Zamascikov, Sergei. "Gorbachev and the Soviet Military." Santa Monica, CA: RAND Corporation Library Collection Papers P–7410, January 1988.

Zegvold, Walter, and Christian Enzing. *SDI and Industrial Technology Policy: Threat or Opportunity?* London: Francis Pinter, 1987.

Ziemke, Caroline F. "Rethinking the 'Mistake' of the Past: History's Message to the Clinton Defense Department." *Washington Quarterly, 16,* 2 (Spring 1993): 47–60.

Zuckerman, Mortimer T. "The Gorbachev Effect." *U.S. News and World Report, 109,* 2 (July 9, 1990): 29–30.

Index